LEADERSHIP & DISCIPLINE

FROM BATTLESPACE TO BOARDROOM

Ebenezer K. Agyemang

BLACK MASK LTD
2020

Published by

BLACK MASK LIMITED

P. O. Box CT 770 Cantonments-Accra, Ghana

Email: bmask4u@gmail.com

Copyright © Ebenezer K. Agyemang – 2020

ISBN: 978 – 9988 – 3 – 0234 – 4

Designed and Printed by Black Mask Limited

Dedication

In associating myself with Erik Pevernagie, I state that-
> '............ *One night I dreamed a dream. I was walking along the beach with my Lord. Across the dark sky flashed scenes from my life. For each scene, I noticed two sets of footprints in the sand, one belonging to me and one to my Lord . . . .'*

This project is for leaders who aspire to leave remarkable footprints for others to tread. It is particularly dedicated to my father, Agyemang Bediako, a retired educationist, Brigadier General Fusieni Iddrisu, my first Commanding Officer in the Ghana Army and the late Brigadier General Emmanuel Tetteh-Akunor, my first Course Commander as an Officer Cadet at the Ghana Military Academy for leaving trails for my trace.

Table of Contents

Preface

'. . . . . Your own ease, comfort and safety come last, always and every time . . . . .'
Field Marshal Sir Philip Walhouse Chetwode

Leaders harness the potentials in the resources placed under their authority (command) and care. It has been observed that some choices made through the actions and decisions of person's in positions of power and authority have been inimical to the growth and sustenance of societies and their organisation. This book brings to the fore the gray merge between civil and military decisions and choices in leadership. As will be noted, discipline is that mental attitude and state of training which renders instinctive obedience under all conditions. The military has been touted as the most disciplined institution in the world, the Ghana Armed Forces not excepted. In recent times, a decline in the standards of discipline has been observed. Consequently, civil establishments would have a lot to gain when their leadership and decision choices are evaluated from the perspective of the military.

The book is in nine chapters. The first chapter looks at a generic concept of discipline and honour in military service. It delves into the author's personal experiences during his days at the Ghana Military Academy as a regular career officer. In particular, he brings to the fore how officers are moulded and conditioned in an environment where discipline is held in high esteem and self-comfort is a luxury. He also attempts to identify why standards and discipline seemed to be falling and professes solutions for its improvement. Chapter Two is a continuation of Chapter One, and examines how discipline could be upheld for institutional survival. Chapter Three covers choices and behaviours in leadership. The chapter adds the central role of decision in every leadership endeavour. Chapter Four also looks at skills and types of intelligence in leadership.

In particular, cognitive intelligence in leadership is comprehensively treated, and ends by emphasizing the adaptability quotient as the additional trait that every effective and resilient leader must have in our rippled and technologically endemic environment. Chapter Five considers some traits of leadership with special focus on humility and hubris. The chapter delves into the effect and impact of these traits in team behaviour and organisational health. Chapter Six looks at some 'contaminated' choices in leadership which leads to the creation of toxic environments at all workplaces. Chapter Seven then exposes the reader to the concept of Battle Space and management decision. Here some ideas from the military are borrowed for the good of the civil manager. Chapter Eight looks at generational cohorts and examines how millennials are impacting organisation growth. Chapter Nine examines the concept of morale and its impact of organisation success. It highlights the fact that, whether good or bad, our performance and actions will depend on the choices, direction and decisions made by leaders.

Acknowledgements

Firstly, I would like to express my gratitude to my talent whisperers and mentors; Deputy Director of Immigration Kojo Oppong-Yeboah of Ghana Immigration Service, Emmanuel Kwadwo Duku of Ghana Accreditation Board, Peter Oteng Darko of Centre for Agriculture and Rural Development and Captain Victor Abbey (Rtd) of V5 Consultancy for their continuous support for this work. Their exemplary fortitude and guidance helped in the writing of this book.

Furthermore, I would wish to express my unqualified gratitude to Lepowura Alhaji Mohammed Nuru-Deen Jawula, former GFA President and Chairman of Premier League Management

Committee, Maj Albert Don Chebe (Rtd), CEO of GN TV and Opia-Mensah Kumah, a UN Diplomat, and Prosper K. Agordjor for their insightful review of the book. It is also dedicated to all my Commanders in the Ghana Armed Forces, especially Major General JN Adinkrah, Major General William Omane-Agyekum and Brigadier General F. Iddrisu, for sowing in me the seed of resilience and fortitude which has yielded these results.

I would also wish to thank the rest of my team at CrossBridge Leadership Institute, Centre for Risk and Resilience Management, Retina Training Group, Mining Intelligence and Investigation Group and Africa Centre for Mining Governance for their support and encouragement. I was indeed incentivized by their sheer offer of alternate views which widened the research from various perspectives

To all my intake mates of Ghana Military Academy Regular Career Course 37 & Short Service Commission/Special Duty 36, my Cohort 2 Doctoral mates at SBS Swiss Business School/Nobel International Business School and authors from whose work ideas were borrowed, please accept my profound gratitude for leaving a trail for my trace.

Finally, I thank my wife Pat, and children, Aba and Nana, for trading their happiness for the completion of this work.

Ebenezer K. Agyemang
August 17, 2020

Chapter One

Discipline and Honour in Service

'The safety, honour and welfare of your country come first, always and every time. The honour, welfare and comfort of the men you command come next. Your own ease, comfort and safety come last, always and every time'.
Field Marshal Sir Philip Walhouse Chetwode

Centrality of Discipline in Military Leadership

Many leadership qualities have been observed throughout history. Some were adopted by bad leaders while others were exhibited by good and effective leaders. In either case, the characteristics of those in charge correlated to their ability to accomplish their goals. Those same traits determined how much or little their followers looked up to them for inspiration. With the hindsight provided by history, we can now put issues in perspective to learn and understand the effect of each trait and use the lessons learnt from the experiences of others to develop admirable leadership strengths for today and years to come.

Discipline has been defined as a specific form of instruction, which develops self-control, character, and efficiency. It is that mental attitude and state of training which renders instinctive obedience under all conditions. Military discipline or leadership, therefore, is the manner of leading and directing troops. It is that mental attitude and state of training which renders obedience instinctive under all conditions. Without discipline, an army is nothing more than an assemblage of volunteers, incapable of uniting for a collaborative defence, eager only for plundering and chaos. Discipline is founded upon respect for, and loyalty to properly constituted authority. It is discipline which unites military personnel under the orders of the officers, to which they owe a blind obedience for everything related to the service. It involves the ready subordination of the will of the individual for the good of the group.

The quotation cited at the beginning of this chapter is known as the 'Chetwode Motto', and is attributed to Field Marshal Philip Chetwode who was the Commander-in-Chief of the Indian Army and was instrumental in the 'Indianisation' of the Indian Defence Force. The quotation which stirs so much passion in all officer cadets and alumni is derived from an address he gave to the Military Academy in 1932. These words from his speech have become immortalized and even serve as the *'Honour Code'* of the Ghana Military Academy. 'The Code' is to be a key reminder to every officer, even in days after commissioning, to consider 'nation above self' in all endeavours.

Military bearing, which correlates to having or projecting a commanding presence and a professional image of authority, therefore needs to radiate aspects of the *Honour Code* at all times. In essence, it is the manner in which the military leader behaves or comports himself or understands his position, environment or situation. The leadership development field manual of the United States Army, equally provides a doctrinal framework which covers methods for leaders to develop other leaders, improve their organizations, build teams, and develop themselves. For most people in the civil environment, their job is what they do; in the military it more deeply defines who they are. Members of the military and their families share a unique bond, professional ethics, ethos, and value system. With this in mind, military personnel, especially the officers, are expected to observe a sense of calmness even in the most stressful situations. Ultimately, military bearing and discipline are key essentials in the soldier's life. This is not only because that is how the army wants them to act, but also because they are ways to tell other soldiers who they are and where they stand in the code and law of the Armed Forces. Minute details on everything that the officer does, refining the endless search for perfection in performing daily tasks and duties, practising obedience by following orders, and taking the initiative on self-improvement are some examples of military discipline.

Memories of Training at the Ghana Military Academy

Even though I am not an ancient veteran, my days at the Academy resonates each time I pass by the gate of the Military Academy and Training Schools (MATS). I recall countless times when I was subjected to physically rigorous punishment because I had not properly dressed my bed, or not done a task to its minutest detail. Through these punishments and the intentional creation of discomfort, my colleagues and I learnt to perfect and accomplish goals more easily. There were occasions during which my failure to adhere to instruction affected my colleagues as well. Esprit d'corps, fellow feeling and concern for a colleague were paramount in all endeavours we undertook. The steeple chase runs, map reading exercises, long treks, mountaineering, jungle training, range exercises, airborne training and others, built the needed cohesion, team work, military bearing and discipline in the officer-cadet. Our seniors also shared similar stories with us; some we found to be extreme, but we later grew to appreciate them. There were a number of occasions when some of my colleagues contemplated quitting. Interestingly, anytime they confided in a colleague, they discovered that their plight was not as much as half the pain and stress felt by the comforter. Fellow feeling, empathy, conviviality and care kept us moving, with each passing day, and celebrated as a milestone. 'No pain, no gain', what makes the grass grow ...., 'undue haste makes waste', 'behave a local', 'combatants', 'arear-front, 'gorri-gorri-gorri', and 'ahoo…., ahoyaa…' were some of the refreshing slogans and quotes that kept us going.

We would complain of fatigue, but the 'road runs' later became our source of energy and inspiration. The songs were infectious and the choreographed musical presentations and renditions either on the walk or run, were spectacles to behold. From 'amatuule, amaatule' to 'kenkeynemane Soja' through Maaley maaley- maaley wa' to 'when I go heaven' were too infectious and inspirational for anyone to quit. The overnight remembrance ceremony or celebration of our heroic 'Lt Mensah's' funeral in a mosquito infested outer environment was in itself, a solemn spectacle to behold. I do not think any officer cadet who participated in the funeral celebration would ever forget the exceptional stagecraft exhibited by our seniors and the full participation of junior cadets. One would grow to accept that the training caused the seniors to craft a near perfect scenario for such an occasion. We could not quit because we seemed to share the same pain! I remember a medical officer cadet coming to me to prescribe medicine for the cure of 'her' swollen leg! That was the extent to which we trusted our fellows for the most effective advice, just for our survival. The mention of river 'Kosiko' at the Ghana Armed Forces Jungle Warfare School at Achiase is enough for anyone to reminisce some experiences from the School. Military ethics, discipline, bearing and morale kept us indoors during the 22 months stay at the Ghana Military Academy. Indeed, for one to 'feel' Accra, you must just wake up in the night and watch the blinking lights in the distance. That was the standard which could guarantee commitment to the national cause borne out of pride and undiluted loyalty to the colours.

There was this 'heaving bar' or 'un-doored gate', at the Military Academy. It was yet another constant reminder of the central role of self-discipline and adherence to order. The inscription on the bar, weird as we initially found it, was later found to be apt! *'Abandon all hope of normal life all ye who pass this gate'*. How could anyone abandon hope of 'normal' life? What was the definition of 'normal' in the military? Was it a gate? a punishment bar? a heaving bar? or a gate without a door?   I asked initially. But I grew to know and appreciate that, indeed, one's meal could only be guaranteed after 'successfully' passing through the 'un-gated' heaving bar. I say successfully, because the 'seniors' would devise or orchestrate all manner of 'tricks', including physical training exercises for execution before one could be guaranteed his/her meal. 'Give me ten pushups, give me 20 heave ups, go round the block, sing louder… etc., were some of the demands that guaranteed one's qualifications for a meal. Indeed, the mental posture, character and trait of the senior cadet on duty and his colleagues on 'restriction' were yet other keys to the 'ungated' heaving bar. We saw some of our seniors as 'devil incarnates' and therefore in dread of our survival when they were on duty.

In the course of time, we grew to understand that, indeed, life at the Academy was not the 'normal' normal – sleeplessness, fatigue, unfinished jobs, extra care, tidiness, brisk walking and marching in teams became our portion. It was at the Academy that I 'discovered' that the 24 hours in a day was not enough for our comfort. We were told, and indeed we grew to appreciate that, anytime you appeared to have time on your hand, it meant you might have forgotten something! We grew, however, to appreciate that they were part of the exercises for our 'toughening' and the development of our 'mental agility'. Indeed, it was at the military academy that I first came across what was called 'annoyance parade'. This practice was meant to 'root out' that negative character trait that caused some persons to be infuriated at the least provocation. The living area of the Officer Cadet (Cadet Lines) was not fenced with any brick wall or concertina, but was seen as if it was a kind of a Biblical Jericho wall, or the fence of the office of the Bureau of National Investigation (BNI) of Ghana. We saw Accra to be very far yet it was so near. Discipline and self-denial made the mind to believe this. Military ethics, discipline, fellow feeling, high morale and bearing kept us indoors during our 22 rigorous and treacherous months' stay at the military academy. We were taught and mentored to be disciplined in order to stand the demands ahead, for God and country.

At the Military Academy, our first Course Commander, who unfortunately did not complete our formative career path with us, was instrumental in moulding us to develop resilience and a positive leadership mindset. He was an officer commissioned at Royal Military Academy, Sandhurst in the United Kingdom. On return and through his career path, he seemed to have discovered that a lot of time was being 'wasted' on other issues that were not critical to our professional and mental development. He therefore set forth to engender some change in the environment which had been used to develop an ex-ante strategy of 'working on the brute as against the brain'. He told us to 'read not weed'. By this, he encouraged and indeed admonished us, to focus on the core academic and professional development rather than focusing on unrelated issues. He also guided us not to 'major on the minors.' 'Majoring on the minors', I grew to understand, meant that we focused on what was irrelevant and beneficial on any endeavour (the minors). We were made to 'cut the fat' and avoid all 'time wasters'. If you say that someone or something is a time waster, you mean that they cause you to spend a lot of time doing something that is unnecessary or does not produce any benefit. In friendship and in building our social capital, he enjoined us to avoid anyone who causes us to waste time doing something that does not achieve any good result. We were to focus on what is relevant at all times and behave in a selfless, humane and empathetic manner towards our colleagues and subordinates at all times.

The late Brigadier General's advice and mentorship, I would say, has been part of my yearning to contribute to knowledge in leadership. The General was right! It is not strange for the officer, and the military person, to be empathetic and caring. After all, command and leadership embodies complete subordination of one's interest to the common good of all. In the military, we are told that time is the non-renewable factor of development and achievement of set objectives. Everything else can be recreated with varying costs, but time is irretrievable. According to Waheed, Shahzad and Khurshid, 'no morning can be repeated, no noon and no evening can come again'.

In my study, I found some research very instructive on the topic of time wasters. It has been discovered that the effective exploitation and utilization of time has a positive effect on the regular function and development of an organization. However, individuals waste time for many reasons. A study at the University of Cape Coast in Ghana by Sefenu in 2001, for example, concluded that, time wasting among Senior Administrative Personnel in the Central Administration was very high. The study revealed that up to 50% of official time was lost by the personnel. According to Brain Tracy, the average worker has admitted in a research to wasting about three hours of their workday on non-work-related tasks. That is three times as much time as employers had suspected, costing businesses about $759 billion in wasted salaries every year. A report issued by Salary.com in 2019, indicated that about 4% of workers admit to wasting as much as half of their workday doing things that have nothing to do with their jobs. Available statistics reveal that about 64% of workers use the internet for personal issues during the workday and 50% make personal phone calls or send texts during office hours. Additionally, some 60% of workers admit to making online purchases when they are supposed to be working, and many more play video games. Nevertheless, the use of time for personal issues is not the only workday waster affecting businesses.

We should note that, twenty years ago, cell phones were not a problem at work. Now, everyone has one, and it is becoming more of a distraction in the company. In the security services, including the military and the police, it has become a liability. A recent research by LearnStuff.com, and collaborated by American Express found that, social media at work costs companies an estimated $650 million each year because of lost productivity. Some in-office time wasters that employees report include gossip (42%), social interaction with co-workers (32%), snacks and breaks (27%), meetings (23%) and in-office noise distractions (24%). Thirty-one percent of employees admit to wasting 30 minutes a day at work. That number should not be surprising, but what was surprising was that, 4% of employees admitted to wasting 4 or more hours a day at work. That makes up nearly half the work day! One report also estimates that if every employee in the United States wastes a mere 36 seconds per day, the cost is an astronomical US$120,484,000 every year! Interestingly, the average American worker, for example, wastes two hours and five minutes each day - not counting lunch - translating to a productivity loss of more than $759 billion a year. While it has been dubbed the 'new smoke break', employees tend to be sucked into it and lose track of time. The General cautioned us to avoid time wasters, and he was right. The case of Ghana and many developing countries is worse. These have been so because many people lack self-discipline and many organisations do not have strict systems to control time wastage.

Discipline has always been the cornerstone upon which the tradition, name, fame, and valour of the armed forces is built. Leaders within the Ghana Armed Forces, just like their counterparts around the world, have the competitive advantage; the service possesses qualities that technology cannot replace nor can they be substituted by advanced weaponry and platforms. The modern military therefore demands trained and ready units with agile, proficient leaders. Developing our leaders is integral to our institutional success for today and tomorrow. It is an important investment to make for the future of the military because it builds trust in relationships and units, prepares leaders for future uncertainty, and is critical to readiness and our Army's success [1]. Leader-development programmes must recognize, produce, and reward leaders who are inquisitive, creative, adaptable, and capable of exercising mission command borne out of trust in excellence. Leaders must exhibit a commitment to developing subordinates through the execution of their professional responsibility to teach, counsel, coach, and mentor subordinates. Successful, robust leader development programmes incorporate accountability, engagement, and commitment; create agile and competent leaders; produce stronger organizations and teams; and increase expertise by reducing gaps between knowledge and resources.

The Leadership Development Process

Military leadership-development has been noted to be the deliberate, continuous, sequential, and progressive process, founded on military values that grows soldiers (officers) and military civilians into competent and confident leaders capable of taking decisive action even in the midst of confusion. Leadership development is to be achieved through the lifelong synthesis of the knowledge, skills, and experiences gained through the training and education opportunities in the institutional, operational, and self-development domains [2]. Leadership development, therefore, involves multiple practices

---

[1]. Field Manual, No. 6-22, Washington, 2015

[2]. Army Regulation 350–1, Army Training and Leader Development, Department of the Army, 2014

that ensure that people have the opportunities to fulfil their goals, and that the military has capable leaders in position and ready for the future. The practices include recruiting, accession, training, education, assigning, promoting, broadening scope, and retaining the best leaders, while challenging them over time, with greater responsibility, authority, and accountability. A military leader, by virtue of assumed role or assigned responsibility, is expected to inspire and influence people to accomplish organizational goals. Army leaders motivate people both inside and outside the chain of command to pursue actions, focus thinking, and shape decisions for the greater good of the organization.[3] These occur through leadership which is the process of influencing people by providing purpose, direction, and motivation to accomplish the mission and improve the organization.[4]

Military leaders assume progressively broader responsibilities across direct, organisational (Unit), and strategic levels of leadership. To maintain 'good order and discipline' commanders at all levels are given widespread authority over the personal affairs of their subordinates and held personally responsible to resolve any issues that could potentially affect the performance of duty. The military develops its officers at all echelons to understand and practise the mission command philosophy to lead and execute unified land operations. The Army expects officers to integrate leader-development practices with collective and individual training to accomplish the Army's missions and develop subordinates for future responsibilities. They routinely operate direct-level interactions with others and work at the organizational and strategic levels to plan, prepare, execute, and assess leader development policies, systems, and practices. Warrant officers serve at all echelons as the primary integrators and managers of Army systems. They bring an

---

3. Headquarters Department of the Army, ADP-22 Army Leadership, August 2012

4. Ibid

unequalled depth of knowledge, experience, and perspective in their primary areas of expertise. Warrant officers at all echelons are to understand and practise the mission command philosophy to execute unified land operations. Non-Commissioned Officers (NCOs) are responsible for setting and maintaining high-quality standards and discipline while conducting daily missions and making intent-driven decisions. NCOs serve as standard-bearers and role models vital to training, educating, and developing subordinates.

Through training, coaching, mentoring, counselling, and informal interaction, they guide the development of soldiers on everyday basis and play a role in the development of junior officers. NCOs, at all echelons, understand and practise the mission command philosophy to execute unified land operations. NCOs advise officers at all levels and are an important source of knowledge and discipline for all enlisted officers. Army civilians provide crucial continuity that complements the roles of soldiers. Civilian employee leaders also require a broad understanding of military, political, and business-related strategies, as well as, high levels of managerial, leadership, and decision-making skills. Army civilians create and practise leader development for other army civilians and support the development of military personnel while serving as supervisors, mentors, and instructors. At all echelons, army civilians should understand and exercise the mission command philosophy while providing mission-based capabilities to support army missions. Cultural and individual mindsets that promote continuous learning are the cornerstone for creating and sustaining an agile army. Through activities in the institutional, operational, and self-development, domains, personnel obtain education, training, and experiences in order to grow and be able to succeed in positions of greater responsibility.

The Transitional Leadership Challenge

The military in Ghana, and many other militaries across Africa, are said to be in transition. This is especially so when telecommunication, bio-related pandemics, peacekeeping, hybrid counter insurgency and low intensity internal security operational deployments have come to affect the traditional role of the institution. History has shown that leadership lessons can be lost during a transition period. Soldiers deserve good leaders. The distinction between managers and leaders is crucial and clear; managers are efficient and leaders are effective [5]. Military leaders have to be good stewards of the institutional values and professionals in and out of the barracks and mission area. General Marshall, for example believes values and professionalism go hand in hand. He noted that, after WW I, the success of the United States of America came from the courage of the individual leaders and soldiers and not by the 'soundness' of centralized leadership doctrine. [6] He argued further that it is essential for the leader to know from personal contact the mental, moral, and physical state of his troops, the conditions with which they are confronted, their accomplishments, their desires, and their needs.

For military organizations and the leader to survive in the transitional period, there are six transition points spanning the full range of organizational levels. These include: [7]

▢ **Leading at the Direct Level**: Initial-entry soldiers and civilian transition from a focus on self to providing direct leadership to others. Junior leaders learn how to plan daily tasks and activities, understand organizational constructs, and how to interact with subordinates, peers, and superiors. In Ghana

---

5. Warren G. Bennis and Burt Nanus, Leaders: Strategies For Taking Charge, 2nd ed. (New York: Harper Business, 1997.

6. Pogue, George C. Marshall: Education of a General: 250.

7. Field Manual 6-22 (Leadership Development), Op sit

for example, learning is fashioned to happen in one of three ways:

a. In training which replicates the challenge of war;

b. Through doctrine, backed by study positive attitudes related to trust, accepting advice, and accepting feedback will pay dividends during this phase and into the future; and

c. Through experiences during combat, including peace enforcement.

- **Leading Organizations**: The second transition occurs when leaders begin to lead at the organizational level. This level begins at platoon, company, battery, troop, staff, Unit, Command and similar organization levels for army civilians. Direct level leadership still occurs at this level, but the leaders become leaders of leaders and will rarely be performing individual tasks, unless out of emergency or in undermanned organizations. Coaching subordinate, direct-line leaders and setting a positive example as a leader are two characteristics that stand out for managers.

- **Leading Functions**: The third transition is from leading an organization (as a leader of direct-line leaders) to leading functions. This level involves directing functions beyond a single individual's experience path. Operating with other leaders of leaders and adopting a longer-term perspective are key characteristics of this phase. Functional leaders typically include majors, mid-level warrant officers, and mid-level NCOs.

- **Leading Integration:** A fourth transition occurs when leaders assume command and leadership responsibility for battalion and similar sized generating force organizations. These leaders must become more adept at establishing a vision, communicating it, and deciding on goals and mission outcomes. They need to find more time for reflection and analysis and value the importance of making trade-offs between future goals and current needs.

- **Leading Large Organizations**:   A fifth transition happens when leaders operate at the brigade equivalent and higher levels of operational and institutional organizations. These leaders develop strategy for organizational and strategic-level operations. They are operating outside their experience paths while leading others operating beyond theirs as well. Leaders in this phase will only be successful by valuing the expertise and success of others and operating within the multiple layers of their organization. Humility is a desired characteristic of organizational and strategic leaders who should recognize that others have specialized expertise indispensable to success. A modest view of one's own importance helps underscore an essential ingredient to foster cooperation across organizational boundaries. Even the most humble person needs to guard against an imperceptible inflation of ego when constantly exposed to high levels of attention and opportunities.

- **Leading the Enterprise**: A final step occurs in the transition to serving as an enterprise leader. Enterprise leaders are to be long-term, visionary thinkers who spend considerable time interacting with agencies beyond the military. This level of leadership must be willing to relinquish control of the pieces of the enterprise to strategic and lower-level leaders.

Leadership and the Levels of War

There is no agreed definition of war today; among the multitude offered, none works across time and cultures. And that is simple, if we are thinking of conflict between groups of humans with some organisation and not that with other species. The situation is complicated by the host of what could be characterised as "non-traditional conflicts" to which the term is applied and has long been applied. Some have resulted in killings; others have not. The classic instance of the use of the term *war* across much of history is that of conflict over religion, both between religions and, more profoundly, between good and evil. A different and far more recent instance of a use of the term *war* that very much overlap with violence is that of 'war on terror.' With an overlap, but less of an overlap, there is 'war on drugs' and 'war on crime,' let alone cancer, poverty, among others. This flood of 'wars' leads to a normalisation of the term in English. In functional terms, war can be seen as both organised and non-organised large-scale violence. This definition separates war from say the actions of an individual, however violent the means or consequences. It also separates war from non-violent action, however much, as in "direct action," it can be an aspect of coercion. The definition also creates a gap with large-scale violence in which the organisation is not that of war, for example, football hooliganism. Hooligan groups plan for "battle" with each other. Each of these points and caveats can be detailed and qualified, but they draw attention not only to fundamental issues of definition, but also to real difference.

War can also be approached in cultural, social and ideological terms, namely as the consequence of bellicosity. [8] The historical context of the term *war* has left an indelible imprint on the minds of strategic leaders and the general public. This imprint limits one's ability to view warfare as anything other than armed conflict between nations. The *Stanford Encyclopaedia of Philosophy* states that "war should be understood as an actual, intentional and widespread armed conflict between political communities.[9] On the first page of *On War*, Carl von Clausewitz defines war as "an act of force to compel our enemy to do our will" [10].Most would agree that these are understandable and

---

8 Jeremy Black, What is War? See also https://defenceindepth.co/2018/06/11/what-is-war/ .

9 Brian Orend, "War", The Stanford Encyclopedia of Philosophy (Fall 2008 Edition), ed. Edward N. Zalta, accessed September 18, 2012, http://plato.stanford.edu/archives/fall2008/entries/war/.

10 Carl von Clausewitz, On War, ed. and trans. Michael Howard and Peter Paret (Princeton, NJ:

accurate definitions in the general context of what the average person thinks when they hear the word war. The military historian, John Keegan offers a useful characterization of the political-rationalist theory of war in his *A History of War*. It is assumed to be an orderly affair in which states are involved, in which there are declared beginnings and expected ends, easily identifiable combatants, and high levels of obedience by subordinates. The form of rational war is narrowly defined, as distinguished by the expectation of sieges, pitched battles, skirmishes, raids, reconnaissance, patrol and outpost duties, with each possessing their own conventions. As such, Keegan notes that the rationalist theory does not deal well with pre-state or non-state peoples and their warfare. However, from the strategic perspective, these definitions are arguably too simplistic to convey the complexity of war and the many facets which contribute to national success in the international arena.

Today's strategic leaders conceptualize and define war in a broader perspective. The new definition encompasses three attributes: the complex characteristics and nuances of war fought in a global society, a broader interpretation of who engages (or should be engaged) in war, as well as how wars may be fought and won in the future. Terrorism and violent aggression conducted by non-state actors require strategic leaders to rethink these traditional characteristics of warfare and the definition of war itself. War is no longer limited to "conflict between states or nations," nor is it fought solely between political communities as the Global War on Terrorism has proven.[11] As Joseph Nye illustrated, "In today's global information age…more things are happening outside the control of even the most powerful states."[12] In 2006, "161 billion gigabytes of digital information were created and captured;"

Princeton University Press, 1976), 75

[11] Merriam-Webster, War, 2012.

[12] Joseph S. Nye, The Future of Power, (New York, NY: Public Affairs), 113.

about "3 million times the information in all the books ever written."[13] This connectivity has driven globalization down to the individual and small group level; enabling non-state actors to think, act, and locate themselves globally; in some cases without ever leaving their home because of technology.[14] A strategic leader's concept of war must necessarily be more encompassing, and also more complex. War is the coherent execution of all means to bring about sufficient adherence to a nation's will in the international (global) arena; resulting in armed conflict only when all other means fail. [15] War is an exercise in domination. It is a lethal adventure applied to expendable populations as some are removed from the land. It may be prompted by religious, economic, and political considerations.

Modern military theory divides war into three levels, which are the strategic, operational, and tactical levels [16,17,18]. This is not different from civil practice. Military leadership therefore transits through the tactical, operational and strategic levels. Although this division has its basis in the Napoleonic wars and the American Civil War, modern theory regarding these three levels was formulated by following the Franco-Prussian War. It has been most thoroughly developed by the Soviets (Russians). The three levels allow causes and effects of all forms of war and conflict to be better understood, despite their growing

---

13 Ibid, 115.

14 Thomas L. Friedman, The World is Flat: A Brief History of the 21st Century, 2005 (New York, NY: Farrar, Straus and Giroux).

15. https://smallwarsjournal.com/jrnl/art/what-is-war-a-new-point-of-view

16. Chris Bellamy, "Trends in Land Warfare: The Operational Art of the European Theater," Defence Yearbook 1985 (London: Brassey's Defence Publishers, 1985), 227–28;

17. Lt Col Clayton R. Newell, "The Levels of War," Army, June 1988, 26–2924–28; and Col Wallace P. Franz, "Maneuver: The Dynamic Element of Combat," Military Review, May 1983, 2–12.

18. Clayton R. Newell, "Modern Warfare: Balancing the Ends, Ways and Means," Army, August 1986,

complexity. It be borne in mind that; the boundaries of the levels of war and conflict tend to blur and do not necessarily correspond to levels of command. Nevertheless, in the Ghanaian system, the strategic level is usually the concern of the National Security Council (NSC)) and the highest military commanders, while the operational level is usually the concern of theatre commanders, and the tactical level is usually the focus of the sub-theatre commanders. Each level is concerned with planning (making strategy), which involves analysing the situation, estimating friendly and enemy capabilities and limitations, and devising possible courses of action.

Corresponding to the strategic, operational, and tactical levels of war and conflict are national (grand) strategy with its national military strategy subcomponent, operational strategy, and battlefield strategy (tactics). Each level also is concerned with implementing strategy, which must be re-evaluated constantly (and usually on the basis of incomplete information) because warfare is dynamic. Therefore, a key to success in war and other conflicts is the ability to adapt rapidly to the changing situation and to exploit transient opportunities rather than strictly adhering to a predetermined course of action. The ability to adapt and exploit requires extraordinary judgment, a "feel" for the situation and knowing what to do and how to do it. The exercise of this good leadership and judgment is the art of war at each level.

a. **The Strategic Level**: The strategic level focuses on defining and supporting national policy, and relates directly to the outcome of a war or other conflict as a whole. Usually, modern wars and conflicts are won or lost at this level rather than at the operational or tactical levels [19]. The strategic level applies to all forms of war and conflict from military activities short of war through insurgent,

---

[19]. Allan R. Millett and Williamson Murray, "Lessons of War," The National Interest, Winter 1988–1989, 83–95.

conventional, and nuclear warfare. This level involves a strategic concept, plans for preparing all national instruments of power for war or conflict, practical guidance for preparing the armed forces, and leadership of the armed forces to achieve strategic objectives. Determining US national security strategy is the responsibility of the NCA. The armed forces contribute through the Chairman of the Joint Chiefs of Staff and the Service Commanders, especially to the military component of the national security strategy.

b. **The Operational Level**: The operational level is concerned with employing military forces in a theatre of war or theatre of operations to obtain an advantage over the enemy and thereby attain strategic goals through the design, organization, and conduct of campaigns and major operations. In war, a campaign involves employment of military forces in a series of related military operations to accomplish a common objective in a given time and space. In activities short of war, a campaign consists of a series of related military, economic, and political operations to accomplish a common objective in a given time and space. Commanders should design, orchestrate, and coordinate operations and exploit tactical events to support overall campaign objectives. Where and when to conduct a campaign is based on objectives, the threat, and limitations imposed by geographical, economic, and cultural environments, as well as the numbers and types of military resources available. The essence of the operational level of war is discovering the enemy's strategy and developing a counterstrategy. This corresponds with Clausewitz's idea that the enemy is 'an animate object that reacts'. Operational strategy as "the art and science of planning, orchestrating, and directing military campaigns within a theatre of operations to achieve national security objective. [20]

c. **The Tactical Level**: In the traditional sense, the various operations that make up a campaign are themselves made up of manoeuvres, engagements, and battles. From this perspective, the tactical level translates potential combat power into success in battles and engagements through decisions and actions that create advantages when in contact with or in proximity to the enemy. Tactics therefore deal with the details of prosecuting engagements and are extremely sensitive to the changing environment of the battlefield [21]. Thus, in nuclear and conventional warfare, the focus of the tactical level is generally on military objectives and combat. However, combat is not an end in itself; it is the means to achieve goals set at the operational level. Drew and Snow, define battlefield strategy or tactics as the art and science of employing forces on the battlefield to achieve national security objectives. The classic differentiation between tactics and higher levels of strategy [or levels of war] remains relevant in the sense that tactics govern the use of forces on the battlefield while grand strategy, [national] military strategy, and operational strategy brings forces to the battlefield . . . .. Tactics are concerned with doing the job 'right,' and higher levels of strategy are concerned with doing the 'right' job. [22]

Interestingly, business tends to use the same approach when dealing with the three levels. In business and its management, the typical military distinction does not play out very well. In business management, strategy can be formulated at three

---

20. Army FM 100-5, Operations, June 1993, 4-1–4-6.

21.

22. Dennis M. Drew And Donald M. Snow, Making Twenty-First-Century Strategy; An Introduction to Modern National Security Processes and Problems. Air University Press, November 2006

levels, namely, the corporate level (military strategic), the business level (military operational), and the functional level (military tactical). At the corporate level, strategy is formulated for the organization as a whole. Corporate strategy therefore deals with decisions related to various business areas in which the firm operates and competes, including aspects of the supply and production value chain. At the business unit level, strategy is formulated to convert the corporate vision into reality. At the functional level, strategy is formulated to realize the business unit level goals and objectives using the strengths and capabilities of the organization. There is a clear hierarchy in levels of strategy, with corporate-level strategy at the top, business-level strategy being derived from the corporate level, and the functional-level strategy being formulated out of the business level strategy. In a single business scenario, the corporate and business level responsibilities are clubbed together and undertaken by a single group, that is, the top management, whereas in a multi business scenario, there are three fully operative levels. [23]

a. **Corporate Level:** Corporate level strategy defines the business areas in which your firm will operate. It deals with aligning the resource deployments across a diverse set of business areas, related or unrelated. Strategy formulation at this level involves integrating and managing the diverse businesses and realizing synergy at the corporate level. The top management team is responsible for formulating the corporate strategy. The corporate strategy reflects the path toward attaining the vision of your organization. For example, your firm may have four distinct lines of business operations, namely, automobiles, steel, tea, and telecom. The corporate level strategy will outline whether the organization should compete in or withdraw from any of

---

[23] https://seprianhidayatamin.wordpress.com/2016/04/23/7-the-three-levels-of-strategy/

these lines of businesses, and in which business unit, investments should be increased, in line with the vision of your firm.

b. **Business Level:** Business-level strategies are formulated for specific strategic business units and relate to a distinct product-market area. It involves defining the competitive position of a strategic business unit. The business level strategy formulation is based upon the generic strategies of overall cost leadership, differentiation, and focus. For example, your firm may choose overall cost leadership as a strategy to be pursued in its steel business, differentiation in its tea business, and focus in its automobile business. The business-level strategies are decided upon by the heads of strategic business units and their teams in light of the specific nature of the industry in which they operate.

c. **Functional Level:** Functional-level strategies relate to the different functional areas which a strategic business unit has, such as marketing, production and operations, finance, and human resources. These strategies are formulated by the functional heads along with their teams and are aligned with the business-level strategies. The strategies at the functional level involve setting up short-term functional objectives, the attainment of which will lead to the realization of the business-level strategy. For example, the marketing strategy for a tea business which is following the differentiation strategy may translate into launching and selling a wide variety of tea variants through company-owned retail outlets. The realization of the functional strategies in the form of quantifiable and measurable objectives will result in the achievement of business level strategies as well.

These levels are invoked in the planning for business sustainability. Strategic planning is an organization's process of defining its strategy, or direction, and making decisions on allocating its resources to pursue this strategy. Generally, strategic planning deals, on the whole business, rather than just an isolated unit, with at least one of three key questions of what to do, who to do for, and how to excel. Operational planning is the process of linking strategic goals and objectives to tactical goals and objectives. It describes milestones, conditions for success and explains how, or what portion of, a strategic plan will be put into operation during a given operational period. An operational plan addresses four questions including:

i. Where are we now?

ii. Where do we want to be?

iii. How do we get there?

iv. How do we measure our progress?

Tactical planning is short-range planning emphasizing the current operations of various parts of the organization. Short range is generally defined as a period of time extending about one year or less into the future. Managers use tactical planning to outline what the various parts of the organization must do for the organization to be successful at some point one year or less into the future. Tactical plans are usually developed in the areas of production, marketing, personnel, finance and plant facilities. Because of the time horizon and the nature of questions, mishaps potentially occurring during the execution of a tactical plan should be covered by moderate uncertainties and may lie closer to the control of management (next year shipping prices, energy consumption, but not a catastrophic black-out, etc.) than strategic ones. Those mishaps, in conjunction to their potential consequences are called 'tactical risks'.

Since senior management generally have a better understanding of the organization as a whole than lower level managers do, senior management generally develops strategic plans. Because lower level managers generally have a better understanding of the day-to- day organizational operations, they would usually develop tactical and operational plans. Because strategic plans are generally long term and are surrounded by more uncertainties in terms of their occurrence and consequences (with an exception being tailings management planned until closure, and after closure) they are generally less detailed than tactical plans. However, despite their differences, strategic, tactical and operational planning are integrally related. Managers need both tactical and strategic planning programmes, and these programmes need to be closely related to be successful.

In the military, interaction with colleagues, superiors, subordinates, families, civilian employees, other security agencies, the wider populace including higher civil authority and security actors all form part of the transition processes in developing the leadership trait of the military leader. Even though military Commanders, Generals and strategists have revealed some key traits that must be exhibited by their leaders. The position of General Eisenhower will be instructive for our purpose. According to General Eisenhower, what soldiers expect from their leaders include:

- Honest, just, and fair treatment.
- Consideration due them as mature, professional soldiers.
- Personal interest takes in them as individuals.
- Loyalty.
- Shielding from harassment from 'higher up'.
- The best in leadership.
- That their needs be anticipated and provided for.
- All the comforts and privileges practicable.
- To be kept oriented and told the 'reason why'.
- A well-thought-out programme of training, work and recreation.
- Clear-cut and positive decisions and orders which are not constantly changing.
- Demands on them commensurate with their capabilities – not too small, not too great.
- That their good work be recognized, and publicized when appropriate. [24,25]

Lieutenant General Moore, a veteran of the Korean war, on the other hand, gave four principles of conduct needed in battle for leaders. [26] In the first of his four interrelated principles, he states that the leader can either inspire confidence in his unit or contaminate the environment and his unit with his attitude and actions. The leader must therefore:

- Be visible on the battlefield.

---

24. General Bruce C. Clarke, "General Bruce C. Clarke: A Study in Leadership and Training," ed. Missouri U.S. Army Training Center Engineer and Fort Leonard Wood (MO,1980), ii.

25. Major Gregory W. McLean A Monograph, U.S. Army, Fort Leavenworth, Kansas

26. Connelly, On war and leadership: the words of combat commanders from Frederick the Great to Norman Schwarzkopf: 214.

- Exhibit determination.
- Demonstrate the will to win.
- Remain calm and cool.
- Show no fear.
- Ignore the noise of war (dust, smoke, explosions, screams and yell of the wounded and dead)
- Never give a hint of uncertainty.

These characteristics were very relevant when the Severe Acute Respiratory Syndrome Coronavirus 2 (SARS-CoV-2) infected people in a number of countries in late 2019 and the greater part of 2020. During this period, leadership across the globe was tested in real time. Countries and institutions whose leaders (Presidents, Heads of State, Directors, Commanders, etc.) demonstrated these traits were able to bring the pandemic to an appreciable level of control. In the modern sense, war may not necessarily be the combat between or among belligerents but anything that will hinder the realisation of human safety, security and economic potential can be routed through 'war'.

Conversely, General Ulmer and his team drew conclusions on the behaviours validated by officers returning from theatres of combat. They therefore selected twelve (12) behaviours, which were considered as the most important factors for leader success in combat. [27] These leadership traits referred to as the 'Big 12' were meant to help define the differences between a 'good' and a 'bad' leader. These are that the leader:

- Keeps cool under pressure.
- Clearly explains missions, standards, and priorities.
- Sees the big picture; provides context and perspective.
- Can make tough, sound decisions on time.
- Adapts quickly to new situations and requirements.
- Sets high standards without a 'zero defects' mentality.

---

27. Lieutenant General Walter F. Ulmer, "Leader Behavior: How to Identify Good Leaders," Armor 2006.

- Can handle 'bad news.'
- Coaches and gives useful feedback to subordinates.
- Sets a high ethical tone; demands honest reporting.
- Knows how to delegate and not 'micromanage'.
- Builds and supports teamwork within staff and among units.
- Is positive, encouraging, and realistically optimistic.

These are the traits of leaders when leading men and women in combat, not a long drawn out vignettes or definitions, which takes two to three pages to set out.

As has been noted by Schoomaker and Brownlee, the adversaries of today, regular and irregular, will be well armed, well trained, well equipped, committed, believing in a course and often ideologically inspired. They will be patient, and they will adapt. [28] The military must therefore overmatch their training and the development of the leader- officers and men. Speed and adaptability in combat is what gives the military its competitive edge over the enemy. We must learn faster, understand better, and adapt more rapidly. It is to this end that Francis Harvey, former Secretary of the Army in the US said that leaders in this century' 'need to be pent-athletes, multi-skilled' who can thrive in uncertain and complex operating environments. Additionally, they are to be innovative and adaptive experts in the art and science of the profession of arms. In essence, the military needs leaders who are decisive, innovative, adaptive, culturally astute, effective communicators and dedicated to lifelong learning [29].

---

28. Peter J. Schoomaker and R.L. Brownlee, 'Our Army at War - Relevant and Ready… Today and Tomorrow. A game Plan for Advancing Army Objectives in FY05 and Beyond,' *Thinking Strategically*, 28 October 2004.

29. Department of the Army, *Field Manual (FM) 6-22 Army Leadership*, (Washington, DC: Government Printing Office, 2006), 2-4, Figure 2-2.

Military Leadership as a Process

Leadership is a process, which can be intuitive because soldiers and officers have to be framed and moulded in character. [30] General Bradley in applying leadership for combat indicated that 'just as the diamond requires three properties for its formation; carbon, heat, and pressure, successful leaders require the interaction of three properties of character, knowledge, and application. Like carbon to the diamond, character is the basic quality of the leader. Nevertheless, as carbon alone does not create a diamond, neither can character alone create a leader. The diamond needs heat. Man, therefore, needs knowledge, and preparation. The third property, pressure, acting in conjunction with carbon and heat forms the diamond. Similarly, one's character attended by knowledge, blooms through application to produce a leader'. [31] General Odeirno, who once commanded troops in Iraq defined his intent, priorities, principles, and his leader expectations. These were captured in some eight (8) points of leader expectation. [32] To him, the leader must:

- Have a vision and lead change.
- Be the formation's moral and ethical compass.
- Learn, think, and adapt.
- Balance risk and opportunity to retain the initiative.
- Build agile, effective, high performing teams.
- Empower subordinates and underwrite risk.
- Develop bold, adaptive, and broadened leaders.
- Build and encourage nested communication – up, down, and laterally, tell the whole story.

---

[30]. General U.S. Army Edward C. Meyer, 'Leadership: A Return to Basics," Military Review LX, no. July NO. 7 (1980).

[31]. General of the Army Omar N. Bradley, 'Leadership," Parameters Winter (1972): 7; Edward C. Meyer, "Leadership: A Return to Basics.'

[32]. Chief of Staff of the Army General Raymond T. Odeirno, "Marching Orders, 38th Chief of Staff, U.S. Army, America's Force of Decisive Action ", ed. United States Army (Washington D.C.: United States Army, 2012).

At the organizational level, leadership is an act of influence between at least two people in the pursuit of organizational goals or objectives. Leadership style, therefore, is the pattern of behaviour used by a leader as recognized by those who are led. Therefore, effective leadership is a combination of three factors: Leader, Follower, and Situation. This is summed up as:

$$EL = f(L: F: S)$$

Where:

EL	=	Effective Leadership
L	=	Leader
F	=	Follower
S	=	Situation

In my experience and training as a military officer, the formula is not exhaustive. I am of the conviction that the Situation is also composed of two elements of Environment (En) and Time (Tm) and moderated by Technology (Te). The formula, therefore, should stand as:

$$EL = f(L: F: S \{En \times Tm\}/Te)$$

Where:

EL	=	Effective Leadership
L	=	Leader
F	=	Follower
S	=	Situation
En	=	Environment
Tm	=	Time
Te	=	Technology

Technology has come to affect the action of leaders so much that nothing can literally be done in secret against any group of persons. Technology will expose the act and thus help court local and international pressure to be brought upon the perpetrating leader, if he seeks to abuse his followers. Organizational effectiveness is also defined by near-term accomplishments. This means that the leader's effectiveness will be defined by the sum of all the parts in the bracket.

Observed Deterioration of Standards

Interestingly, the observance of the deterioration of standards in military service is not a recent phenomenon. General John McAllister Schofield, who held major commands during the American Civil War, figured this out in the late 1800s. In 1899, the Secretary of the Army in the United States, Elihu Root stated, among others, that 'the Army was defective and needed improvement and it ought to be improved.' [33] Schofield in his 'definition of decline' notes that the discipline which makes the soldiers of a free country reliable in battle is not to be gained by harsh or tyrannical treatment. On the contrary, such treatment is far more likely to destroy than to make an army. It is possible to impart instruction and give commands in such a manner and such a tone of voice as to inspire in the soldier no feeling, but an intense desire to obey, while the opposite manner and tone of voice cannot fail to excite strong resentment and a desire to disobey. The one mode or the other of dealing with subordinates spring from a corresponding spirit in the breast of the commander. He who feels the respect which is due to others cannot fail to inspire in them regard for himself, while he who feels, and hence manifests, disrespect toward others, especially his inferiors, cannot fail to inspire hatred against himself'. [34,35] Although today's army is not defective, leaders in 1939-41 had much more operational experience with combat and specifically with leadership in combat, much more than today's leaders. The military and civil leadership have come to the crossroads yet again. Leaders in the Ghana Armed Forces (GAF) may have operational experience, which cannot be lost to future warriors.

---

[33]. Kretchik, U.S. Army Doctrine: from the American Revolution to the War on Terror: 151.

[34]. https://www.themilitaryleader.com/quotes/schofield-on-discipline/

[35]. Major General John M. Schofield in an address to the Corps of Cadets, August 11, 1879.)

The GAF leadership experience missions in the World, West African Peace Enforcement tours, and the various hybrid peacekeeping operations across the globe are important experiences.

In 2009, the Chief of the Defence Staff of the Ghana Armed Forces, Lt Gen Blay during an Army Regimental Sergeant Majors' (RSMs) Annual Convention at 6 Infantry Battalion, decried the falling standards of discipline, traditions and values of the GAF.[36] Later in 2014, some retired officers of Ghana Military Academy Intake VIII, visited the Academy to share their experiences and challenges with the cadet officers as part of their 50th anniversary celebration. On that occasion, Rear Admiral Jonathan Yanful Adoko, the President of the Intake, told the officers the importance of good leadership qualities in their chosen career. He thus urged them to work on such virtues in order to become leaders of the military. Lieutenant Colonel Awudu Rahman, a member of the Intake also advised the officers not to get themselves involved in politics as the duty of the military man or woman is to protect democracy as well as ensure the peace and stability of the nation. [37] Interestingly, in 2015, some 501 recruits were sacked from the Ghana Army Recruits Training School (ARTS) for what was classified as 'misbehaviour and a threat to national security' [38] occasioned by gross indiscipline.

In 2017 during the graduation ceremony for Special Cadet Intake III, a call for knowledge upgrade and enhanced professional competence to deal with national security challenges was made by the President of Ghana. The President reiterated that the

---

[36]. https://www.ghanaweb.com/GhanaHomePage/NewsArchive/CDS-decries-falling-standards-of-discipline-in-GAF-161434

[37]. https://www.newsghana.com.gh/millitary-officers-urged-to-be-discipline/

[38]. https://www.myjoyonline.com/news/2015/December-30th/sacked-501-recruits-the-inside-story.php

prevailing global dynamics and the new forms of security challenges could only be dealt with by security personnel who would adopt innovative strategies and adhere to ethical standards. Personnel, therefore, were required to be prepared mentally, physically and professionally to meet that challenge. [39] Officers' training, which translates into the disciplined lifestyle is expected to be anchored on dedication to duty, personal and professional integrity, and diligence in safeguarding the country's image. Discipline is to be a learned behaviour. It is a state of order and obedience that is a result of regulations and orders. For any unit to achieve their objective, they must be disciplined. Discipline is training that develops, moulds, strengthens, or perfects the mental faculties and character. It involves placing group goals above one's own, being willing to accept orders from higher authority, and carrying out those orders effectively. We are taught that military discipline is that mental attitude and state of training which renders instinctive obedience under all conditions. It is founded upon respect for, and loyalty to properly constituted authority. While it is developed primarily by military drill, every feature of military life has its effects on military discipline.

I am not a very old 'veteran'. However, I find it regrettable to note that, one of the most discussed topics about the military and the security services in general, has been the steady decline of the standard of discipline, bearing and leadership in recent times. Generally, there has been an observed steady decline or reduced discipline and incidence of poor bearing in today's Ghanaian society. It is imperative to note the observed fall in standards of virtues, values, discipline, family ties, loyalty, sincerity, selflessness, etc., in the service. Most personnel want to take short cuts to achieve success and acquire wealth. Discipline, however, is to help separate the 'sheep from the

---

[39]. https://www.graphic.com.gh/news/general-news/enhance-competence-to-deal-with-security-challenges-prez-tells-armed-forces.html

goats.' During disasters and crises, (earthquakes, floods, riots, or any other calamity) where the civil institutions are unable to cope, the military is usually called in as the only reliable institution available for any day. The morale of the personnel in the Armed Forces in recent times has been dependent on:

    i.   the environment of their social circle;

   ii.   their comfort zone, including the living conditions, food, recreation and leave;

  iii.   the Security of their family;

  iv.   their salary and other enumerations including allowances;

   v.   the general bearing and sharp outlook;

  vi.   self-respect based on how seniors and peers are viewed and the status in society; and

 vii.   the posture of the general populace towards their contribution to national good.

Proximal Reasons for Dwindling Discipline and Standards

Governments and the military high command have strived to provide what is needed to guarantee high morale and maintain discipline but the standards continue to fall. Why then have the standards of discipline gone down? The following are some of the reasons cited to have combined to affect the standards of bearing and discipline in the military:

1. **An Officer's Tenure within the Battalion**: The average Infantry Officer spends more than 50 per cent tenure outside the battalion on missions, doing professional courses and staff and instructional tenures. The case of the other ranks could be worse. The number of operations and the rate of rotations is another source of worry. Today, the trend is for officers to take some years of study leave and do management or other vocational courses, which will help them rehabilitate and transit well into civil life after

retirement. The average soldier is now retiring at the young old age of 40 – 45 years. To further compound matters, there is an acute shortage of officers and junior commissioned officers. The middle rung officers are therefore being stretched to breaking point.

2. **High Stress Levels**. Deployments to support civil authority, such as Operations Calm Life, Gong Gong, Vanguard, Cow Leg, with no specific end point of mission creates high levels of stress among personnel. Some of these environments could be hostile with a 'no mistake' tag attached. This puts a heavy responsibility on the officer's shoulders. Commanders at all levels feel the stress. This aspect will have to be addressed if we wish to overcome lapses in discipline. When officers and other rank leaders rub shoulders with their subordinates, they bond with them. They know you; you know them. 'Know your men and they will follow you to hell and back.'

3. **Rapidly Changing Social Values**: The officer and soldier are both parts of the same society. There are always some rotten apples in the basket. These are more the exceptions than the rule. The GAF have a glorious past on which is based the traditions and values of a regiment or a battalion. The situation in the army grows worse every day: information coming in from all sides indicates that the army is systematically falling apart. As has been noted by Castells, in the last quarter of the twentieth century, a technological revolution centered on information has transformed the way we think, produce, consume, trade, communicate, and even how we make love. [40] The availability of information technology around the world is linking up valuable people and activities while switching off

---

[40]. Castells, M. (2000). The Rise of the Network Society, The Information Age: Economy, Society and Culture, Vol. I. Oxford: Blackwell Publishing Ltd.

from conventional networks of power and wealth. To a large extent, cyberspace is the manifestation of postmodern society whereby novel technologies have created a new social environment and a new reality. We are now living in an era of simulations, where humans are constantly "substituting signs of the real for the real". [41] The line between reality and unreality is blurred, and in the postmodern world, it is difficult to tell the real from those things that simulate the real. [42]

4. **Civil Control:** It is true that the military is expected to be subservient to civil authority, but the extent of control has been far too invasive. There have been occasions where without proper planning, the civil authority has sanctioned the deployment of personnel. Additionally, there are recorded situations where civil authority has tended to dictate the shape of the disciplinary board. In Ghana, the fear of a coup d'état has led to situations where successive governments have been 'tightening' their grip over the military.

5. **Weak Troop Welfare and Support Systems**: By regulation, the soldier is highly restricted in what he can do. A study of military culture and regimentation reveals a stark difference to what his civil counterpart can do. Military culture incorporates unity, a sense of purpose and direction, and values that you find in most civilian career fields. Overall, military culture is a unique one; [43] one that presents distinctive challenges for its service members and their family members. [44,45] While the military itself can be

---

41. Baudrillard, J. (1995). 'Simulacra and Simulations'. Michigan: University of Michigan Press

42. Ritzer, G. (1996). Postmodern Social Theory. New York: McGraw-Hill Publishing

43. Luby, C. D. (2012). Promoting Military Cultural Awareness In An Off-Post Community Of Behavioral Health And Social Support Service Providers. *Advances in Social Work, 13*, 67–82.

44. Brown, M., & Lettieri, C. (2008). State policymakers: Military families. Retrieved from

viewed as a profession, the military extends into the service members' personal realms as well, affecting everyday lifestyle as well as the lifestyle of family members [46]. Rank and order are rigid in the military, with service members expected to show respect for and compliance with their superiors. This authoritarian structure may be mimicked in the military family's home life as well. Overall, a service member's rank determines how much is earned financially, how much education is provided, the level of access to resources and the expected amount of responsibility. There are clearly defined rules and expectations for military service members and their families, including etiquette guidelines for spouses and children regarding dress, mannerisms and behaviour in public. Military families are directed where to live, when they can travel and with whom they can socialize. Additionally, higher ranking service members exercise authority over the family's personal life.

6. **Unrewarding Self-Sacrifice:** Imbedded deeper within military culture is the notion of self-sacrifice. Guided by the ideal that the individual is secondary to the unit, military family members face numerous deployments, relocations and separation from one another. These challenges are expected and anticipated, as they are a constant reality for military families in times of war and peace. For example, the deployment cycle is continuous, affecting family members as they prepare for, experience and reunite after the deployment. In the midst of these challenges, over half

---

https://workfamily.sas.upenn.edu/
sites/workfamily.sas.upenn.edu/files/imported/pdfs/policy_makers15.pdf

45. Gooddale, R., Abb, W. R., & Moyer, B. A. (2012). *Military culture 101: Not one culture, but many cultures*. Retrieved from
http://www.citizensoldiersupport.org/lib/resources/ORNC%20Military%20Culture%20101%20 Workshop%2014%20Sep%2012.pdf

46. Cozza, S. J., & Lerner, R. M. (2013). Military children and families: Introducing the issue. *Military Children and Families*, 23(2), 3–11

of military family members have reported that they are satisfied with the military lifestyle, emphasizing their commitment to routinely facing and overcoming challenges.

7. **Political Infiltration**: It is very common to find military leaders aligned to political parties. This situation has been observed to affect the delivery and morale of personnel. Even though not common, some personnel are deployed and or promoted by virtue of their perceived political leaning. Additionally, some persons are recruited or enter the various military institutions not based on merit, but on some 'protocol' arrangements. The 501 recruits who were sacked in 2015 were reported to have had such effrontery to complain about the intensity of the training because some of them were well connected with some political authority or an executive power.

8. **Effect of Peacekeeping Operations**: Ghana for instance, has been acclaimed to be among the countries to provide peacekeeping globally. It is true that the troops have been delivering on set objectives, but the flipside has not been beneficial. Peacekeeping has led to conflict in doctrine and approach. It has even led to dilution of the basic training of the personnel. For example, while the military is more biased towards using UK standards in training, the new incidence of Africa Contingency Operations Training & Assistance (ACOTA) leans more towards the US doctrine. The cumulative effect is some confusion among the personnel when they are deployed to deal with real situations. Additional to this, the way and manner the military personnel dress up has been affected, over time — all because of peacekeeping and influence from other doctrines.

9. **Globalisation and Internet Communication Technology**: Globalisation, aided by ICT has made the world very small. It has indeed aided interaction and inter communication through the removal of physical barriers. It has enhanced connectivity and helped the service to pass on information in real time. Conversely, it brought in its wake attitudes and actions among personnel which could be considered as inimical to 'good order and discipline'. What has been observed to be a major contaminant has been the internet and attendant social media platforms. Electronic gadgets which can easily be procured are common on the Ghanaian market. Personnel are also able to afford complex gadgets when they travel on peacekeeping missions. Friends and family members could equally procure one for them. It is regrettable to note, these gadgets and related ICT programmes and platforms are negatively affecting the general output of personnel. These days, it is not uncommon to find personnel on duty not only glued to the phones, but with their ears, which are supposed to be one their senses to guarantee alertness, plugged with earphones. Attention and alertness at duty post has, largely, been taken for granted. The mobile phone, tablet and the android application have affected the general bearing and discipline among personnel. Additional to the above has been several instances of alleged misconduct by uniformed personnel on social media, especially those in the junior ranks. Leadership must consistently educate and remind personnel on the appropriate use of social media. Educational awareness of the young officers and soldiers through formal and informal channels for the proper use of social media as well as its negative side effects must be created. Perhaps a policy or guidelines for the use of such media of communication and connectivity must be developed as soon as possible.

10. **High Uncertainty after Retirement**: The length of time spent in service by the personnel is shorter that what is practised in the service. Various reasons have been given to justify that. Because the personnel would leave at a relatively early age, and there is no plan to get them employed in the civil or private sector, their anxiety and uncertainty increases. The service does not have any structured plan to train the personnel to fit into the civil stream. Some personnel are specialist in the service, including weapon instructors, artillery and pure infantry. They may know their job but may not be able to fit into the civil environment.   Consequently, when they are close to the end of their tenure, their general approach to work becomes questionable.

11. **Counter Insurgency and Other Internal Security Operations:** The deployment of soldiers as part of the security mix to deal with internal duties hitherto reserved for the police has also been a major contributory factor to the decline in discipline. For example, their continuous deployment for Operation Calm life, Operation Cow Leg and other illegal mining related operations have created command and control problems. Personnel of the units that were in the regions or areas endowed with mineral wealth had had cause to complain about their constant absence from home for the most part of the year. The personnel of the 2 Battalion, 4 Battalion, 6 Battalion of Infantry and Air Borne Force were reported to have a minimal aspect of military touch in the barracks and unit administration due to their long stay outside the barracks.

12. **Mixed and Convoluted Doctrinal Exposure**: This aspect is very important when one puts into perspective the exposure of personnel who are sent for training in friendly countries with different concepts and doctrines. It

becomes unclear to many personnel which doctrine they are engaged in, especially at the lower level of professional development.

13. **Generational Gap in Leadership**: Many officers can be classified as the millennials, born between mid-1980s to 2000. In the same vein, others could be classified as 'digital natives', while the commanders could safely fit into the 'digital immigrant' category. These different age groups, in practice, have differing value attachment, career paths and technology styles, making them 'unknown' to some employers. The millennials make up 75% of the global workforce. Interestingly, Africa has the highest youth population in the world with 200 million people aged between the ages of 15-24. Africa's working-age population is projected to increase from 705 million in 2018 to almost 1.0 billion by 2030. As millions of young people join the labour market, the pressure to provide decent jobs will intensify. The current trend indicates that this figure would double by 2045, according to the 2012 African Economic Outlook report prepared by experts from the African Development Bank (AfDB) [47]. In Africa, millennials comprise 37 percent of the population, making Africa the most youthful continent on the planet. As more and more young people join Africa's workforce, they are increasingly influencing production and consumption patterns in the region.

Millennials are demanding a new approach to organizational structures. Young professionals reject the old top-down management concepts that many corporations continue to support. Moreover, staff turnover within this age group is expected to be the highest in emerging and frontier markets, between 2016 and 2020. Technology has made a big change for

---

47. GeoPoll Straw Poll Survey

the new generations. They are the 'Digital Natives' and 'Digital Immigrant's, [48] proposed by Prensky. Today's young personnel have not just changed incrementally from those of the past, nor simply changed their diction, clothes, body adornments, or styles, as has happened between generations previously. 'Digital natives' who are mostly young officers, are comfortable in the digital age, because they grew up using technology. 'Digital Immigrants', (Senior officials) on the other hand, are those who were born before the 1980s and are fearful about using technology. Digital natives are 'native speakers' of the digital language of computers, video games and the Internet. Most of them are 'technosexuals' and therefore spent their lives surrounded by and using computers, videogames, digital music players, video cams, cell phones, and all the other toys and tools of the digital age. The officers of today are being socialized in a way that is vastly different from their colleagues.

According to Prensky, the numbers are overwhelming: over 10,000 hours playing videogames, over 200,000 emails and instant messages sent and received; over 10,000 hours talking on digital cell phones; over 20,000 hours watching TV, over 500,000 commercials seen—all before the kids leave college. Computer games, email, the Internet, cell phones and instant messaging are integral parts of the lives of the present-day officer. In addition, there maybe, at the very most, 5,000 hours of book reading. Perhaps the clearest case of this is the staff use of social media, particularly Facebook. 'Digital Native' officers are used to receiving information really fast. They like parallel processing and multi-tasking. They prefer their graphics before their text rather than the opposite. They prefer random access (like hypertext). They function best when networked. They thrive on instant gratification and frequent rewards. They prefer games to 'serious' work. Because of interaction with technology,

---

48. Martina Čut, Digital natives and digital immigrants — how are they different

'digital natives' think and process information fundamentally differently. Besides year of birth, there are some other differences between digital natives (young officers) and digital immigrants (senior officers), which include the following:

i.   A digital immigrant will call to ask if an email has been received while a digital native will check to see if you opened their snapchat. While both populations are immersed within the technological world, the digital native has fully adapted to the new ways of the 'World Wide Web'. While a digital immigrant may be active on social networks such as Instagram or Snapchat, a digital native will know how to utilize beyond their intended "photo sharing" capabilities.

ii. A digital native streams everything online; a digital immigrant owns the boxed DVD set. Not long ago, TV fans would rejoice over ownership of every single episode of their favourite show.

iii. A digital immigrant has the book; and a digital native has a 'kindle'. Digital natives have a deep appreciation for hard copies, where digital immigrants are likely to write a note on their phone rather than with a pen and notepad.

iv. A digital immigrant is connected with their friends on Facebook; a digital native never lost touch. Since digital natives grew up within the social media boom, they have been adding to their online network of connections since they were young. There is quite a span of time since digital immigrant's old neighbourhood days and the first Facebook friend request. This makes digital immigrants more appreciative of the use of this tool as a way to reconnect with old friends.

v.   A digital native reads things on their phone; a digital immigrant does same on their laptop or in printed form. We have quickly transformed into an on-the-go society.

Digital natives are professional multi-taskers, checking their email, listening to a podcast, and all the while brushing their teeth, eating, running, walking, reading, driving, learning, etc.

Summary

The concept of discipline and leadership in military service is paramount to the development of the personnel and sustenance of the institution. This is because, discipline drives behaviour, which in turn influences the success of every endeavour. In particular, the military profession requires the officer to uphold discipline in high esteem and to consider self-comfort as a luxury. The officers and men are therefore moulded in such an environment to consider 'country before self'. Interestingly, standards and discipline seemed to be falling, not only in the service, but in many areas of human endeavour. Using the aged long admonishment of leadership by military commanders, including Field Marshal Sir Philip Walhouse Chetwode, other experts, and the experience of the author gained through training and working exposure, some proximal reasons for the falling standards have been identified. The chapter also looks at the process and definitions of leadership. The chapter ends with some professed solutions to the creeping canker that is eating away discipline, which is the bedrock of military ethos. This sets the tone for the subsequent chapters.

Chapter Two

Upholding Discipline for Organisational Survival

Organizational discipline is the practice of self-restraint and learning to follow the best course of action which may not be ones' desire.
It acts as the backbone of the organization structure and maintains order
Ravinder Jit and Anju Bharti [49]

Maintaining Discipline in the Era of Ripples

An organisation is a consciously coordinated social unit, composed of two or more people, which functions to achieve a common goal. Organisational behaviour, in principle, looks at the actions and attitudes that people exhibit within the organisation. Organizational discipline is the practice of self-restraint and learning to follow the best course of action, which may not be ones' desire. Organizations thrive on teamwork, and without discipline teams cannot function properly. It acts as the backbone of the organizational structure and maintains order. Organizational discipline can thus be explained as a system of conducting the organizational proceedings by its members who abide by the guidelines laid out by the organization. It imbibes a sense of obedience towards the organization that works instinctively under different circumstances. The boardroom, where the group of people who manage a company or

---

49 Ravinder Jit and Anju Bharti, Servant Leadership and Organizational Discipline: A Qualitative Study

organization have their meetings, is where leadership crystallises. Decisions are made, takeovers are undertaken, mergers are decided, remunerations are approved and future direction of organisations are all made in the boardroom. As a leader, there are countless demands, opportunities and choices placed before you. Managing other people at whatever level, the leadership style matters.

Whether you are running a large global firm, in charge of a small project team, or setting out in an entrepreneurial venture, it is the way you communicate and connect to other people that can, and will, make or break your success. The key is to make every connection count so that you can lead as it matters. You make hundreds of decisions, ranging from the subconscious and mundane to the complex and life-changing each day. Each decision is a drop that creates a ripple effect on those around you. A ripple effect influences results in the organization and beyond. No matter your title, your generation or your background, leadership is a choice. Our actions relate to, and impact legacy, which often comes later in life, as we look back at what we have accomplished and contributed. Leaders must recognize the "ripple effect" of what they say and do each day. It matters because each and every leadership choice you make has some kind of a 'ripple effect' that spreads out to your team and to the organization as a whole.

Every organization is a living ecosystem in which everything and everyone is connected, directly or indirectly. Therefore, everything that happens within that system has an impact, a reverberation. It might be almost undetectable, or it might be a shock wave. The closer to the source, the more directly the impact is felt. Moreover, just as every drop of a pond water is an integral part of the entire pond, everyone within the organization is an integral part of the entire organization. Su and Wilkins contend that 'the more senior you are, the more visible you are. The higher your performance, the greater the impact of your ripple and the mark that you leave'. Leaders, therefore, need to pay very close attention to their 'responsibility pond', whether it is healthy or toxic. They have a role to play in the health or illness of their part of the ecosystem. As leaders, we need to know how to ensure that the ripples we make have the intended impact, whether it is running meetings, handling conflicts, making confident decisions, or instituting needed changes. To have an effective and efficient military, it is of first importance that all officers and NCOs be well disciplined. The ripple effect is a great visual understanding of a leader's influence on others throughout an organization. They must constantly keep in mind the principle that example is one of the best methods for influencing people. They must themselves have the mental attitude and state of training which renders obedience and proper conduct instinctive under all conditions.

All staff members must realize that they cannot expect respect and obedience from others unless they themselves are obedient and respectful to their officers and others in authority. When an order is received, the first and only thought should be to carry it out as quickly and carefully as possible. Roxana Bahar Hewertson highlights this fact by stating that, 'every organisation is effectively a 'living ecosystem' - through which everything and everyone is connected, directly or indirectly.' Hewertson notes that, "leadership today is far too much about gaining status, popularity, money, power and not enough about inspiring and developing people or creating a healthy culture and future that builds and sustains a company, our communities, or our world."[50] Thus everything happening within that system has an impact; and of course, the closer it is to the source, the more heavily that impact is felt. The correct standard behaviour must be displayed if the leader expects

---

[50]. Roxi Bahar Hewertson,2014, Lead Like it Matters...Because it Does: Practical Leadership Tools to Inspire and Engage Your People and Create Great Results, McGraw-Hill Education

discipline to be maintained. After all, the standard we pass on is the standard we accept. We must, therefore, set the right standards so other would emulate. Some of the useful tools available may include:

a. **Setting the Example**. Because of the leader's grade and position, they must see themselves as a role model. Whether they realize it or not, others are constantly watching and imitating their behaviour. Sometimes, people learn to imitate less than desirable behaviour. For example, if the officer shows less than acceptable grooming standards, the cadets, recruits and soldiers would eventually do the same. Because he is a role model, consciously and continually, he must set a positive example.

b. **Gaining Knowledge**. The officer leader must know his job, understand its importance, and realize how it contributes to the success of the unit. The leader must strive to improve and upgrade their knowledge.

c. **Knowing the Unit's Requirements**: Knowing that a regulation or standard exists is not enough; understand why it exists. The leader must have an in-depth understanding of the legal and regulatory instructions and administrative procedures of the unit and the service.

d. **Communicating**: The leader must understand the information being given out. Communication represents the key element in the normal functioning of every military or civil organisation. Nowadays, productive communication assumes a vital role, because the complexity of modern warfare produces larger leading structures made at the same time multiplying the possible sources of obstacles of the essential intelligence flow. Having in mind the Maslow pyramid, communication manifests itself in two different ways: nonverbally (willingly or unwillingly) and verbally (orally and written). Taking into consideration the nonverbal communication, first, it is important that it must not be underestimated as a useful intelligence source, because, as Frank Tippet argues in his work 'Why so much beyond words', 'maybe almost 20% of the human communication is verbal. Most of the time, the largest part of the communication process consists of nonverbal signals. Each needs to reinforce the other. Officers should not say one thing and then do something else. The nonverbal communication means are the following:

i. **Facial Expressivity:** It could reveal whether an individual is alert, bored, tired, frustrated, careful, etc.

ii. **Body Movement:** Hiding the facial expressions can be easily learned, but it is very hard and uncommon to hide the unconscious signals related to certain body movements; a trained eye can tell whether a person is stressed, even if the facial expression is a relaxed one;

iii. **Gestures Language:** Certain gestures are of a very conventional nature, yet they are not necessarily perceived identically by different communities or people;

iv. **Voice Inflexions:** Besides the meaning of words, the tone and the voice inflexion are very important in learning a foreign language. This is because they contribute substantially to the connotation of the words, knowing at the same time that every language has its own particular inflexion;

v. **Artistic Expression:** Is a very important form of communication; painting, sculpturing and other artistic forms gather their strength through the use of symbols;

these symbols can communicate messages with a higher strength than messages communicated through words; it is a very effective way of communication, and every propaganda institution or publicity service is aware of this fact;

vi. **Silence:** We all know that silence often means approval. Yet this is not necessarily, and always correct; silence can also mean disapproval, indifference, perplexity, interest, and so on. A correct evaluation of the silence of an individual belonging to a group could be very important for the leader of that group. As for verbal communication (oral or written), we have to admit that language is a means through which a person reveals or hides its own intentions (hostile, neutral, friendly), anxiety, fear, frustration or satisfaction. The capacity of perceiving the verbal and nonverbal communication is mandatory in any kind of environment. It is important to understand that an effective communication process is at the base of every military strategy. As the Chinese strategist, Sun Tzu indicated, 'the supreme art of war is the domination of the enemy without a fight'. A military leader's effectiveness is measured partly by his communication skills and how well people understand you.

The Essence of Communication

Communication means transferring messages from one to another through any medium. There are various levels in communication such as intrapersonal communication, interpersonal communication, group communication and mass communication. Mass communication plays the vital role because it reaches a very large audience. Basically, mass communication has two forms; one is interpersonal communication and another one is media communication. There are, however, some eight forms of communication which the leader must acknowledge and master. These are intrapersonal, dyadic, group, public and mass communication.

i. **Intrapersonal Communication**: Intrapersonal communication is communication which happens with one's self. Here both Source (sender) and receiver is only one. So, the feedback works without any interruption. For, example, a person can communicate with himself through pain, thinking, feelings and emotion, etc.

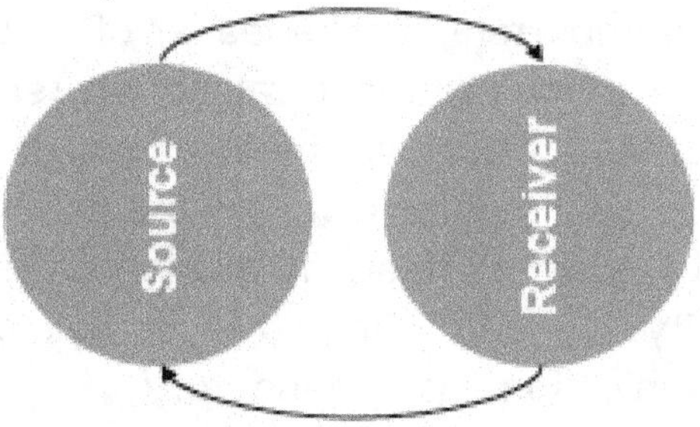

ii. **Dyadic Communication**: In Dyadic communication, two persons are involved in this communication process. Here the source becomes a receiver and receiver become the source because of the dynamic communication process in which the feedbacks are shared between Source Receiver.

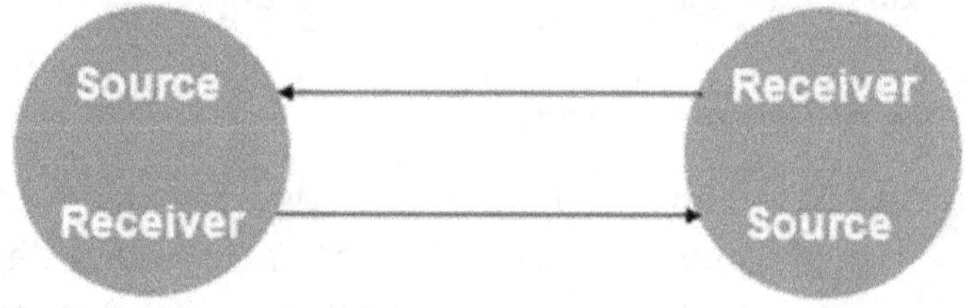

iii. **Public Communication**: More than two members involved, and the communication process will become a group communication. If a minimal number of persons is involved, the group communication is called as small group communication. In this communication process, everyone becomes a Source as well as Receiver through sharing information and giving feedback to one another.

iv. **Small Group Communication:** Where more than two members are involved in the communication process, it will become a group communication. If the least number of persons are involved in the group communication, it is called small group communication. In this communication process, everyone becomes a Source as well as Receiver through sharing information and giving feedback to one another.

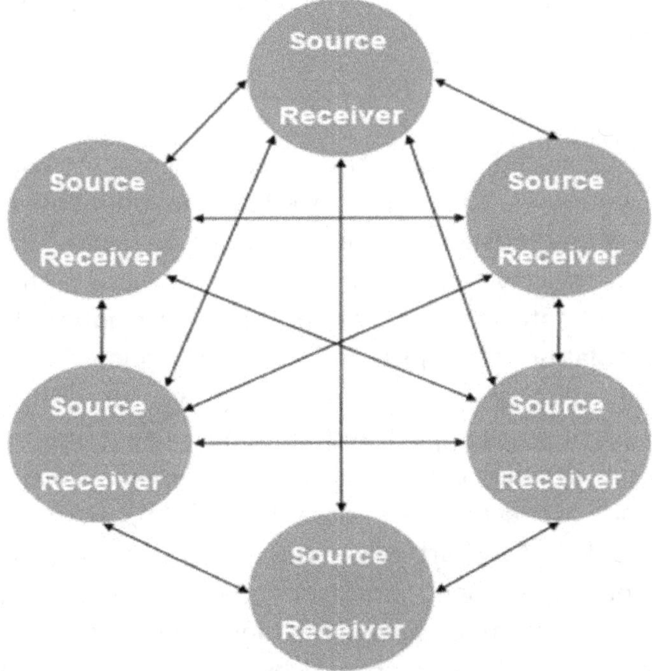

v. **Mass Communication:** The term 'mass communication' and 'mass media', were coined in the early 20th century to describe the then new social phenomenon. It was a key feature of the emerging modern world that was being built on the foundations of industrialism and popular democracy. Mass communication, basically, has a large audience, and the members of this audience cannot all be grouped together in one place, so there is the need for certain tools or technology for the communication process. The early mass media (newspapers, magazines, phonogram, cinema and radio) developed rapidly to reach formats that are still largely recognizable today, with changes mainly of scale and diversification as well as the addition of television in the mid-twentieth century. In mass communication, there is no direct access with the receiver. Therefore, for that, there is the need for media such as newspaper, radio, television and internet. Here, audience feedback is very limited or delayed.

It should be noted that, in the current complex environment, communication is to be perceived as multidimensional. The defining characteristics is their capacity to reach the entire population rapidly and with much the same information, opinions and entertainment; the universal fascination they hold; their stimulation of hopes and fears in equal measure; the presumed relation to sources of power in society; the assumption of great impact and influence. There are, of course, many and continuing changes in the spectrum of available media and in many aspects of their content and form, and one purpose of this book is to chart and assess these changes. Having a happy, healthy, engaged workforce goes far beyond providing free food, gym memberships and a ping-pong table. While those perks are sure to be appreciated by employees, they don't do much in the way of motivating or retaining them. What it really comes down to is the employee-employer relationship.

Data released in 2014 by Virgin Pulse revealed exactly what employees need to love their job and a large part of that is a good relationship with their employer. In fact, nearly 60 percent of the more than 1,000 full-time employees surveyed said their relationship with their employer positively impacts their focus or productivity at work, and 44 percent said it positively impacts their stress levels. [51] It is noteworthy that nearly 50 percent of the 7,200 adults surveyed in a recent Gallup study left a job "to get away from their manager." When it comes to an engaged workforce, the manager-employee relationship is key. It is time to re-evaluate the employee-employer relationship. Make it clear that socializing is encouraged, so long as it doesn't get in the way of employees' performance. Help your people connect and build friendships by issuing office wide competitions that encourage teams to come together or promote interdepartmental connections. Challenges can be business-goal related, or something more creative like seeing who can make it to the gym or take the stairs each day. The key to any good relationship is communication that goes both ways. Unfortunately, employees did not appreciate that their bosses were really listening. Those who show employees some love could win them over for the long haul.

---

[51]. Virgin Pulse, Labor Of Love: What Employees Love About Work & Ways To Keep The Spark Alive, 2015 Survey Report

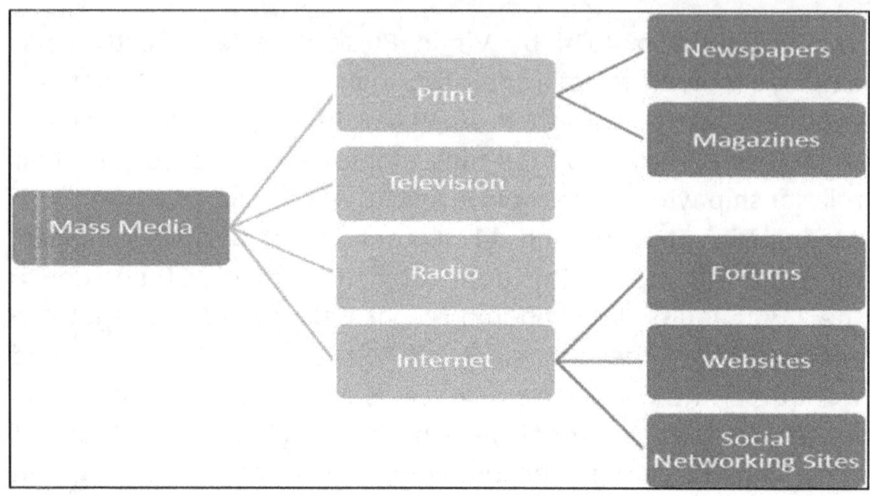

By offering tools, programmes and resources that help them make progress on meaningful work, show how they relate to the company's mission and goals, they connect with the areas of life where they are most looking for support. By this, one will help drive their most productive, focused selves at work and beyond. According to a survey of over 1,000 full-time employees across the US, 81% of employees would rather join a company that values "open communication". [52] In particular, younger employees feel "unheard". When asked why they did not share feedback with bosses, 29% of millennials said managers were "too busy to listen", while 28% said their managers "don't ask us to share these things." Meanwhile, 17% of millennials feel their "feedback isn't taken seriously." Every day, social life is strongly patterned by the routines of media use and infused by its contents through the way leisure time is spent, lifestyles are influenced, conversation is given its topics and models of behaviour are offered for all contingencies. Gradually, the media have grown in economic value, with ever larger and more international media corporations dominating the media market, with influence extending through sport, travel, leisure, food and

---

52. http://www.prweb.com/releases/2015/03/prweb12565921.htm

clothing industries, and with interconnections with telecommunications and all information-based economic sectors.

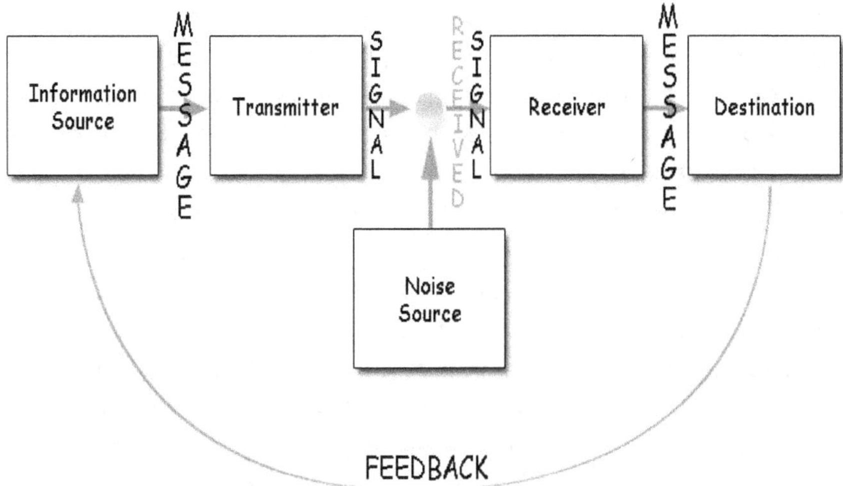

The basic steps of leadership or managerial communication are:
i. The forming of communicative intent – (the speaker generates an idea)

ii. Message encoding– (the speaker encodes an idea or converts the idea into words or actions)

iii. Transmission of the encoded message as a sequence of signals using a specific channel or medium– (the speaker transmits or sends out a message)

iv. Reception of signals- (the receiver gets the message)
v. Reconstruction of the original message
vi. Interpretation and making sense of the reconstructed message - (thereceiver decodes or interprets the message based on the context)
vii. The receiver sends or provides feedback.

Leaders and managers are to note that the various means of communication are intended to drive a certain attitude or behaviour change. As has been noted by Mcquail, the field of media theory is also characterized by widely divergent perspectives. A difference of approach between the left (progressive or liberal) and the right (conservative) tendencies can sometimes be discerned. Leftist theory is, for instance, critical of the power exercised by the media in the hands of the state or large global corporations, while conservative theorists point to the 'liberal bias' of the news or the damage done by media to traditional values. There has also been a difference between a critical and a more applied approach to a theory that does not necessarily correspond to the political axis. Lazarsfeld referred to this as a critical versus administrative orientation. [53] Critical theory seeks to expose underlying problems and faults of media practice and to relate them in a comprehensive way to social issues, guided by certain values. Applied theory aims to harness an understanding of communication processes to solving practical problems of using mass communication more effectively. [54] However, two other axes of theoretical variation can also be distinguished. Four main approaches can be identified according to two dimensions: media-centric versus society-centric; and culturalist versus materialist.

One of these separates 'media-centric' from 'society-centric' (or 'socio-centric') approaches. The former approach attributes much more autonomy and influence to communication and concentrates on the media's own sphere of activity. The media-centric theory sees the mass media as a primary mover in social change, driven forward by irresistible developments in communication technology. It also pays much more attention to

---

53 Lazarsfeld, P.F. (1941) 'Remarks on administrative and critical boammunication research studies', Philosophy and Social Science, IX (2).

54 Windahl, S., Signitzer, B. and Olson, J. (2007) Using Communication Theory, 2nd edn. London: Sage.

the specific content of media and the potential consequences of the different kinds of media (print, audio-visual, interactive, etc.). the socio-centric theory mainly views the media as a reflection of political and economic forces. Theory for the media is a special application of broader social theory. [55] Whether or not society is driven by the media, it is certainly true that mass communication theory itself is so driven, tending to respond to each major shift of media technology and structure.

The second, horizontal, dividing line is between those theorists whose interest (and conviction) lies in the realm of culture and ideas and those who emphasize material forces and factors. This divide corresponds approximately with certain other dimensions: humanistic versus scientific; qualitative versus quantitative; and subjective versus objective. While these differences partly reflect the necessity for some division of labour in a wide territory and the multidisciplinary character of media study, they also often involve competing and contradictory ideas about how to pose questions, conduct research and provide explanations. These two alternatives are independent of each other, and between them, they identify four different perspectives on media and society.

The dimensions and types of media theory.

Source: McQuail [56]

Mcquail [57] identifies four types of perspective, which can be summarized as follows:

---

[55]. Golding, P. and Murdock, G. (1978) 'Theories of communication and theories of society', Communication Research, 5 (3): 339–56.

[56]. Denis McQuail, McQuail's Mass Communication Theory. 6th edition SAGE Publications Ltd, 2010

[57] Ibid

a) **A Media-culturalist Perspective.** This approach takes the perspective of the audience member in relation to some specific genre or example of media culture (e.g. reality TV or social networking) and explores the subjective meaning of the experience in a given context.

b) **A Media-materialist Approach.** Research in this tradition emphasizes the shaping of media content, and therefore, of potential effects, by the nature of the medium in respect of the technology and the social relations of reception and production that are implicated by this. It also attributes influence to the specific organizational contexts and dynamics or production.

c) **A Social-culturalist Perspective.** Essentially this view subordinates media and media experience to deeper and more powerful forces affecting society and individuals. Social and cultural issues also predominate political and economic ones.

d) **A Social-materialist Perspective.** This approach has usually been linked to a critical view of media ownership and control that ultimately are held to shape the dominant ideology transmitted or endorsed by the media.

e) **Social Media:** Is also instructive to note that social media has also presented a new dimension to the communication processes to leadership. The phenomenon has even likened the advent of social media to the Industrial Revolution (though a bit exaggerated in my mind), bringing with it an era of change and progress. It is a common thread connecting millions of people worldwide, and it is changing how we communicate and connect. As has been noted by Audrey Willis, there are currently 2.8 billion social media users worldwide. This means that over a third of the world's population is using some form of social media to communicate, making social media marketing an imperative tactic for boosting leads for higher education programmes. Facebook, for example, has over 2.01 billion monthly users, and 88 percent of 18-29-year-olds use this platform. Facebook should always be a top priority for higher education marketers. It is allowing people to connect with anybody, from their best friends to distant relatives, as well as share their personal thoughts, pictures, videos, blogs and links. Twitter, on the other hand, has 328 million monthly users with 36 percent of 18-29-year-olds on it. [58] Using this platform seems the next best way to reach potential students.

Leadership must understand that no matter what platform we look at or access, social media as a whole has informed and shaped millennial culture through gifs, sound bites, chats, brief moments, and temporary flashes of content. Social media has created a sense of urgency and a need to share. In basic communication, humans transmit information and receive instant feedback. The integration of texting, messaging and emailing, however, has enabled senders and receivers to sit and dwell before responding. Instagram Stories and Snapchat have changed the game by making messages and content available to view for only 24 hours. Additionally, it is providing an inside perspective of faraway places and events. Facebook Live for example, has ended up revealing a lot about our society, from police shootings to a look at the increasing rate of opioid overdose deaths.

---

58 https://techcrunch.com/2017/06/27/facebook-2-billion-users/

Trust cognitive onion model in social media communication.

Source: Cheng, Fu and Vreede [59]

There are many ways to integrate the social media into organizational communication and any model has a number of variables that would be unique to the organization. However, there is one common denominator. Integration requires thinking differently. In developing a working model to integrate the social

---

[59] Xusen Cheng, Shixuan Fu, Gert-Jan de Vreede, Understanding trust influencing factors in social media communication: A qualitative study. International Journal of Information Management, 2017

media into a public relations-driven communication plan. Experience has shown that the social media tends to be too cumbersome for most public relations departments (and outside firms) to manage; Leaders and managers should maintain, manage, and promote the organization's blog. This may include market intelligence (which is shared with the public relations team), but primarily consists of content development and content distribution that adds value for stakeholders. They may also maintain, manage, and develop the organization's social networks. This includes online programmes and information sharing that nurtures true engagement and two-way communication in real time. It may also include identifying forums beyond popular social networks where people ask questions that need to be answered. And, in this model, we should allow for advertising support specifically designed to drive customers toward networks where they can be engaged. A blogger outreach occurs directly and indirectly as bloggers may source content from the organization's blog or develop relationships with the social media team via any number of social networks. [60]

Barriers to Communication

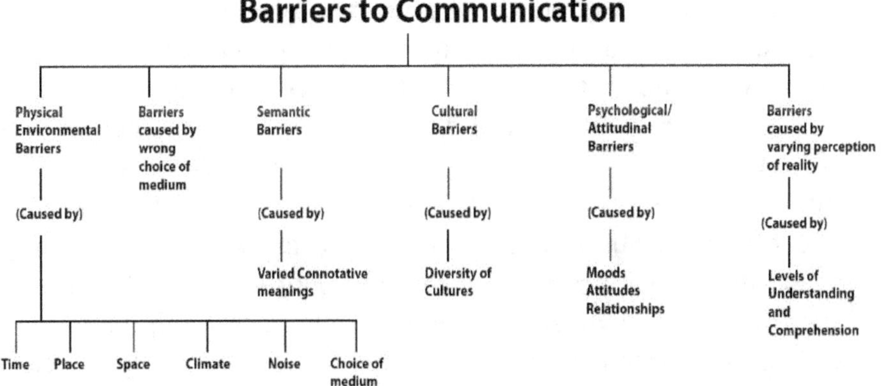

As has been cautioned by PwC, before adding social media to your business continuity management programme, it is important to have a clear plan for how the tools can best be leveraged and by whom. Make sure your team includes digital communication experts who can lead your social media monitoring and response. A 2014 survey on Social Media in the Workplace revealed that 88% of businesses are using the social media in some form. Much of the focus to date has been about creating policies for appropriate employee use of the social media vs. broadening how the tools can be used for crisis management. While employee misuse of social channels is a concern, this fear has slowed the expansion of social media for legitimate business purposes. There are many ways social media can be used to improve crisis management and overall organizational resiliency. [61]

Despite the good intention for social media platforms, there has been a plethora of negative issues that has been brought to the media space since their inception. In May 2020, for example, the UN launched a programme dubbed, "Verified", to combat the growing scourge of COVID-19 misinformation by increasing the volume and reach of trusted, accurate information. The UN notes, with worry, that misinformation spreads online, in messaging apps and person to person. Its creators use savvy production and distribution methods. To counter it, scientists and institutions like the UN needed to reach people with accurate information they can trust. 'Verified', is managed by the Department of Global Communications, and provides information around three themes: science — to save lives; solidarity — to promote local and global cooperation; and solutions — to advocate for support to impacted populations. It will also promote recovery packages that tackle the climate crisis and address the root causes of poverty, inequality and hunger. [62]

---

61 https://www.missionmode.com/social-media-business-continuity/

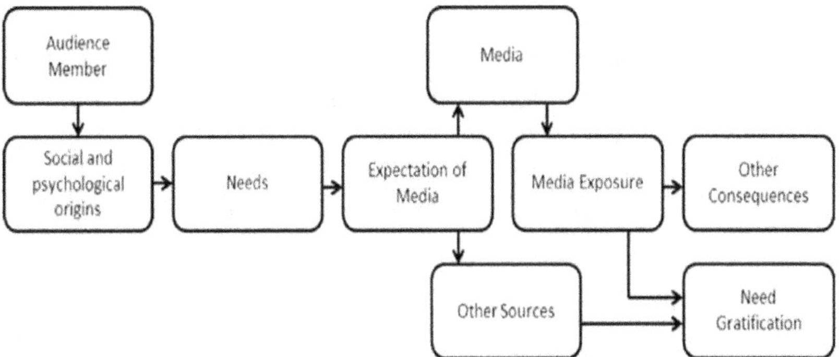

The communication process according to Katz, Blumler, and Gurevitch.

The initiative is calling on people around the world to sign up to become "information volunteers" to share trusted content to keep their families and communities safe and connected. Described as digital first responders, the volunteers will receive a daily feed of verified content optimized for social sharing with simple, compelling messaging that either directly counters misinformation or fills an information void. The Department is partnering with other UN agencies and country teams, influencers, civil society, business and media organizations to distribute trusted, accurate content and work with social media platforms to root out hate and harmful assertions about COVID-19. The UN recognizes that, in many countries, the misinformation surge across digital channels is impeding the public health response and stirring unrest.[63] The new UN initiative aims to push back against the tide of lies and hate that has risen in tandem with the COVID-19 pandemic, by empowering people worldwide to share accurate information to

---

62 https://www.un.org/africarenewal/news/coronavirus/covid-19-united-nations-launches-global-initiative-combat-misinformation

63 https://news.un.org/en/story/2020/05/1064622

help save lives and promote global solidarity. Under Verified, information will be provided around three themes: science – to save lives; solidarity – to promote local and global cooperation; and solutions – to advocate for support for populations that have been impacted by COVID-19. [64]

Building blocks of information behaviour on SLSSs as a flowchart

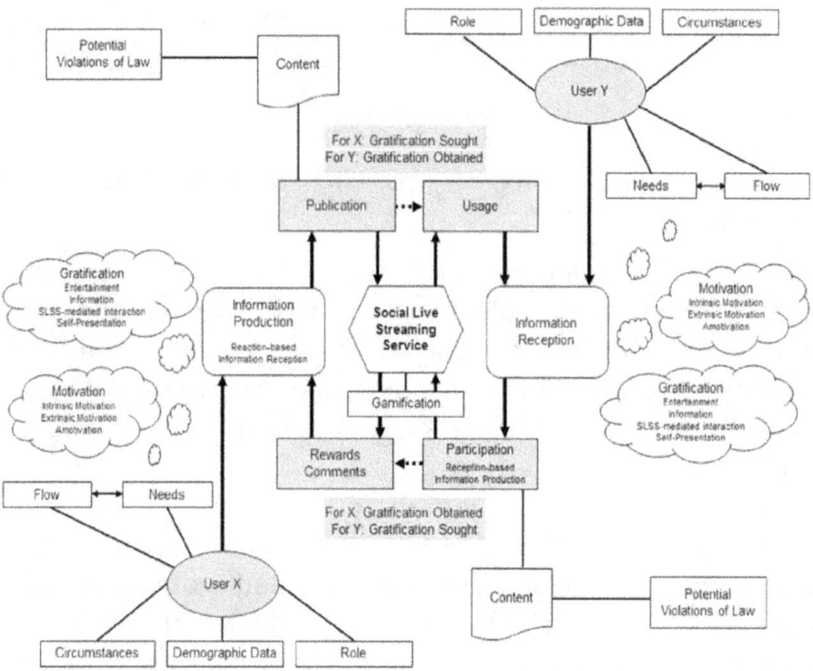

The initiative is a collaboration with Purpose, one of the world's leading social mobilization organizations, and is supported by the IKEA Foundation and Luminate. UN has observed a disturbing effort to exploit the crisis to advance nativism or to target minority groups, which could worsen as the strain on societies grows and the economic and social fallout kicks in", she added. "The Verified 'initiative also seeks to work to address this trend with hopeful content that celebrates local acts of

---

64 https://news.un.org/en/story/2020/05/1064622

humanity, the contributions of refugees and migrants, and makes the case for global cooperation." As the COVID-19 pandemic spreads, another virus is infecting our lives; misinformation. Millions of people are being exposed to dangerous claims that COVID-19 doesn't exist, or that a miracle cure has been found, or that the virus emerged as a result of a plot to destroy humanity or make profits. A tsunami of hate, xenophobia, scapegoating and scare-mongering has been unleashed.

Infodemics, which are an excessive amount of information about a problem, which makes it difficult to identify a solution. They can spread misinformation, disinformation and rumours during a health emergency. [65] It is an overabundance of information – some accurate and some not – that makes it hard for people to find trustworthy sources and reliable guidance when they need it. Infodemic refers to a large increase in the volume of information associated with a specific topic and whose growth can occur exponentially in a short period of time due to a specific incident, such as the current pandemic. In this situation, misinformation and rumors appear on the scene, along with the manipulation of information with doubtful intent. In the information age, this phenomenon is amplified through social networks, spreading farther and faster like a virus. [66]

Misinformation, on the other hand, is false or inaccurate information deliberately intended to deceive. In the context of the current pandemic, it can greatly affect all aspects of life, specifically people's mental health, since searching for COVID-19 updates on the Internet has jumped 50% – 70% across all generations. Infodemics can hamper an effective public health

---

[65] https://www.un.org/en/un-coronavirus-communications-team/un-tackling-%E2%80%98infodemic%E2%80%99-misinformation-and-cybercrime-covid-19
[66] Office Of The Assistant Director, Understanding The Infodemic And Misinformation In The Fight Against Covid-19, PAHO

response and create confusion and distrust among people. Many false or misleading stories are fabricated and shared without any background or quality checking. Much of this misinformation is based on conspiracy theories, some introducing elements of these into seemingly mainstream discourse. Inaccurate and false information has been circulating about all aspects of the disease: how the virus originated, its cause, its treatment, and its mechanism of spread.

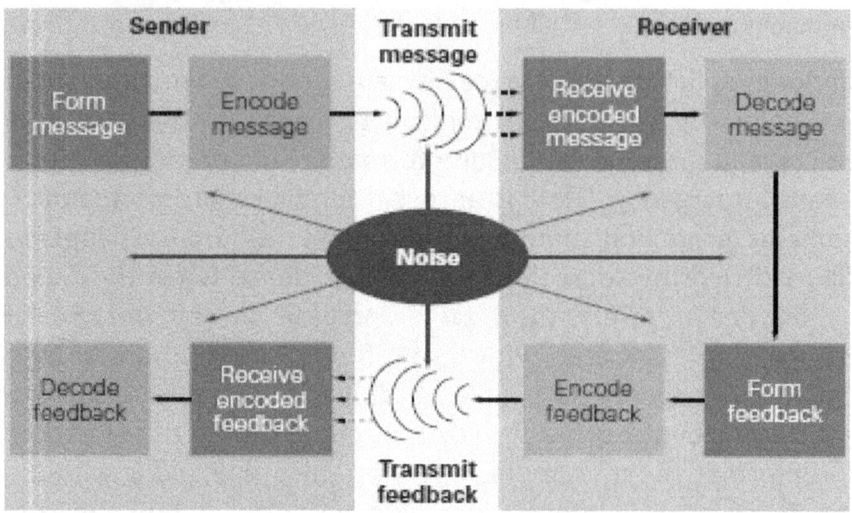

Misinformation can circulate and be absorbed very quickly, changing people's behavior, and potentially leading them to take greater risks. All this makes the pandemic much more severe, harming more people and jeopardizing the reach and sustainability of the global health system. From selling fake coronavirus cures online to a cyberattack on hospitals' critical information systems, criminals are exploiting the COVID-19 crisis. [67] This 'infodemic' is proliferating and are potentially deadly in the working space. We cannot cede our virtual spaces to those who traffic lies, fear and hate. [68] In the consideration

---

[67] Zarocostas, J. (2020). How to fight an infodemic. The Lancet, 395(10225), 676.
[68] https://www.un.org/en/coronavirus/good-communication-saves-lives

of leaders and managers, communication should be seen as any of the following:

i. As a one-way process from sender to receiver.

ii. As a two-way process between actors.

iii. As an omnidirectional diachronic process of meaning development itself. [69]

According to the UN, 'good communication saves lives'. Many organisations could replicate the UN efforts and also recruit digital responders to assist in its drive to ensure effective communication and also enforce media sanity. Strategic communication is said to examine how organizations use communication purposefully to their mission.

f. **Enforcing Moral and Ethical Standards**: 'Ethics' is concerned with building up a coherent set of 'rules' or principles by which people ought to live. Sometimes the vicissitudes and complexities of life mean that these simple rules are sometimes put to the test. Ethics is often used in connection with the activities of organisations and with professional codes of conduct. Consistently and continually correct anyone who is not complying with the Code of Service or the ethics of the profession, policy and regulations. Morality, on the other hand, is most often used in connection with the ways in which individuals conduct their personal, private lives, often in relation to personal financial probity, lawful conduct and acceptable standards of interpersonal behaviour (including truthfulness, honesty, and sexual propriety). Treat people fairly, when two service personnel make the same mistake, both must be corrected at the same time, in the same way. Inconsistency erodes the cooperation you have with your team because they will not know what

---

[69] Betteke van Ruler (2018) Communication Theory: An Underrated Pillar on Which Strategic Communication Rests, International Journal of Strategic Communication, 12:4,367-381, DOI: 10.1080/1553118X.2018.1452240

you expect. You gain commitment from the subordinates when they are a part of a system they believe in, feel is fair, and understand. If personnel realize that it would be morally good to do something, then it would be irrational for them not to do it. The 'Chetwode standard' will have to be applied at all times.

g. **Instilling Discipline and Bearing:** It is generally indicated in an individual or unit by smartness of appearance and action; by cleanliness and neatness of clothes, equipment, or quarters; by respect for seniors; and by prompt and cheerful execution by subordinates of both the letter and the spirit of legal orders of their lawful superiors. There are four main types of discipline which is expected to be adhered to by the soldier at given time and space. These are:

h. **Self-Discipline.** Self-discipline is a willing and instinctive sense of responsibility that leads the officer to know what needs to be done. Getting to work on time, knowing the job, setting priorities, and denying personal preferences for more important ones all measure how self-disciplined you are. This is the ideal situation where the employees themselves are motivated enough to regulate their actions regarding time management, priority setting, etc., and the organization does not have to put in any extra effort to ensure these. This is the highest order of all disciplines because it springs from the values you use to regulate and control your actions.

    i. **Task Discipline.** Task discipline is a measure of how well you meet the challenges of your job. Task discipline requires that you have a strong sense of responsibility to do your job to the best of your ability. In this situation, the employee has to be responsible enough to do their job in the best way possible.

    ii. **Group Discipline.** Group discipline is teamwork. Since most jobs in the military require that several people work effectively as a team, group discipline is very important. Most jobs in an organization require to be worked upon by a team, so group discipline is very important.

iii. **Imposed Discipline.** Imposed discipline is the enforced obedience to legal orders and regulations. It is absolute in emergencies when there is no time to explain or discuss an order. This type of discipline provides the structure and good order necessary throughout your unit to accomplish a task no matter the situation. The purpose of discipline is to enhance adherence to set standards for any activity where people work together toward a common objective. The military depends largely on group cooperation, and cooperation cannot be achieved without discipline. Discipline is the structure and order within an individual or within a group that allows for true cooperation, real support of the mission and the members of the team or organization. It is founded upon respect for, and loyalty to properly constituted authority.

j. **Drills and Ceremony**: Drill is marching; plain and simple. In the olden days, the most powerful, efficient, and developed empires developed ways of moving troops from one place to another without them getting mixed up with other troops. Inspections and other skills that stress attention to detail to make more time for combat skill training. There are a lot of folks that say we need to go back to the basics, i.e., drill and ceremony, because we have lost a lot of the discipline aspect of what it means to be a soldier. The theory was, without drill, masses of soldiers would end up getting lost on the way to battle. The drill and ceremony is going to be interwoven into, when they move to and from places. Movements will not just be lollygagging, non-tactical movements, they will be actually executing some team drill and ceremony as they move to and from the dining hall and through the barracks. The other big piece that needs to be done in Basic Combat Training that helps with the esprit de corps and the discipline aspect and also lends a measure of grit and resilience is drill. These days, military drill is mostly used for military ceremonies, such as military parades, and to instill pride and discipline during military training. Drill is the foundation of discipline in battle, and that its importance has been proven again and again [70]. Regular parades and public displays would require the military as a highly trained, disciplined, and professional force. Even though the parade itself does not provide any useful function on the battlefield, it instills public confidence and pride in the nation's military forces [71].

k. **Reviving Regimentation:** Regiments have core function of raising, equipping and training of troops. Every Regiment has its own characteristic colours, uniform and insignia, and accomplishments in combat zone. They become a fundamental object of allegiance, pride and esprit de corps of its soldiers. The military is unlike any other career, and the demands of military life creates a unique set of pressures on service members and their families. For most people, their job is what they do; in the military, it more deeply defines who they are. For families, military life offers a sense of community with clearly defined rules and expectations. Everything possible must be done to ensure that these aspects of military culture and life, including uniformity, teamwork, anonymity, camaraderie, depersonalization, stoicism, expendability, loneliness, hard work, trust, boredom, and

---

70. https://www.military.com/join-armed-forces/the-importance-of-drill.html

71. *Basic Training for Dummies*, copyright © 2011 by Wiley Publishing, Inc., Hoboken, New Jersey. Used by arrangement with John Wiley & Sons, Inc.

orderliness are engrained. Commanders in the military are responsible for their subordinates' conduct on and off duty.

I. **Reviewing Training and Orientation**: The great object of education is to develop all the faculties of their nature, physical, intellectual and moral, and to endeavour to train and unite them into one harmonious system, which shall form the most perfect character of which the individual is susceptible, and thus prepare them for every period and every sphere of action to which they may be called [72]. If one wishes to understand a nation's interpretation of war and other conflicts, one must understand the professional education of that nation's military. A firm grasp of the professional education of the military is vital because this learning shapes the activities of a nation's military through providing paradigms to interpret war and other conflicts. The mathematician, Gerald Whitrow wrote that 'the primary function of mental activity is to face the future and anticipate the event which is to happen [73]. In this way, staff officers look ahead and attempt to foresee what is to come and organize their services for the roles that they will be assigned by the government. In this fashion, they remove the burden of minutia from military commanders in order to allow those leaders to guide and manage their forces [74]. The need for professional military education is especially pronounced in the army, which to a greater extent than the other services, traditionally relies on the

---

72. https://www.nytimes.com/1862/03/09/archives/military-education-the-propriety-of-introducing-military-drill-and.html

73. Quoted in David Kahn, "Note: The Prehistory of the General Staff," *The Journal of Military History* 71, no. 2 (April 2007): 500.

74. Brigadier General (Retired) James D. Hittle, United States Marine Corps, *The Military Staff: It's History and Development*, 3rd ed. (Harrisburg, PA: The Stackpole Company, 1961).

understanding and application of a common body of knowledge, or in modern terms, doctrine, to conduct effective military operations [75]. Specialised training such as progressive leadership, personnel administration, fraud and corruption, counter terrorism and criminal enterprise, computer forensics and geopolitics must be added to the existing stock of development paradigm, especially for the officer cadet. It should be part of the advance curricular of all second-tier training after commissioning or passing out. Additional to the above, disaster and crisis management must be made a key component of the training and development of the officer. The keys to fostering an effective and harmonious team can be summed up in two words: education and training. Every cadet, recruit and staff member must appreciate the absolute necessity for self-improvement, intense practice, and positive education and training. You remember best what you repeated most. This is one of the basic laws of learning! Practice makes perfect; repetition strengthens corrections. As leaders, we must strive to never let ourselves or our people repeat errors in training.

Forward Looking Actions for the Military

The military in Ghana is touted to be an exemplary and disciplined institution on the mount. Military discipline has been identified as a state of order and obedience existing within a command. Military discipline is the bedrock that enhances self-control, behaviour, and competence. The outcome of this specialised nature of training means adherence to the regulations formulated for the advantage of the team. Military discipline is the code of conduct that governs the operations of

---

75. Allan English, *Understanding Canadian Military Culture* (Montreal & Kingston: McGill Queen's University Press, 2004).

the military in times of operations and at work. Military discipline is unique for every nation and is established for the benefits of the military and of civilians. Ultimately, military bearing and discipline are key essentials in a soldier's life. Self-discipline in the military is demonstrated when soldiers do what is right without being told, even in the absence of the commander. Discipline is created within a unit by instilling a sense of confidence and responsibility in each individual. This is not only because this is how the service wants them to act, but also because these are ways to tell other soldiers who they are and where they stand in the codes and laws of the Ghana Armed Forces. Military leaders must put 'service before self'. To get our military leaders into order, the following traits are suggested to be nurtured:

- The military leaders must bond with their team.
- They must serve the battalion/regiment. Serve their subordinates like they serve them.
- Leaders must ensure subordinates get the same facilities and comfort that they enjoy. It is their lawful right.
- Leaders must give peers and subordinates the respect that they duly deserve.
- Leaders must endeavour to know the men they command. They must make an effort to know their families, their villages, their problems, and try to address their problems. They will earn their love and respect eternally.
- Leaders must be good and upright officers. Remember, reputation is more important than rank.
- They must improve themselves through education, training and development.
- They must take interest in the development of subordinates.
- They must enforce standards by consistently and continually correcting anyone who is not complying with

> the Code of Service discipline or the ethics of the profession, policy and regulations.
> ☐ They must instill discipline.
> ☐ They must trust in God at all times.

As has been noted by General Odierno, [76] decentralized operations require that leaders at all levels understand their environment, learn quickly, make sound decisions, and lead change. Because there are no predetermined solutions to problems, Army leaders must adapt their thinking, formations, and employment techniques to the specific situation they face. This requires an adaptable and innovative mind, a willingness to accept prudent risk in unfamiliar or rapidly changing situations, and an ability to adjust based on continuous assessment. General Omar Bradley [77] once remarked that 'leadership in a democratic army means firmness, not harshness; understanding, not weakness; generosity, not selfishness; pride, not egotism.' This requires personal commitment, constant learning, self-assessment, and passion for soldiers and units.

Being a leader is not about giving orders; it is about earning respect, leading by example, creating a positive climate, maximizing resources, inspiring others, and building teams to promote excellence. Along the way, honest mistakes may be made, but that should be taken as part of the learning process. Officers must internalize military values and ethics, demonstrate unimpeachable integrity and character, and remain truthful in word and deed. Indeed, soldiers trust their leaders. Leaders, therefore, must never break that trust, as trust is the bedrock of the profession. In fairness, we must develop a working culture with a vision to lead change, be the moral and ethical compass of the units under command and in the eyes of the civil

---

[76]. Secretary of the US Army: United States Army Chief of Staff

[77]. General of the Army Omar Nelson Bradley was a senior officer of the United States Army during and after World War II. Bradley was the first Chairman of the Joint Chiefs of Staff and oversaw the U.S. military's policy-making in the Korean War

population, officers must learn, think, and adapt. It is important to balance risk and opportunity to retain the initiative, building agile, effective, high-performing teams, empower subordinates and underwriting risk, developing bold, adaptive, and broadened leaders. It is also imperative to effectively communicate through both horizontal and vertical nesting and telling the whole story without fear or favour. Governments and military leadership in command, staff and strategic positions must continuously provide for the personnel. Peacekeeping should be re-invented so that, any alien behaviour is dealt with before they become contaminants. Recruitment and training practices must be reviewed. Personnel in service must be prepared for civil life. Possible options to employ retiring and retired service personnel may be exploited. Employing them at Training Schools and Staff Colleges may need to be considered. Lessons from the past still apply and must be learnt. The need to take advantage of ICT and information warfare is crucial.

Military discipline is prompt, intelligent, willing, and cheerful obedience to the will of the leader. Its basis is the voluntary subordination of the individual to the welfare of the group. It is the cementing force which binds the members of a unit; which endures after the leader has fallen and every semblance of authority has vanished; it is the spirit of the military team. Discipline establishes a state of mind, which produces proper action and prompt cooperation under all circumstances, regardless of obstacles. It creates in the individual a desire and determination to undertake and accomplish any mission assigned by the leader; and, in the leader's absence, to make and carry out decisions which it is believed he would make if present. True military discipline extends deeper than, and beyond mere outward sign. Nevertheless, proper dressing and smartness in appearance are desirable and conducive to good discipline. However, they are not alone conclusive proof of true discipline. A more positive indication is the behavior of individuals or units away from the presence or guidance of their superiors. In spite of advances in technology and technique, man is and always will be the fundamental element in war. He is most valuable as an individual when he has developed a strong moral fiber exemplified by self-respect, self-reliance, and confidence in his leaders and comrades. We can turn the tide if we could reflect on the reason why people choose to serve their country, even at the peril of their lives. Leadership is paramount to our profession. It is integral to our institutional success today and tomorrow. The ultimate purpose of all military training is effectiveness in battle.

In modern combat, only well-disciplined troops exercising cooperative and coordinated effort can win. Without discipline, a group of men is incapable of organized and sustained effort. With discipline comes the feeling of true comradeship that permits the individual to forget himself and act only in the best interests of the group. An undisciplined military force is a greater danger to the state than to any foreign enemy. Military discipline can be attained only by careful and systematic education and training. All types of training which develop positive qualities of pride, honour, loyalty, confidence, initiative, and teamwork are essential. The basic factor of leadership is character. The influence of the leader is transmitted to his men by his manner and by his action. Since these are controlled to a large degree by his knowledge of the methods of handling men, there is much in this regard which can be learned by the untrained military leader. Sometimes great leaders have to look back in history to find lessons to apply today and future. We should be thinking about what may require us to see beyond current probabilities to create future possibilities. The cultural environment would change, but military ethics and leaders should stand the test of time. The time for review and such endeavour is now.

Summary

Every organization is a living ecosystem in which everything and everyone is connected, directly or indirectly. Therefore, everything that happens within that system has an impact. The organisation therefore, is a consciously coordinated social unit, composed of two or more people, which functions to achieve a common goal. Organisational behaviour, in principle, looks at the actions and attitudes that people exhibit within the organisation. This Chapter examines how discipline could be upheld for institutional survival, especially in the military. The chapter further examines how discipline plays a central role in upholding organisational survival. Teamwork, communication, and some forward-looking guidance for the revitalization of discipline is brought to the fore. It is held in this chapter that, without a good culture grounded on discipline, teams, including that of the military and civil organisations, cannot function properly.

Chapter Three

Behaviours and Choices in Leadership

'The exercise of command relies on professional mastery,
which is built on ability gained through training,
education and the experience of command'.
Army Doctrine Publication 6-22

The Centrality of Decision in Leadership

Our life is gauged by the threats we face and, life must be considered as a war. On that premise, we can say that we are constantly facing threats, direct and indirect, known and unknown. For our purpose, it is important to see threat as anything that can derail the achievement of a goal. A threat may also be conceived as any activity directed against, or detrimental to the interests of any business entity or individual, and includes any other activity performed in conjunction with any activity relating to espionage, sabotage, terrorism or subversion, but does not include any lawful advocacy, protest or dissent not performed in conjunction with any such activity. Additionally, it may be any activity directed at undermining, or directed at or intended to bring about the destruction of one's interests by unlawful or hostile means. This may include any act or threat of violence or unlawful harm that is directed at, or intended to achieve, bring about, or to promote any industrial, social or economic objective, or change in one's business model. It covers any conspiracy, incitement or attempt to commit any such act or threat; and is detrimental to the interests of the individual, community or organisation, and is clandestine or deceptive or involves any threat whatsoever to our individual or collective interest.

Command, in the military, is the authority, responsibility and accountability vested in an individual for the direction, coordination, control and administration of military forces. Professional mastery requires an excellent and comprehensive understanding of a profession's vast body of knowledge that is complemented by the recognised ability to apply that knowledge unerringly to achieve the desired objective [78]. The exercise of command relies on professional mastery, which is built on ability gained through training, education and the experience of command. The manoeuvrist approach relies on adaptive, decisive and independent-minded commanders supported by professional and versatile staff. The effective use of their staff gives commanders freedom of action to focus on the key issues rather than be distracted or overwhelmed by detail. Commanders rely on staff for frank advice to ensure that plans are robust. For this reason, commanders who cultivate 'yes men' are unable to apply a manoeuvrist approach effectively. Commanders need to be highly effective leaders and managers to achieve their mission. Every military unit has a warfighting philosophy. In the military, the essence of the operational art is to be able to identify beforehand what is going to be decisive in an operation, and an understanding of what shaping operations are needed to permit decisive success. The warfighting philosophy is derived from multiple sources, including its understanding of the national character, the nature and history of warfare, the utility of land forces and their role in national military strategy. It also takes account of the nature of future conflict, the resources likely to be assigned, and the

---

[78]. Sanu Kainikara, Professional Mastery and Air Power Education. Royal Australian Air Force Air Power Development Centre, Working Paper 33

expectations of the people. This warfighting philosophy must ensure that the Army retains strategic relevance while maintaining tactical superiority. Timely and effective decision-making is a pre-requisite for success in operations. The aim of battle procedure is to ensure that troops are given orders in sufficient time to prepare, and that they are properly briefed prior to starting an operation. Decision-making is a key part of battle procedure. On the one hand, decision-making can be intuitive; on the other, it can be the result of detailed analysis of a problem.

Where time is a significant constraint, the commander/leader will have to rely more heavily on his intuition, and it may be that only one Course of Action (COA) can be developed. Where time is not as pressing a constraint, the commander/leader will probably wish to develop several COAs. In either case, the decision-making process seeks to answer a number of simple questions, which can be applied at every level of command. As the level of command gets higher and operations become more complex, so does the need increase to apply tools and techniques for decision-making to ensure that plans for the application of combat power are both integrated and synchronized. The way the military or defence experts make decisions is based on the operational art. The Combat Estimate aims to ensure that a timely, enemy focused and effect-based plan is produced. It is a thought process, not a rigid series of drills. To be effective, the commander/leader must make timely decisions and take the appropriate action. He should continually strive to decide and act faster than the enemy. The planning process must support this. The plan must be flexible enough to react to a changing enemy picture.

The military sees their decision-making process, called the 'estimate', as a planning tool consistent with the 'manoeuvrist approach' and associated philosophy of mission command. It is designed to guide the thought process. The manoeuvrist approach seeks to shatter the enemy's cohesion through a series of actions orchestrated to a single purpose, creating a turbulent and rapidly deteriorating situation with which the enemy cannot cope. The manoeuvrist approach focuses commanders at every level on exploiting enemy weaknesses, avoiding enemy strengths and protecting friendly vulnerabilities. At all times, the commander is seeking to undermine the enemy's centre of gravity. The manoeuvrist approach is based on the manoeuvre theory, which is a way of thinking about warfare rather than a particular set of tactics or techniques, and its essence is defeating the enemy's will to fight rather than his ability to fight. Manoeuvre theory emphasises the centrality of the human element in warfare. It relies on speed, deception, surprise, and the application of firepower and movement. Mission command enables commanders to use initiative and empowers subordinates to capitalise on opportunities. It precludes the use of prescriptive plans and rigid orders that attempt to predict enemy actions. Commanders are, therefore, required to train their subordinates in an environment that fosters initiative and mission command.

Mission command does not preclude centralised control where circumstances warrant such an approach. Commanders should maintain regular personal contact with their subordinate commanders during all stages of an operation. This contact allows a commander to confirm progress, issue orders and develop first-hand knowledge of the enemy, terrain and any local intelligence that might be useful in future planning. During battle, commanders should locate themselves where they can best get a 'feel' of the situation in order to influence the outcome through timely decision-making. Commanders and their subordinates must understand that command presence and personal contact are not meant to undermine trust and initiative. In particular, commanders will have to manage the temptation to interfere with their subordinates' actions, given the growth of situational awareness that has been created by the increased availability of information.

Rather than focusing exclusively on the destruction of an adversary's capability through attrition warfare, this approach resolves to shatter the enemy's 'morale' and 'will' to fight through ingenuity and skilfulness.[79] It concentrates one's own strengths against an opponent's identified vulnerabilities and applies all conceivable ways to overwhelm their capacity to make timely and well-informed decisions. The manoeuvrist approach does not just target the physical component of an adversary's fighting power, it also applies direct and indirect methods to undermine the conceptual and moral components of that power.

By attacking the morale and the will of the adversary, the manoeuvrist is able to gain momentum, tempo and agility, which, in turn, enable him not only to achieve operational initiative on the battlefield but also to progress toward a strategically decisive victory. The fundamental tenets of the manoeuvre theory concentrate on applying strength against weakness; recognising and exploiting war's inherent characteristics of friction, danger, uncertainty and chaos; and, focusing friendly planning on defeating the enemy plan rather than defeating the enemy forces. Importantly, the manoeuvre theory regards war as a competition based in time and space rather than on spatial position alone in which the ability to maintain a higher tempo of operations relative to the enemy's creates opportunities for defeating the enemy's centre of gravity. The manoeuvre theory is based on a profound understanding of the enemy, and particularly how the enemy's perceived strengths can be undermined.

The manoeuvrist theory also assumes a detailed knowledge of friendly forces, and the neutral or non-combatant parties within

---

79. Great Britain Ministry of Defence Development, Concepts, and Doctrine Centre (DCDC), Joint Operations, Joint Doctrine Publication 01 (Shrivenham, UK: DCDC, 2004), para. 315

and outside the battlespace. This allows the commander and his staff to divine the precise nature of the problem or given mission first, and then to create a plan that achieves the effect required. It is purposed to construct a workable plan, based upon a winning concept, which reflects all relevant circumstances and a sound rationale for military operations. One critical issue that has been identified to have contributed to the collapse or poor performance in many areas of human endeavour has been decision-making. Decision-making is critical for the success of any human enterprise.

The military has identified this as key to success, and therefore, spend time in rigorously interrogating any intent. The military calls this process an Estimate. It is the process through which leader-managers identify and resolve problems and capitalize on opportunities. It may be said to be a subset of planning in the broader sense. It must be noted that every decision must be qualified as being rational for a successful outcome. Decision is thus meant to be a commitment that will involve further action and perhaps the use of resources with the aim of achieving a desired (uncertain?) outcome. It means that, to meet the test of time, a decision should be made by the most informed people and by authorized people. This caveat of being informed and authorized has been found to be one of the greatest banes to African development, especially when we look at political leadership. Additionally, it has transcended into African entrepreneurship especially when it borders on one-man ownership companies.

In Ghana, this was manifested when a wave of collapses and mergers caught up with a number of banks. One of the reasons for the non-performance was the uninformed nature of Boards, the lack of capacity, and by extension authorisation of these members to make rational decisions. Selecting the course of action in the business environment in most African countries is not rigorous. This may explain, in part, why most family-owned companies do not survive when the pioneer fades away. Family businesses are widely seen as the backbone of the economy – they create wealth, they provide jobs, they are locally rooted and connected to their communities and they seem to be around for long periods of time. Family conflicts, incompetent members of the next generation and flamboyant lifestyles are just some of the more frequent criticisms about family businesses. Each multi-generational family business develops its own particular history, which is made up of both gains and pains, but it is essentially based on a culture of resilience and the unshakable commitment to succeed over the long term. Each family business is basically a story about people: entrepreneurs and their families whose personal values and visions leave an indelible imprint on the businesses that they have created and that subsequent generations continue to manage.

In the mid-1990s, Joseph Bower and Clayton Christensen introduced the framework of Disruptive Change into the social sciences domain to help explain one of the most consistent patterns in businesses, 'the failure of leading companies to stay at the top of their industries when technologies and markets change. [80] According to Bower and Christensen:

> 'Research shows that most well-managed, established companies are consistently ahead of their industries in developing and commercializing new technologies, from incremental improvements to radically new approaches, as long as those technologies address the next-generation performance needs of their customers. However, these same companies are rarely at the forefront of commercializing new technologies that don't initially meet the needs of mainstream customers and appeal only to small or emerging markets. . .'

---

80. Joseph Bower and Clayton Christensen, "Disruptive Technologies: Catching the Wave," Harvard Business Review, January–February 1995, p. 43

The technological changes that damage established companies are usually not radically new or difficult from a technological point of view. They do, however, have two important characteristics: First, they typically present a different package of performance attributes, ones that, at least at the outset, are not valued by existing customers. Second, the performance attributes that existing customers do value, improve at such a rapid rate that the new technology can later invade those established markets. Only at this point will mainstream customers want the technology. Unfortunately, for the established suppliers, by then, it is often too late: the pioneers of the new technology dominate the market. Disruptive technologies introduce a very different package of attributes from the one mainstream customers historically value, and they often perform far worse along one or two dimensions that are particularly important to those customers. [81]

Writing on why African family businesses collapse after the founders fade, Peter Mutua of Business Daily concluded that poor planning by entrepreneurs leave a vacuum that sparks rows when they die or lose control. [82] The reason may be bound on a number of factors. The first and most prevalent being the lack of a clear succession plan from one generation to the next. A PricewaterhouseCoopers survey shows that half of family businesses sampled did not have a succession plan in place, and only half of those that did had designated a specific person to take the reins. Entrepreneurs can become hesitant to place their passion in the hands of another, or simply become too caught up in the day-to-day challenges of the business. However, succession can require a multi-stage process of growing involvement and it is crucial for predecessors to dedicate time to

---

81. Ibid., pp. 44–45.

82. .https://www.businessdailyafrica.com/lifestyle/pfinance/Why-African-family-businesses-collapse-after-founders-fade/4258410-2247560-xahb7p/index.html

creating a business roadmap. Planning cannot be done in isolation of the family; if it is, you are planning to fail. Advisers typically make the mistake of promoting planning only with the controlling generation. The close second being the emergence of factions among family members, and the distant third being the insistence on an operation model which has either been overtaken by time or which heirs cannot deftly manoeuvre. Mutual support among relatives is key to instilling loyalty towards the family business.

Many families lack procedures that help to manage conflict in an objective and productive way, so seeking outside help is often necessary to help the family out of seemingly unresolvable issues. It is when parents die, grow old or lose control of their enterprises that cracks are sure to emerge among even the closest siblings. The size of these cracks is exponentially related to the size of the estate parents accumulated. If not attended to, such cracks can and will eventually lead to the collapse of the entire family business. The family enterprise forms the backbone of the many economies, with families owning or controlling 80 per cent of all businesses. However, research shows that 30 percent survive into the second generation while even fewer continue to the third. The success of family businesses inevitably comes down to the fine art of integrating and balancing the needs between ownership, family and business [83]. Another factor is the lack of trusted advisers. While lawyers, accountants, financial planners, therapists, etc., have formidable technical skills, many require a more sophisticated level of understanding around business families and their unique challenges. Trusted advisers should be able to work collaboratively with other disciplines to provide the best outcome for the family and avoid giving conflicting advice.

---

[83]. Leah Golob, Ten Reasons Why Family Businesses Fail

The next is different visions between generations. Generational conflict can hinder the growth of the business, especially if there is a disagreement in core values and missions. The next generation should be careful not to reject established work methods and entrepreneurial vision, just as predecessors should demonstrate flexibility in exploring new management strategies and ideas for innovation. Governance challenges also contribute to the demise of family businesses. Business families do not need to just consider corporate governance. In addition to corporate oversight, they require family and shareholder governance infrastructure. Family governance requires family meetings, councils or assemblies, which require time and commitment. It is crucial to communicate and create a flow of information between owners, the business and the family. Many members fear raising sensitive issues, losing control or sharing too much information. Without governance, members are confronted with exclusion and secrecy, assumptions and procrastination as well as the exclusion of family members outside the business. Every family member has an investment in the business and the overall assets of the family, whether they are active in the management of the business or its assets. Because the business and assets impact lifestyle, health, and happiness of everyone in the business family, the 'let's deal with business as a business approach' seldom works for the family. A forum outside of business for family – both married into and born into the business, and shareholders to deal with issues is critical. There is also the need to examine the interest of unprepared next generation leaders. In successful transition cases, the next generation is not parachuted into a top position. It is important for successors to learn the ropes and learn all aspects of the business. The business should create guiding principles outlining requisite education and experience before making offers of employment. Good planning creates motivation that can sustain the family and business through various trials that arise. Businesses should be careful to balance the needs of family and business; family considerations can restrict the strategic aggressiveness within the business, yet strategic planning should include more than just finances. Not using their 'familiness' advantage. 'Familiness' refers to the unique resources embedded in a family business. Many of the world's oldest and most respected businesses are family owned. By identifying the family with the business, the firm can promote a brand of security, loyalty and commitment. Fundamental principles of business are not applicable.

Traditional business education is not catered to meet the complex demands of a business family. Central issues like family dynamics, succession planning, family governance and communication are often overlooked in Masters in Business Administration (MBA) programmes, business degrees and continuing education courses. Families wanting to ensure successful succession of their businesses should seek specialized education in the business family field. There is no business model, no matter how innovative or novel that can find application throughout the course of history. New models will overtake the old, and younger, more vigorous, innovative and daring organisations will burst onto the commercial scene. The first is entirely the fault of the leader, the second the fault of the heirs and the third a combination of various factors, some of which have no known remedies. Poor succession planning is another setback. Many Africans typically do not like to think or talk about death, grave misfortune or permanent disability. Nobody would wish for any of these, but they are some of life's risks and realities. Therefore, we must always consider, and plan for them. Finding the right successor to take the reins of a business is a conscious, deliberate and calculated process (or decision) that should not be left to chance, or emergency situations. When parents are alive, healthy and in control, most families enjoy relatively stable relationships among siblings [84].

Their death, however. creates the friction leading to disintegration and eventual collapse. In sum, generational transition, governance, and succession result in predictable paradigm changes. It all boils down to planning which is a key function of effective leadership.

In the military, on the other hand, combat functions describe the range of actions that land forces must be able to undertake to apply land power. They are fundamental to the manoeuvrist approach and are generated through the synergies created by the combined arms team and joint task forces. The combat functions allow a force to react positively to a changing situation by seizing the initiative, and defeating the enemy.

The combat functions are illustrated below:

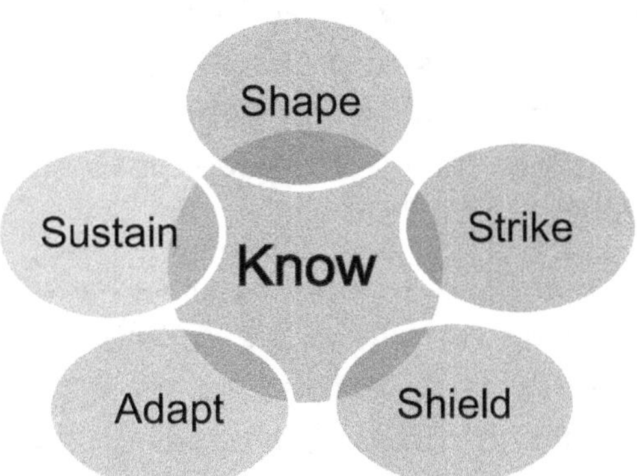

a. **Knowing**. To know is to possess the capacity to predict, detect, recognise and understand the strengths, vulnerabilities and opportunities available within the battlespace. Knowledge links the other combat functions, and is derived from information and understanding. Information is gained from the army, joint, coalition and civilian command, control, computers and communications;

---

84. Joachim Schwass, Family Businesses: Successes and Failures. International Institute for Management Development Global Family Business Center, 2013

intelligence, surveillance, and reconnaissance assets (C4ISR) assets. Fully integrated C4ISR systems with real-time or near real-time links provide forces with a crucial advantage. When information is analysed, interpreted and understood, it becomes knowledge. Understanding is a cognitive process that is enhanced by professional mastery. The use of knowledge and the achievement of a knowledge edge provide forces with a distinct advantage over the enemy.

b. **Shaping**: To shape is to engage in actions that enhance the friendly force's position, delay the enemy's response, or lead the enemy into an inadequate or inappropriate response in order to set the conditions for decisive action. Shaping can take the form of disruption or dislocation, by preventing the enemy from using terrain or key capabilities, or by constraining the enemy's freedom of action. Shaping can also include measures to prepare the friendly force so that consequent action can be more effective, such as enhancing mobility corridors. Actions to shape the battlespace may include movement and physical strikes.

c. **Striking:** To strike is to apply tailored effects in a timely fashion. Striking requires the precise integration and application of force at selected points in the battlespace to achieve specific outcomes. It depends on the capacity of the force to orient, organise, move and apply physical and non-physical effects. Since the strike function can involve moving units through the battlespace and applying effects, it forms a substantial portion of the army's application and procedural-level doctrine.

d. **Shielding:** To shield is to protect friendly forces and infrastructure. Shielding is achieved by measures that include avoiding detection, and protection against physical or electronic attack. A wide variety of activities contribute to shielding, including signature management, movement, fire, physical protection, information operations, counter-reconnaissance operations, operational security procedures, active and passive air defence, and deception. As the combat component of force protection, shielding is most effective when it is supported by a continuous and accurate assessment of threats and risks, and early warning.

e. **Adapting**: To adapt is to respond effectively to a change in situation or task. The chaotic nature of war results partially from actions by two forces that are constantly trying to dislocate or disrupt each other. This constant search for symmetry leads to a dynamic and chaotic battlespace. The presence of non-combatants adds to this dynamism. Success in this environment requires rapid and continual adaptation of procedures and plans. Adaptation rests on professional mastery, mental agility and flexible organisations.

f. **Sustaining**: To sustain is to provide appropriate and timely support to all forces from deployment, through the completion of assigned missions, to redeployment. It includes the provision of stocks, replacement of weapon systems and reinforcement. Sustainment of one's forces is a joint responsibility that will be challenged by the enemy. The dispersion of units throughout the battlespace exacerbates the problem. Resupply and maintenance systems that exploit situational awareness and incorpor-ate modular replacement allow anticipatory planning that enhances freedom of action

Elements in Leadership Decision Process

Every decision making must be guided by some basic elements. These elements, which are listed below must drive the process. They include the following:

a. **Values:** This helps to define the direction and philosophy of the endeavour, shows the importance of the endeavour, and gives the acceptable course of action and desired outcome.

b. **Options**: The options are the anticipated impacts and comebacks on the decision and how various counteractive and alternate plans can be implemented to ensure sustainability and business continuity.

c. **Probabilities and Risk:** Murphy's Law tends to explain why things go wrong. It states that whatever will go wrong will go wrong. Nature sides with its own inherent flaw. Every solution breed new problems or risks

d. **Information**: Information collection is hardest in time of crisis when time is pressing. Information supremacy is now seen as key to military success in the West, leading to information-based warfare/network centric warfare, etc. There is the need for information from and about 'stakeholders' i.e., those affected by a decision and who can influence the outcome of a decision. Information is derived from numerous sources: print and broadcast media, internet, diplomatic service, intelligence services. Do not shoot the messenger,' encourage the delivery of accurate information, not just that which is nice to hear.

e. **Time Available**: Decision-making has a time factor. Decision-making requires evaluating alternatives that differ on a number of attributes. During this evaluation process, selection of options depends on the duration of the options, the duration of the expected delay for realizing the options, and the time available to reach a decision. Time and decision making has a relationship. There are three elements of time which impacts the decision making process. The first relates to the timing of making decisions. The second is the availability of time for making the decision. The third is the time for implementation of the decision. The successful outcome of the decisions take place when these three timings are properly considered in the decision making process. There are several interactions between time and decision making. Time is always present and is a prominent dimension in all decision making actions. Decisions take time to make. They are made to be implemented in future time. The consequences of decisions develop over time, and these consequences are sometimes thought about and debated for a long time afterwards. Knowledge and experience of the decision maker has a big influence on the time taken for the decision making. While knowledge plays a major role in speedier decision making, the same cannot be applicable in case of experience. In case of experience, the memories can be distorted, or the environment for decision making may have undergone certain changes and may include certain different aspects. The longer is the timing of previous experience the higher is the distortion expected.

The Decision Theory

Almost everything that human beings do involves taking decisions. Therefore, to theorize about decisions is almost the same as to theorize about human activities. Modern decision theory has developed since the middle of the 20th century through contributions from several academic disciplines. Although it is now clearly an academic subject of its own right, decision theory is typically pursued by researchers who identify themselves as economists, statisticians, psychologists, political and social scientists or philosophers. This means that there are many different ways to theorize about decisions, and therefore, also many different research traditions. This text attempts to reflect some of the diversity of the subject. Decision theory is the study of how choices are and should be made in a variety of different contexts. Decision problems arise for agents - entities with the resources to coherently represent, evaluate and change their environments in various possible ways typically within the context of ongoing personal and institutional projects, activities or responsibilities. These projects together with the environment, both natural and social, provide the givens for the decision problems the agent faces: her resources for acting, her information and often her standards for evaluating outcomes, as well as the source of the problems she must respond to. Lastly, for agents to face a genuine decision problem they must have options: actions that they are capable of performing and equally of foregoing if they so choose. Some examples will illustrate the variety of forms such problems can take.

A decision maker or decision-making body has a number of options before them: the actions they can take or policies they can adopt. The exercise of each option is associated with a number of possible consequences, some of which are desirable from the perspective of the decision maker's goals, others are not. Which consequences will result from the exercise of an option depends on the prevailing features of the environment? Decision making is the process of making choices by identifying a decision, gathering information, and assessing alternative resolutions. Using a step-by-step decision-making process can help you make more deliberate, thoughtful decisions by organizing relevant information and defining alternatives. This approach increases the chances that you will choose the most satisfying alternative possible. In the military, it is a process of choosing among two or more courses of action for a given situation. Making decisions is a part of everyday life. Some consider it an art, others a proficiency. Intelligence is to allow leadership to take informed decision. In a classical decision environment, there are certain processes that need to be followed as a guide both in the civil and military environment. These are the following:

<table>
<tr><td align="center">Civil Narrative</td></tr>
</table>

Option 1	Option 2	Option 3: (Mid-Point)	Civil Narrative
Identifying The Incident	Identifying opportunities and diagnosing problems	Identify the Goal or Problem that Requires a Decision	The first step in the decision making process is the clear identification of opportunities or the diagnosis of problems that require a decision. An assessment of opportunities and problems will only be as accurate as the information on which it is based.
Defining The Problem At Hand.	Identifying objectives	Gather Information and Alternatives Associated With Choices	Objectives reflect the results the organization wants to attain. Both the quantity and quality of the desired results should be specified, for these aspects of the objectives will ultimately guide the decision maker in selecting the appropriate course of action.
Gathering Information.	Generating alternatives	Analyse the situation	Once an opportunity has been identified or a problem diagnosed correctly, a manager develops various ways to solve the problem and achieve objectives. The alternatives can be standard and obvious

			as well as innovative and unique.
Formulating And Evaluating Options	Evaluating alternatives	Develop options/ Weigh the evidence. Acceptability and desirability	The fourth step in the decision-making process involves determining the value or adequacy of the alternatives generated. Predetermined decision criteria such as the quality desired, anticipated costs, benefits, uncertainties, and risks of each alternative may be used in the evaluation process.
Making The Decision	Reaching decisions	Evaluate alternatives. Evaluate for feasibility	Decision making is commonly associated with making a final choice. Although choosing an alternative would seem to be a straightforward proposition, in reality the choice is rarely clear-cut.
Orders/ Instructions Formulated	Choosing implementation strategies	Select a preferred alternative	The bridge between reaching a decision and evaluating the results is the implementation phase of the decision-making process. The keys to effective implementation are:

			Sensitivity to those who will be affected by the decision. Proper planning and consideration of the resources necessary to carry out the decision
Communicating The Decision	-	Act on the decision	Communicate decision to wider force for their understanding and seek their buy-in. Some decision may engender change so it is important they are brought on board.
Activity	-		Initiate the activity for which the decision has been arrived at
Evaluating The Effect Caused By The Decision	Monitoring and Evaluating	Review your decision	No decision-making process is complete until the impact of the decision has been evaluated. Managers must observe the impact of the decision as objectively as possible and take further corrective action if it becomes necessary.

The Military Narrative of Decision Making

The military process and narrative is relatively different but more detailed. The military fathoms the decision-making process as a systematic way of problem solving for any scientific research area. The military decision-making process (MDMP) is a proven analytical process for designing operations, troop's movements, logistics or air defence planning. The MDMP is a way of the army's analytical approach to problem solving. Decision making in uncertainty (rippled) environment is about making choices between alternatives whose results are not predictable. The MDMP, which is the military's problem solving approach can be used in many situations and even for non-military problems. It is a standard method of information evaluation and working to reach a solution. It has proven a useful and elastic method in many situations. There are seven steps in military decision-making according to the literature on decision-making. These are receipt of mission, mission analysis, course of action development, course of action analysis, course of action comparison, course of action approval and orders production. Each step of the process needs input of previous steps. Decision makers use inputs of every previous step in order to construct decisions. The proposed MDMP framework is demonstrated by the flow chart below:

Suggested Military Decision Making Process

This as indicated in the table below:

Military Decision Making Process: Estimate	
Estimate Process	**Military Narrative**
Review of Situation	To set the strategic context within which the Estimate is to be conducted
Identify and Analyse the Problem	Identifying and analysing the problem to allow the Commander to deduce what he has to do, within what Context, and Why; thereby focusing his mind. ☐ What is the intention of Commanders one and 2 up, and what is your role in their plans? ☐ What are your specified and implied tasks? ☐ What constraints are there on my freedom of action? ☐ Has the situation changed? Using the four questions to identify and understand purpose, tasks, constraints, freedoms – usually in terms of resources including Rules of engagement, time and space, and politics. ☐ Object Analysis The enemy (in terms of culture, doctrine, objectives, options, Course of Action (COAs) using Centre of Gravity (CoG) ☐ Friendly Forces, Resources, & the Dispute.
Formulation of Potential Course of Action (COAs)	Requests for Information (RFI) ☐ Commander's Critical Information Requirements (CCIR) ☐ Clarification To launch the Staff from Initial Analysis on to Factor Analysis within potential COAs.
Development and Validation of COAs	COA Development proposed to articulate COA in sufficient clarity and detail to allow comparison for a decision to be made, and for Staff and subordinate HQs to develop into a workable plan. COA Statement ☐ Endstate, Mission, Enemy (Operational) & CoG defined. ☐ Description of What is Decisive * Decisive and Shaping Operations within a 'Concept of Operations.
COA Evaluation	The COA development process should be included in a COA Ontology. These are assumptions, objectives, restraints, constraints, Endstate, Centre of Gravity/decisive points, lines of operation, tasks (assigned, implied), risks, available assets, area of operations, criteria for success, timeline, force capabilities, command and control structures. These are to allow the Commander to select the appropriate COA.

Commanders Decision	The commander's decision cycle underpins and supports the preparations process. It helps the commander and staff understand the environment and focuses both staff actions as well as information flow. It includes staff procedures required to prioritize and resource planning efforts, maintain the flow of orders and directives that reflect commander's intent, ensure unity of effort, and evaluate progress. The commander's decision cycle is a process that assists the commander in focusing the staff to support his critical decisions and actions rhythm.
Draft Plan	An Operation Plan is any plan for the conduct of military operations in a hostile environment prepared by the commander of a unified or specified command in response to a requirement. Draft Plan is a concept format in an abbreviated format that would require considerable expansion or alteration. The general criteria for approval of an operation plan are adequacy, feasibility, acceptability, and consistency with doctrine. Combining the criteria of feasibility and acceptability, the review ensures the mission can be accomplished with available resources and without incurring excessive losses in personnel, equipment, material, time, or position.
*Wargame	It is a strategy game that deals with military operations of various types, real or fictional. It may refer to a simple theoretical study or a full-scale military exercise
**Final Plan Execution ***Enemy Course of Action	**Approving and Ordering of operations *** What: The type of operation, such as attack, defend, reinforce, or conduct retrograde * When: The (earliest) time the action will begin * Where: The sectors, zones, axis of attack, avenues of approach, and objectives that make up the COA * How; The method by which the threat will employ his assets, such as dispositions, location of main effort, the scheme of manoeuvre, and how it will be supported * Why: The objective or end state the threat intends to accomplish

Prevailing Decision Making Process

In our current nuetralistic setting, decision making is offset by a number of factors which makes it difficult. In part, the following strategic assumptions must guide our actions;

    a.   Uncertainty, ambiguity and missing data/information.

b. Shifting and competing goals.

c. Action feedback loops (real-time reactions to changing conditions).

d. Time stress.

e. High Stakes.

f. Different Organizational goals and norms.

The above assumptions will drive the decision-making process as depicted below.

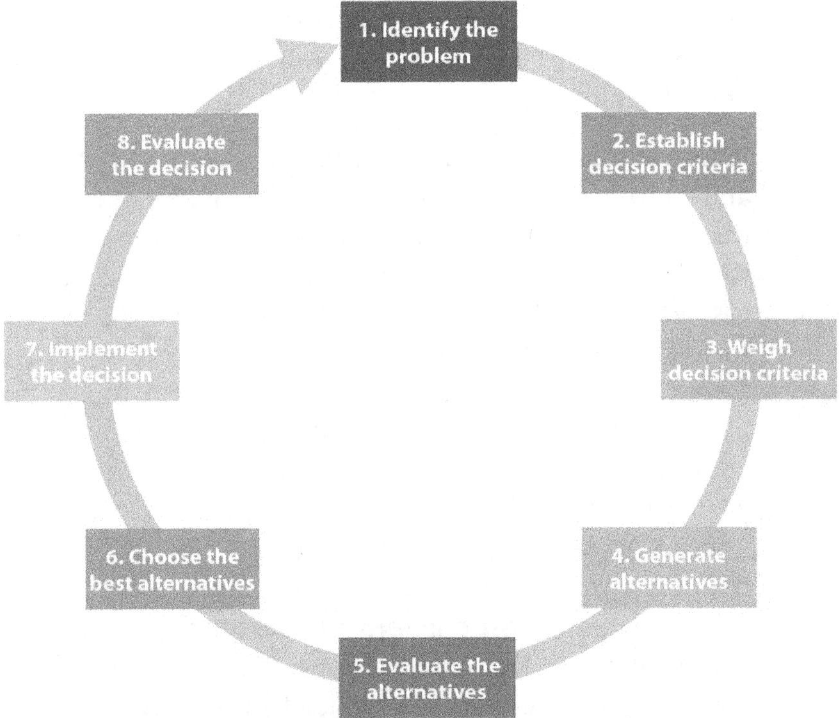

a. **Identify the Decision**: You realize that you need to make a decision. Try to clearly define the nature of the decision you must make. This first step is very important.

b. **Gather/Collect Relevant Information**: Collect some pertinent information before you make your decision: what information is needed, the best sources of information, and how to get it. This step involves both internal and external "work." Some information is internal: you will seek it through a process of self-assessment. Other information is external: you will find it online, in books, from other people, and from other sources.

c. **Identify the Alternatives/Options:** As you collect information, you will probably identify several possible paths of action, or alternatives. You can also use your imagination and additional information to construct new alternatives. In this step, you will list all possible and desirable alternatives.

d. **Weigh the Evidence/Judge:** Draw on your information and emotions to imagine what it would be like if you carried out each of the alternatives to the end. Evaluate whether the need identified in Step 1 would be met or resolved through the use of each alternative. As you go through this difficult internal process, you will begin to favour certain alternatives: those that seem to have a higher potential for reaching your goal. Finally, place the alternatives in a priority order, based upon your own value system.

e. **Choose Among Alternatives:** Once you have weighed all the evidence, you are ready to select the alternative that seems to be the best one for you. You may even choose a combination of alternatives. Your choice in Step 5 may very likely be the same or similar to the alternative you placed at the top of your list at the end of Step 4.

f. **Take Action/Act**: You are now ready to take some positive action by beginning to implement the alternative you chose in Step 5.

g. **Review your decision and its consequences**: In this final step, consider the results of your decision and evaluate whether or not it has resolved the need you identified in Step 1. If the decision has not met the identified need, you may want to repeat certain steps of the process to make a new decision. For example, you might want to gather more detailed or somewhat different information or explore additional alternatives. [85,86]

The first general theory of the stages of a decision process was put forward by the great enlightenment philosopher Condorcet (1743-1794) [87] as part of his motivation for the French constitution of 1793. He divided the decision process into three stages. In the first stage, one "discusses the principles that will serve as the basis for decision on a general issue; one examines the various aspects of this issue and the consequences of different ways to make the decision." At this stage, the opinions are personal, and no attempts are made to form a majority. After this follows a second discussion in which "the question is clarified, opinions approached and combined with one another to arrive at a small number of more general opinions." In this way, the decision is reduced to a choice between a manageable set of alternatives. The third stage consists of the actual choice between these alternatives [88].

The commander will frequently start his analysis with his orders and a map or chart, before his staff develop the intelligence preparation of the battlefield (IPB) tools needed to give him detailed information. At this early stage, accurate information on general locations of legally-protected persons, objects, installations and areas will help to shape his initial thoughts. The decision-making procedure should ensure that accurate

---

85. https://www.umassd.edu/fycm/decision-making/process/

86. https://www.projectmanager.com/blog/decision-making-process

87. Condorcet ([1793] 1847), "Plan de Constitution, presenté a la convention nationale les 15 et 16 février 1793", Oeuvres, vol. 12, pp. 333-415.

88. Ibid

information is available at appropriate levels of notice, to inform this early decision-making phase. While analysing a superior's orders, i.e. extracting and deducing the immediate superior commander's intent, the tasks (specified and implied) necessary to fulfil the mission, the applicable constraints and the potential changes in the situation, the tasked commander needs to assess whether he may lawfully execute the given mission within the applicable legal framework. He should, therefore, be conscious of his obligations. The analysis of both specified tasks (i.e. those stated in the directives or orders received by the subordinate from his superior commander) and implied tasks (i.e. other activities that have to be carried out in order to achieve the mission) enable the commander to identify what he should do to accomplish his mission. This analysis is also an opportunity for the commander and his staff to check the legality of the different tasks and to identify those measures (both actions and constraints) which will be necessary to ensure the tasks are executed in accordance with the law. These necessary actions will translate into missions to subordinates. On completion of his Mission Analysis, the commander gives direction on the completion of the Estimate (Commander's Planning Guidance and the plan for staff work) and may also seek any necessary clarification required. He continues to review his mission throughout the estimate process and subsequent execution. Course of Action (COA) development is based on the direction given by the commander after mission analysis. The Commander's Planning Guidance is, therefore, an opportunity for the commander, at an early stage, to direct the staff to design COAs. The decision-making process should provide concrete measures for the commander, in his guidance to his staff, to:

a. Clarify the constraints, in time, space, rules of engagement, resources, movements, humanitarian effects, etc., which the commander wishes to impose in order to avoid, or in any event minimize the humanitarian impact of his operations;

b. Specify the procedures he wishes to establish in order to control the targeting process, including the identification of legitimate military objectives and the assessment of proportionality in attacks, in particular the appropriate level at which decisions on proportionality should be made;

c. Specify the factors, including issues of proportionality, distinction and humanitarian impact, the commander wishes to be used in evaluating the COAs.

Beyond his given mission, a number of factors, such as the enemy, the environment, his troops and the timing, shape the commander's decision and his operation. During the evaluation of these factors, the identification of their legal and humanitarian implications in addition to their military significance is key for enabling LOAC rules to be applied effectively in the execution of the mission. Relevant information is directly derived from the intelligence preparation of the battlespace (IPB). Its accuracy and prompt delivery, therefore, directly affects the planning and conduct of operations. The analysis of the local geography and demography, in addition to their direct input in determining the elements of the envisaged COAs, should also highlight specific elements that play a role in the application of the legal rules. This analysis must be complemented by an evaluation of the existing humanitarian situation and of the possible consequences of planned or ongoing operations. Without timely and accurate information on the human element of the environment the commander will not be able to meet his obligations to distinguish between military objectives and combatants on the one hand and legally protected persons, objects, installations and areas on the other hand. Similarly, he will not be able to accurately assess proportionality in his operations. A correct understanding of the human dimension of the battlespace and of the potential collateral damage resulting from his operations permits the commander to fix limits to the planned or ongoing COA. These Intelligent Preparation of the Battlespace products should include, in particular:

a. The provision of a detailed analysis of potential opposing forces and military objectives;

b. The provision of a detailed analysis of all legally protected persons, objects, installations and areas within the area of operations;

c. The elements of identification of the opposing forces, including the distinction of their protected members (i.e. medical and religious personnel);

d. The location, movements and situation of personnel, installations and transport means of the enemy's non-combatant units (i.e. medical and religious personnel);

e. The location of POW camps and military or civilian internment camps (i.e. under enemy control);

f. The legal status of the police forces, civil defence units and other organized national services (i.e. members of the armed forces or not);

g. Locations and concentrations of the civilian population (e.g. towns, villages, hamlets, shelters, camps for refugees, displaced persons or civilian internees);

h. The possibility, at the outbreak of the hostilities, of having to face elements of a hostile "levée en masse" and acting as combatants and how they are to be dealt with;

i. The likelihood of direct participation in hostilities by civilians;

j. The presence, location, situation and movements of UN personnel (civilian or military) and humanitarian organizations, if any;

k. Objects indispensable for the survival of the population (e.g. drinkable water, food stocks and their storage, agricultural areas, etc.);

l. Civilian medical installations or facilities, permanent or temporary, and their personnel;

m. Cultural objects (buildings or objects of high cultural value with their recognized level of protection and their personnel);

n. Works and installations containing dangerous forces in the legal meaning (i.e. nuclear power plants, dams and dykes) as well as other specific facilities presenting an equivalent threat (e.g. chemical industry, petrol installations) and their personnel;

o. Areas with special status (e.g. demilitarized or neutralized zones, non-defended localities, diplomatic representations) and their personnel;

p. The necessary coordination mechanism for the continuous and prompt updating and sharing of this information throughout the planning and conduct of the operation with the relevant cells, including in particular the targeting team.

q. The nature, situation, deployment and combat power of the enemy are essential elements of information permitting the commander to correctly assess his possible COAs and hence their potential impact on the humanitarian situation. The IPB will include a terrain analysis and this will frequently allow identification of enemy avenues of approach or movement corridors. A development of this analysis will allow the IPB to give an indication of potential civilian movement corridors, particularly as they relate to potential enemy COAs. This analysis should in turn inform the development of the commander's own COAs.

Time Factor in Decision Matrix

Time, often linked to space, will inevitably constrain the possible COAs. In the military, the commander or his staff has to assess the timing of each task identified. Timing includes both the sequence of tasks and the duration of each, as far as this can be realistically assessed before contact with the enemy. In particular, the commander will be focused on generating tempo – achieving his objectives at a greater rate than his opponent does. However, the commander needs also to consider the tempo of his operations relative to the responses of the civilian population. Therefore, in addition to analysing the likely timelines which can be predicted for enemy action, a similar analysis is required for the reaction of the civilian population to the effects of the conflict. The duration of military operations in any particular area will be an important factor in assessing the extent to which the civilian population will be impacted. Thus, an accurate assessment of duration, linked to the humanitarian infrastructure analysis addressed during the IPB, could impact have on the commander's proportionality decisions during the planning process. The decision-making procedure or manual should address the tasking of staff resources to consider:

a. The time necessary for precautions to be taken to avoid, or in any event to minimize, the risk to legally-protected persons, objects, installations and areas in the planning and conduct of operations (e.g. time and means necessary for an effective warning of the population prior to an attack, time necessary for civilians to take shelter or be evacuated, conditions for a possible ceasefire for civilians to re-supply themselves with medicine, food and water);

b. Possibility for an attack to be scheduled when legally protected persons, objects and areas are less at risk;

c. The time required to ensure that precautions to protect legally protected persons, objects and areas, including mission-specific training for troops if required, are completed;

d. The timeline of likely movements or displacements of the civilian population;

e. The endurance of the humanitarian support infrastructure under the additional pressures, which will be imposed by the planned military operations (e.g. days of supply of medical facilities including medicines and fuel, capacities of water supply systems both in situ and on potential population displacement routes, adequacy of food stocks which cannot be re-supplied due to fighting).

Most writers on management think that management is basically a decision-making process. George Terry therefore, defines decision-making "as the selection of one behaviour alternative from two or more possible alternatives." Mcfarland, on the other hand, defines 'a decision is an act of choice wherein an executive form a conclusion about what must be done in a given situation. A decision represents behaviour chosen from a number of alternatives." They argue that it is only through making decisions that an organisation can accomplish its short-term and long-term goals. The person making the decision weights what options are available, considers the factors of the situation, and chooses, to them, the best solution and applies it. A decision is an act of selection or choice of one action from several alternatives. Decision-making can be defined as the process of selecting a right and effective course of action from two or more alternatives for the purpose of achieving a desired result. Decision-making is the essence of management. When managers make decisions, they exercise choice.

a. They decide what to do on the basis of some conscious and deliberate logic or judgement.

b. When making a decision, managers are faced with alternatives. An organisation does not require a wise manager to reach a decision when there are no other possible choices. It does require wisdom and experience to evaluate several alternatives and select the best one.

c. When taking a decision, the managers have a purpose. They propose and analyse the alternative courses of action and finally make a choice that is likely to move the organisation in the direction of its goal.

At every level, the commander is responsible, after staff work or an individual estimate, for the ultimate decision on the course of action and the tasking of subordinates. This responsibility covers the military, command, individual and legal aspects and extends throughout the full execution of the mission through the commander's permanent control function. The commander must choose among the different possible COAs the one which presents, in his view, the most efficient manner to fulfil his mission. However, when a choice is possible between equally efficient COAs, preference must be given to the one entailing the least potential impact on legally protected persons, objects, installations and areas. Therefore, the proposed courses of action must be legal and presented with their associated risk of collateral damage and an assessment of proportionality. The decision-making procedure should give the commander the tools to enable him to make such a decision. Decision-making helps to utilise the available resources for achieving the objectives of the organisation. Decision-making is a vital part of any business and a key function of its success. Nothing happens in any kind of organization without decisions being made. According to Drucker 'whatever a manager does, he does through making decisions.' All matters relating to planning, organising, direction, co-ordination and control are settled by the managers through decisions, which are executed into practice by the operators of the enterprise. Objectives, goals, strategies, policies and organisational designs are all to be decided upon in order to regulate the performance of the business. Decision-making is perhaps the most important component of a manager's activities. It plays the most important role in the planning process. When managers plan, they decide on many matters as what goals their organisation will pursue, what resources they will use, and who will perform each required task. Effective and successful decisions make profit to the company and unsuccessful ones make losses. Therefore, the corporate decision-making process is the most critical process in any organization. When it comes to making decisions, one should always weigh the positive and negative business consequences and should favour the positive outcomes.

Summary

A threat may be any activity directed at undermining, or directed at or intended to bring about the destruction of one's interests by unlawful or hostile means. Our life is gauged by the threats we face and, life must be considered as a war. The chapter therefore examines some choices and behaviours in leadership. The chapter also examines the central role of decision in every leadership endeavour. The military sees their decision-making process, called the 'estimate', as a planning tool consistent with the 'manoeuvrist approach' and associated philosophy of mission command. It is designed to guide the thought process. The traditional business education is not catered to meet the complex demands of a business family. Central issues like family dynamics, succession planning, family governance and communication are often overlooked. The elements in the leadership decision process, the prevailing decision making process and essence of time in the decision matrix are examined in this chapter.

Chapter Four

Skills and Intelligence in Leadership

'The future welfare of the country hinges in no small degree upon the right education of superior children. Whether civilization moves on and up depends on the advances made by creative thinkers and leaders in science, politics, art, morality, and religion. Moderate ability can follow, or imitate, but genius must show the way.'
Lewis M. Terman, 1919

Cognitive Intelligence and Leadership

Team member characteristics are generally divided into behavioural proclivities like conflict management style; proximal psychological states like beliefs, values and perceptual patterns; and more distal or deeper general psychological states like intelligence. Psychological states are generally viewed as a significant determinant of perception and subsequent behaviour, and are therefore of interest to both researchers and practitioners, particularly those states that can be reliably shaped by external forces [89]. Social cognitive theory suggests that cognitive processing of social information can influence human performance. Beliefs about one's ability to mobilize sufficient effort, cognitive resources and the behavioural strategies necessary for successful task completion are considered important determinants of performance and satisfaction [90]. Soft skills are a combination of people skills,

---

[89] Graeme. H. Coetzer, Emotional versus Cognitive Intelligence: Which is the better predictor of Efficacy for Working in Teams? 2016 Institute of Behavioral and Applied Management

social skills, communication skills, character traits, attitudes, career attributes, social intelligence and emotional intelligence quotients among others that enable people to navigate their environment, work well with others, perform well, and achieve their goals with complementing hard skills. The *Collins English Dictionary* defines the term "soft skills" as "desirable qualities for certain forms of employment that do not depend on acquiring knowledge which include common sense, the ability to deal with people, and a positive, flexible attitude. The world today is characterized by increasing variety, interdependency and connectivity; complexity, change, ambiguity, seamlessness and sustainability. There is no doubt that more 'intelligent' leaders are needed to deal with these emerging challenges and demands. Nevertheless, the world is relentlessly fast and dynamic. Most of the literature on leadership studies was based on the aforementioned approach, and in most of the relevant studies, the behaviours, skills and personal attitudes of leaders are analysed [91].

One of the leading theories that researchers have begun to recently study more frequently is intelligent leadership theory. The understanding of intelligent leadership allows one to act effectively at various levels of management, from certain individuals to teams, organizations and society as a whole. Intelligent leadership should help each member of a team in their comprehensive personal development and help them develop their self-sufficiency; it raises the intellectual potential of an organization and plays an active role in the creation of intellectual communities. The ultimate goal of leadership lies in the creation of a unique environment, in which economic and ethical aspects are balanced. The success of an increasing

---

90 Bandura, A. (1986). Differential engagement of self-reactive influences in cognitive motivation. Organizational Behavior and Human Decision Processes, 38(1), 92-114.

91. Bass B.M. (2010) Theory, Research and Managerial Application (3rd ed.), New York: The Free Press.

number of organizations today depends on making effective and timely decisions, which are based on sensible leadership. The ability to lead is one of the major challenges of the present and the future, because the way leaders think and the manner in which they act determines the development of the organization [92] . Intelligent leadership is a constructive dialogue between leaders and followers, which facilitates bringing their efforts together to achieve a common vision. Such a process is possible if the organization supports certain corporate values and a culture formulated in an industrial and social macro-environment [93]. The task of intelligent leadership is the creation of abilities, the generation of collective enthusiasm, and the expansion of an organization's knowledge capital. The adoption of such an approach in institutions provides a balance between the current activity and planning for the future. The key qualities of leaders include the ability to negotiate and make decisions, strategic and critical thinking, management of talent and teams with account of values, personalities and personal principles.

As a result of the complexity, rise in innovation, and flexibility of organizations, overall, the literature has begun to consider leadership as both a collective and common action. The perception of leadership has started to move from the traditional roles to the new roles such as team building and group work. This means that leaders now face a real risk of becoming merely the sum total of un-reflected, undigested, constantly and rapidly accumulating experiences and information. There is too little time for reflective living, the sort that provides sufficient 'quiet time' so intelligent leaders can constantly transform experiences into information, information

---

92. Soltani I. (2009) Six Intelligence Of Intelligent Leadership Tool. Compass, vol. 210, pp. 21–27.

93. Rutkauskas A.V., Stasytyteb V. (2013) Leadership intelligence: How to get there? Procedia – Social and Behavioral Sciences, vol. 75 (2013), pp. 52–61. DOI: 10.1016/j.sbspro.2013.04.007

into knowledge, and knowledge into wisdom. Intelligence (from the Latin 'to understand') refers to leaders who can observe, think, judge, act, learn and reflect with a growing understanding as they engage – conceptually and practically with the world. Intelligence is the ability of the mind to comprehend, use thought and reasoning for problem solving, the ability to acquire knowledge and use it practically. Sternberg defines intelligence as the mental abilities necessary for adaptation to, as well as the selection and shaping of, any environmental context [94]. Sternberg offers a triarchic model consisting of:

a. `Academic intelligence (as measured by the classical IQ tests);
b. Practical intelligence (which grows through the accumulation of tacit knowledge for solving practical everyday problems); and
c. Creative intelligence, which involves synthetic abilities to see problems in new ways and to escape the bounds of conventional thinking, but has not been studied as rigorously.

Gardner on the other hand defines intelligence as a set of abilities that are used to solve problems and create products that are valuable within a cultural setting or community. [95]

Successful intelligence is the ability to succeed in life according to one's own definition of success, within one's sociocultural context, by capitalizing on one's strengths, and correcting or compensating for one's weaknesses, in order to adapt to, shape, and select environments through a combination of analytical, creative, and practical abilities [96]. Intelligent leadership involves

---

94. Robert J. Sternberg & Elena L. Grigorenko: (2000) Teaching for Successful Intelligence: Principles, Procedures, and Practices Journal for the Education of the Gifted. Vol. 27, No. 2/3, 2003, pp. 207–228.

95. Sternberg, R. J. (1995). In search of the human mind. Ft. Worth, TX: Harcourt

96. Sternberg, R. J., Grigorenko, E. L., & Jarvin, L. (2001). Improving reading instruction: The triarchic model. Educational Leadership 58(6), 48-52.

cultivating the heart, mind, and soul in order to bring exceptional leadership skills to an organization. Intelligent leadership opens the space for collaboration, consultations and cooperation among faculty members and makes them more tightly linked with the organization by integrating behavioural and professional skills into a single base of knowledge and abilities. Intelligent leadership focuses on the achievement of goals, the management of emotions and feelings, the search for meaning and the development of the spirit of teamwork, which can be effective in expanding the scale of activity at a university, and provide for its comprehensive development. John Mattone in his book *Intelligent Leadership*, accedes that it is no secret that strong organizations have strong leaders. However, in today's increasingly volatile, globalized economy, the need for executives who can collaborate, inspire, and motivate is more acute than ever. Mattone describes a process based on empirical research that uses a leader's inner-core strengths and outer-core competencies. [97]

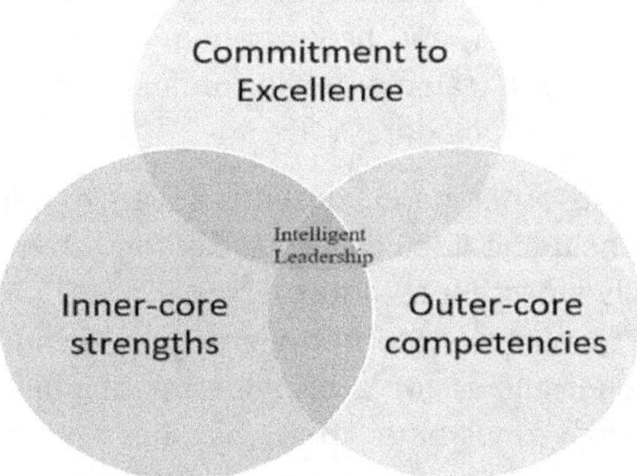

Source: Mattone [98]

---

97. John Mattone, (2013) Intelligent Leadership: What You Need to Know to Unlock Your Full Potential. American Management Association

98 Ibid

Inner-core strengths include traits like character, positive emotions, positive beliefs, self-concept, and values. Outer-core leadership competencies are made up of a person's capabilities, commitment, and connectedness. A leader cannot be focused on the past, but must be able to look realistically at the present situation, with its good qualities and its bad ones. With Intelligent Leadership, a leader not only has a focus on the here and now, but also puts practices into place to ensure the good work outlives its tenure. This involves recognizing and cultivating emerging leadership. Leaders cannot lead effectively unless they know themselves. Any organization that wants continuing success needs Intelligent Leadership. Theoretically, an organization might not require Intelligent Leadership if it were temporary, devoted to a single goal, and ready to disband once that is over, but even that would be short-sighted. Intelligent Leadership is not only devoted to getting excellent results at the particular moment, or the current business quarter, but indefinitely thereafter. Implementing Intelligent Leadership requires, first, finding leaders and future leaders with the potential for greatness, and helping them develop their unique leadership gifts and talents while understanding their own weaknesses so they can address them.

Gardner, on the other hand, outlines seven multiple types of intelligences including linguistic, musical, logical, mathematical, spatial, bodily-kinesthetic, interpersonal, and intrapersonal intelligence [99]. Whereas Sternberg emphasizes mental abilities, Gardner's model allows for a broader set of abilities, such as musical or bodily-kinesthetic, that may have a corresponding biological basis for their functioning and are not typically thought of as mental abilities. Gardner later added naturalistic intelligence, the ability to recognize patterns in the flora and

---

[99]. Gardner, H. (1983). Frames of mind: The theory of multiple intelligences. New York: BasicBooks.

fauna in the wild, and suggested the possibility of an existential intelligence, involving the capacity to address existential questions, pertaining to the fact of our existence as individuals in the cosmos and our capacity to puzzle over that fact [100]. Intelligence is important, but as a stand-alone tool for leadership, it lacks penetrating substance. Cognitive intelligence is the mental quality that consists of the abilities to learn from experience, adapt to new situations, understand and handle abstract concepts, and use knowledge to manipulate or influence one's environment. Here, the circumstances are the objects, or conditions by which one is surrounded. Also, they comprise the complex physical, chemical, and biotic factors, such as climate, soil, and living things that act upon an organism or an ecological community and ultimately determine its form and survival. In addition, they may be the aggregate of social and cultural conditions that influence the life of an individual or community.

Different investigators have emphasized different aspects of intelligence in their definitions. For example, in a 1921 symposium, the American psychologists, Lewis Terman and Edward L. Thorndike differed over the definition of intelligence. While Terman stressed the ability to think abstractly, Thorndike emphasized learning and the ability to give good responses to questions. More recently, however, psychologists have generally agreed that adaptation to the environment is the key to understanding both what intelligence is and what it does. Effective adaptation draws upon a number of cognitive processes, such as perception, learning, memory, reasoning, and problem solving. The main emphasis in a definition of intelligence, then, is that, it is not a cognitive or mental process, per se, but rather a selective combination of these processes

---

[100]. Gardner, H. (1999). Intelligence reframed: Multiple intelligences for the 21st century New York: BasicBooks

that is purposefully directed toward effective adaptation. Thus, the physician who learns about a new disease adapts by perceiving material on the disease in the medical literature, learning what the material contains, remembering the crucial aspects that are needed to treat the patient, and then utilizing reason to solve the problem of applying the information to the needs of the patient. Intelligence, in total, has come to be regarded, not as a single ability, but as an effective drawing together of many abilities. This has not always been obvious to investigators of the subject; however, indeed, much of the history of the field revolves around arguments regarding the nature and abilities that constitute intelligence [101]. Our ability to deal with the various aspects of leadership and change may be considered under the following:

a. **Intelligence Quotient (IQ)**: In total, has come to be regarded not as a single ability but as an effective drawing together of many abilities. This has not always been obvious to investigators of the subject; however, indeed, much of the history of the field revolves around arguments regarding the nature and abilities that constitute intelligence. Schools have taught that good decision-making is about assembling all of the relevant data, analysing the data and then using logical reasoning to come up with the best plan of action. It is all about how to use your brain. Nevertheless, while brain smarts are important, there are two other types of intelligence that make a leader effective. For instance, someone can be intelligent, but awkward with relationships, thus, lacking social intelligence. Someone can be intelligent, but lack self-mastery or character intelligence, and someone can possess superior intellectual capacity, but only from divinity's point of view; this is meaningless. One can have a high I.Q., yet be inept in practical matters.

---

[101]. Robert J. Sternberg, Human intelligence

b. Emotional Quotient (EQ): Most people can recall encountering an individual in a leadership position who was a brilliant thinker, but had great difficulty understanding how to connect with people. These leaders struggle when their team members are unable to commit to a decision, particularly when they see it as the obvious course of action. An individual with a high IQ could influence others by developing an understanding of how to connect with people on an emotional level vs. just using logical reasoning. A case was made that great leaders need to work with both their head and their heart. In 2002, Daniel Kahneman, a Princeton University psychologist, notable for his work on the psychology of judgment and decision-making, as well as behavioural economics won the Nobel Memorial Prize in Economic Sciences. His research that won him the award demonstrated that human beings make decisions first for emotional reasons, and then secondly for rational reasons[102]. The ground-breaking research solidified our notion that both head and heart are critical components in the skill set of an effective leader. For leaders, having emotional intelligence is essential for success. According to Daniel Goleman, [103] there are five key elements to it, which include:

i. **Self-Awareness**: Keeping a journal, and slowing down.
ii. **Self-Regulation**: Knowing your values, holding yourself accountable, and practising being calm.
iii. **Motivation**: Re-examining why you are doing your job; i.e., knowing where you stand and being hopeful, and finding something good.
iv. **Empathy**: Putting yourself in someone else's position. Paying attention to body language and responding to feelings.

---

[102]. Daniel Kahneman, A Perspective on Judgment and Choice, Mapping Bounded Rationality. September 2003 American Psychologist

[103]. Daniel Goleman, 2015, Emotional Intelligence: Why It Can Matter More Than IQ

v. **Social Skills**: Learning conflict resolution, improving your communication skills, and learning how to praise others.

c. Character Quotient (CQ): Character quotient represents the strength of one's character. While your brain may be valuable to someone else (i.e. an employer), your beliefs only hold value to you. Character quotient raises the question of what sum you would command to compromise your beliefs. A person with a high Character Quotient would be unlikely to compromise their beliefs based on temptations such as money or a promotion. This integrity makes them a great asset to your organization. The first step is to recognize the importance of character and its impact on behaviour and decision-making. Once this happens, character can be emphasized as part of a philosophy of building a culture that emphasizes CQ as much as IQ and EQ. By embedding positive principles into organizational culture, an organization can trust their leadership at all levels, and this will increase their effectiveness and overall performance. When identifying people that will drive long-term success and significance, the elements needed to achieve this are:

i. A strong mind (high IQ);
ii. A strong ability to influence people on an emotional level (high EQ);
iii. A strong positive character (high CQ).

In addition to the above, Joel Garcia [104] lists four other aspects considered to be critical for any leader which are wisdom, character, social and spiritual intelligence.

d. Social Intelligence or Quotient: It is the ability to understand humans and act wisely in human interactions. Snow, on the other hand, categorises it as accumulation of knowledge, cognitive abilities and affective sensitivities that enables

---

104. Joel Garcia, Leadership Intelligence: The Four Intelligences of a Leader, Leadership Advance Online– Issue XXII

individuals to navigate their social world. [105] Everyone wants to feel loved and happy at home and at work. The key is healthy relationships. The original definition of social intelligence by Edward Thorndike in 1920 is 'the ability to understand and manage men and women, boys and girls, to act wisely in human relations.' The Mindspa Institute [106] defines SQ as:

> *The extension of Emotional intelligence's relationship management competency. SQ is, thus, your ability to manage your own emotional skills needed to correctly read social situations and other people's emotions and then to react in a manner that is socially acceptable, in order to get others to cooperate and co-exist. Social Intelligence is the essence of human relationships.*

Social intelligence is the capacity to know oneself and to know others. Social scientist Ross Honeywill believes social intelligence is an aggregated measure of self- and social-awareness, evolved social beliefs and attitudes, and a capacity and appetite to manage complex social change.

According to Daniel Goleman, empathy and social skills are social intelligence and the interpersonal part of emotional intelligence. If we want businesses to remain viable and profitable, today's leaders need to build their own networks of interconnected people. Barry Libert, in his book *Social Nation* asserts that people in a Social Nation will support the entity or objective because the leaders support them. Building a Social Nation requires shifts in culture, mindset, and leadership. [107] It is no easy task; it cannot be accomplished without a little prior introspection. How to harness the power of Social Media to attract customers, motivate employees, and grow your business

---

105.

106. The Mindspa Institute is based in South Africa and specialises in skills development

107. Barry Libert, (2010), Social Nation: How to Harness the Power of Social Media to Attract Customers, Motivate Employees, and Grow Your Business. John Wiley and Sons, Inc

is to help leaders and managers get a sense of where their strengths are and how they can improve those and strengthen their other business competencies. Knowing what social skills you have is vital to understanding your own particular brand of leadership. It can improve your ability to make friends, have fans and followers, and ultimately, to succeed in business.

According to Daniel Coleman, social intelligence possesses two components. The first component is social awareness; that is what we sense about others. The second is social faculty, which is what we do with that awareness. In other words, social intelligence is how we read others and approach them to gain the best possible connection. Tim Sanders, author of the book *The Likeability Factor* also asserts that 'likeability is an ability to create positive attitudes in other people through the delivery of emotional and physical benefits. By being likeable, by generating positive feelings in others, you gain as well. The quality of your life and the strength of one's relationships are the product of a choice, but not necessarily the individual's choice[108]. Gifts of likeability may include the following:

i. **Positivity**: This person has an enthusiasm that is contagious. They are upbeat and can get others excited about what they are going to do.

ii. **Activator**: They can make things happen by turning thoughts into action.

iii. **WOO (Winning Others Over) Factor**: They love the challenge of meeting new people and winning them over. They derive satisfaction by 'breaking the ice' and making a connection.

iv. **Communication**: This person finds it easy to put their thoughts into words; they are good conversationalists and presenters.

---

[108]. Tim Sanders, The Likeability Factor How to Boost Your L-Factor and Achieve Your Life's Dreams, Published by Crown, 2005

v. **Empathy**: They can sense the feelings of other people by imagining themselves in their lives or situation.

In other words, social intelligence refers to the ability to read other people and understand their intentions and motivations. It is, basically, the capacity to effectively negotiate complex social relationships and environments. Social scientist, Ross Honeywill, believes social intelligence is an aggregated measure of self-and social-awareness, evolved social beliefs and attitudes, and a capacity and appetite to manage complex social change. According to Sean Foleno, social intelligence is a person's competence to understand his or her environment optimally and react appropriately for socially successful conduct. The social intelligence hypothesis states that social intelligence, that is, complex socialization such as politics, romance, family relationships, quarrels, collaboration, reciprocity, and altruism, (1) was the driving force in developing the size of human brains and (2) today provides our ability to use those large brains in complex social circumstances. That is, it was the demands of living together that drove our need for intelligence generally. Social intelligence is a critical factor in brain growth, social and cognitive complexity co-evolves. Libert, on the other hand, put forth, eight social types, which need to be harnessed for effective social quotient. These are:

1. **Adaptors (Remain Flexible).** The ability to adjust expectations and behaviour on the fly to fit any type of situation is crucial in the fast-paced world of business. Adaptors are comfortable dealing with shifted plans and the unpredictable world of social networks and online communities. They can help identify problem areas quickly and can implement a change in strategy as needed. Leaders must always be prepared to deal with the unexpected. With social media, things move at such an extreme pace that this skill is vital.

2. **Architects (See the Big Picture).** Having a clearly defined mission for how to get to where you want to go is a skill that is often overlooked. In sustaining a social presence, architects keep conversations going by infusing them with this vision. Too often, organizations get bogged down in the details and they lose sight of their overall goals. While the little things certainly matter and help to keep a business running day to day, the big picture should be the ultimate focus. Architects remind us of that purpose, especially when it comes to creating a social strategy.

3. **Collaborators (Work Together).** Being a team player is absolutely essential to the success of any business. Collaborators enjoy being part of a support system of people who share a common purpose. They often measure their own success as a function of the team's success, and they help build social community. Collaborators are also great at revving up team participation. They are not afraid to approach people and build relationships outside an organization's normal sphere of communication.

4. **Connectors (Control the Chaos).** This is the ability to organize the diverse aspects of day-to-day business to achieve results. Connectors integrate a variety of viewpoints and perspectives into a complete composition that encourages social interactions and conversations to run smoothly. Connectors thrive on devising new configurations and assisting in linking discussions through diverse mediums to harmonize an organization's social media strategy with its overall business goals.

5. **Creative Thinkers (Think Innovatively).** Proposing new ideas can rejuvenate a team and keep them from falling into a rut. Creative thinkers come up with new,

inventive ways to tackle familiar challenges. They enjoy being enlightened while collecting new information. Additionally, they are skilled at finding unusual connections among people and content within a Social Nation.

6. **Transparent Individuals (Break Down the Façade).** People who are open and honest are likely to gain trust and respect from others. For transparent individuals, authentic communication is the name of their game — and they encourage their organization to increase its level of transparency by sharing through social media. Social media, by its very nature, is built upon the assumption that online communities will provide a venue for unhindered communication. In fact, it is often scarier for companies to hide information than it is for them to share it. Transparent individuals encourage their organizations to be open and transparent.

7. **Risk Takers (Trying Something New).** Venturing into unknown territory may be scary, but it can also be very rewarding. Risk Takers know that there is much to be gained through trial-and-error learning. They are motivated by progress. Unlike risk-averse naysayers, they would gladly take on the social movement challenge.

8. **Visionaries (Imagine the Possibilities).** Instead of focusing on obstacles, thinking about alternative outcomes and solutions can help energize and inspire others. Visionaries are intuitive. They challenge the status quo in the hope of reaching a better future. They also help identify the next big trends—which is exceptionally vital to building a social strategy. They also add value thanks to their ability to determine long-term, best-case scenarios for an organization's strategy.

d. **Adaptability Quotient (AQ):** Theory U by Otto Scharmer suggests three elements that can help provide a framework: keeping an open mind, so you see the world with fresh eyes and remain open to possibilities; keeping an open heart, so you can try to see any situation through another person's eyes; and, keeping an open will, letting go of identity and ego to sit with the discomfort of the unknown [109]. In essence, it posits that, individuals, teams, organizations and large systems can build the essential leadership capacities needed to address the root causes of today's social, environmental, and spiritual challenges. In essence, we show how to update the operating code in our societal systems through a shift in consciousness from ego-system to eco-system awareness. Adaptability has been proposed by Hall, as a career meta-competency, which along with personal identity forms the core of a protean career. [110] It is, at its core, the capacity to change, including both the competence and the motivation to do so. [111]

The 21st century economy moves faster and demands quicker learning. Also, with massive connectivity within and between organizations, change is rapid and unrelenting. Organizations that can learn and adapt faster than their competitors have an advantage. Amidst political turmoil, technological revolution, energy and health transformations and even private space flight, humanity is facing an intense need to adapt at a pace never before experienced. One of the most helpful ways to cope with change is to think about what could happen before it actually happens. With the accelerating rate of technological change, we are facing more change than ever before, and we can train our brains to better adapt to those changes. Adaptability refers to how well a person reacts to the inevitability of change.

---

[109]. C. Otto Scharmer, 2009, Theory U: Leading from the Future as It Emerges, Berreth-Koehler Publishers, Inc

[110]. Hall, D. T. (2002). Careers in and out of organizations. Thousand Oaks, CA: Sage.

[111]. Hall, D. T., & Chandler, D. E. (2005). Psychological success: When the career is a calling. Journal of Organizational Behavior, 26, 155-176.

Adaptability plays a vital role in success, and as the future of work continues to evolve, acclimating to change can be stressful when you are not prepared for it. Today's businesses are having to find ways to thrive in a rapid, radically changing business environment, including embracing new and more modern business models and more forward-thinking ways of working. In an age of constant technological innovation, the next Uber, Amazon or Airbnb that reshapes their business sector could be just around the corner.

Adaptability Quotient measures a business' ability to greet changes in the marketplace, consumer preferences, and technology. In the definitive treatise of John S. McCallum on the adaptability quotient, entitled 'Adapt or Die', AQ is defined as 'the ability to adjust course, product, service, and strategy in response to unanticipated changes in the market.'[112] The dinosaur metaphor is apt. Sixty million years ago, dinosaurs suddenly disappeared after more than 100 million years on the planet. Paleontologists hotly debate the cause of the dinosaur's extinction, but high on the list of hypotheses is their failure to adapt to rapidly changing climatic, particularly, temperature conditions. If a failure to adapt was the dinosaur's Achilles' heel, then the dinosaur is not alone in the history of evolution. In his landmark 1859 book, *The Origin of Species*, Charles Darwin showed that those species that adapt best to their changing environment have the best chance of surviving, while those that do not adapt do not make it. Since heredity makes children resemble parents, in time, surviving species will have the characteristics of its most adaptable members. According to Darwin, 'it is not the most intellectual of the species that survives; it is not the strongest that survives; but the species that survives is the one that is able to adapt to and to adjust best to the changing environment in which it finds itself. [113] Change

---

[112]. John S. McCallum, Adapt or Die

puts a premium on adapting; the faster the pace of change, the greater the premium. Take away change and there is no need to adapt.

Since the turn of the 21st century, a business' adaptive capabilities have been 'thrown into the spotlight,' though few have turned their attention to it. The Adaptability Quotient is ultimately a variable in the equation of success, but has been frequently overlooked on account of not being well-understood, articulated, or broadcast to a wide-enough audience of business leaders. AQ has been identified as 'the future of work' by the *Fast Company* magazine, while the *Harvard Business Review* describes it as the "new competitive advantage." The business publication *Talent Economy*, reports it could ultimately become as important as either IQ or EQ when it comes to hiring. The *Talent Economy* report is corroborated by a UK study in which 91% of HR decision-makers said that they expect future employees to be recruited based largely on their ability to cope with change and uncertainty. AQ's emergence is the result of trends that are radically reshaping the modern workplace. The shelf life of employee skills is being shortened by technological advancements (a typical business competency now lasts about five years, down from 30 years in 1984), and employees are switching jobs more than ever before.

According to a LinkedIn study, people who graduated between 2006 and 2010 averaged 2.85 jobs in the five years after graduation, compared to 1.6 for people who graduated between 1986 and 2000. Also, according to the most recent data from the U.S. Bureau of Labour, the average employee now spends 4.2 years at a job. That means that if they enter the workforce at age 25 and retire at age 65, they will work at nearly nine different jobs (plus any new roles they might assume within a given company). At the same time, employee skills are becoming

---

[113] Charles Darwin, 1859, On the Origin of Species by Means of Natural Selection, or the Preservation of Favoured Races in the Struggle for Life

out-dated faster than ever before. According to the World Economic Forum, 35% of the skills that employees will require to do their job, regardless of industry, will have changed by 2020. The PwC study 'Adapt to Survive' says that employers will require adaptable employees, many of whom are not currently in the right roles, in order to safeguard against future threats to their business. At least a quarter of workers in OECD countries report a "skills mismatch" with what is required by their current job according to the World Economic Forum. It has been consistently asserted that '...enabling and empowering workers to transform and update their skills is a key concern for businesses and societies across the globe.' The bottom line is that organizations have to be able to quickly adapt to new business realities.

Organizational AQ is a natural by-product of individual AQ, and by encouraging and empowering their employees to adapt, companies can increase their own adaptability and ability to compete. Fostering employee adaptability can be transformative at an organizational level. By investing in their greatest resource, people, companies can unlock trapped potential and create a skilled workforce capable of helping them meet emerging business challenges. To increase workforce adaptability, the focus for organizations should not just be on hiring for a high AQ, but creating a workplace environment that encourages and facilitates the ability to acquire new skills through continuous learning. Human capital and social capital work together to improve the effectiveness and adaptability of our modern organizations. Adaptability is a key competency for career success. Individual adaptability is associated with the accrual of human capital, the organization of the work environment, and the characteristics of individuals. In this turbulent environment, individuals navigate more career transitions and must be adaptable and competent learners. [114]

A conceptual model of antecedents of personal adaptability

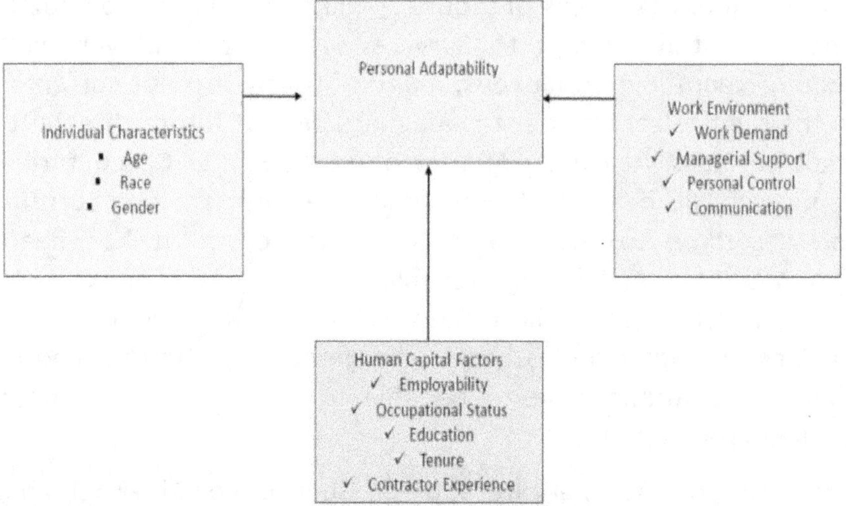

Source: Morrison and Hall [115] and Hall *et al* [116].

New workplace technologies require change and globalization demands the understanding of new sets of cultural rules. Downsizing, rightsizing, and outsourcing all contribute to work transience and affirmation that organizations are not always built from jobs but from elements of work that need to be done. O'Connell, McNeely and Hal have proposed that three groups of factors such as the characteristics of the individual, the characteristics of the work environment, and the measure of human capital are correlates (and perhaps antecedents) of personal adaptability [117]. O'Connell *et al* argue that some

---

[114]. Hall, D. T., & Chandler, D. E. (2005). Psychological success: When the career is a calling. Journal of Organizational Behavior, 26, 155-176.

[115]. Morrison, R. W., & Hall, D. T. (2001). A proposed model of individual adaptability. Unpublished technical report, San Diego, CA.

[116]. Hall, D. T., Zhu, G., & Yan, A. (2002). Career creativity as protean identity transformation. In M. Peiperl, M. Arthur, & N. Anand (Eds.), Career creativity: Explorations in the remaking of work (pp. 159-180). New York: Oxford University Press

[117]. David J. O'Connell, Eileen McNeely, and Douglas T. Hall, Unpacking Personal Adaptability

individual factors such as age, race, and gender might influence adaptability insomuch as these attributes may set expectations according to social norms and produce differences in preferences and treatment in the workplace. The accrual of human capital in terms of occupational status, education, tenure in a work organization, experience working for a contract-based employer, and perceived employability affect one's sense of adaptability. They further contend that aspects of the work environment may increase or diminish one's self-reported adaptability. In this regard, stress researchers, focus on work demand, managerial support, and personal control. [118,119] The receipt of adequate workplace communication may enhance personal adaptability, as suggested by the literature on organizational change and restructuring. [120] It has been noted that, if employability, education, and particular kinds of work experience make people more adaptable, then career coaches or perhaps those involved in leadership development might pay attention to the positive value of those experiences. Likewise, if work design and implementation factors such as personal control, managerial support, work demand, and communication are important in fostering adaptability, then there might be clear implications for action.

Adaptability is the measure of an organism's ability to change in order to adapt to a new environment. It is essentially a measure of adaptation ability. This is being able to change in order to be successful when circumstances in the surrounding environment

---

at Work, Journal of Leadership & Organizational Studies, Volume 14 Number 3 February 2008 248-259

[118]. Karasek, R. A., & Theorell, T. (1990). Healthy work: Stress, productivity, and the reconstruction of working life. New York: Basic Books

[119]. Van Yperen, N. W., & Hagedoorn, M. (2003). Do high job demands create intrinsic motivation, fatigue, or both? The role of job control and job social support. Academy of Management Journal, 46(3), 339-348.

[120]. Brockner, J. (1992, Winter). Managing the effects of layoff on others. California Management Review, pp. 9-27.

change. This includes the ability to be able to handle new climates, diets, expectations, resources, and challenges. While humans and some species (such as coyotes and ravens) are highly adaptable, many species are quite limited in their ability to adapt and survive in a new environment. The ability for people, teams and organizations to adapt to changes in their environments, stay relevant and avoid obsolescence is the defining characteristic between success and failure, growth and stagnation, business and bankruptcy. According to Forbes, adaptable people have the following characteristics:

i.   **Adaptable People Experiment:** To adapt you must be open to change, which means you must have the will, emotional tolerance, mental fortitude, spiritual guidance to not only face uncertainty, but also smack it in the face and press on.

ii. **Adaptable People See Opportunity Where Others See Failure:** To adapt is to grow, to change; and to change you must forego what you once believed to be "right," classify it as "wrong," and then adopt what you now believe to be the "new right".

iii. **Adaptable People Are Resourceful:** You can take away a person's resources, but you cannot remove resourcefulness. Rather than getting stuck on one solution to solve a problem, adaptable people have a contingency plan in place for when Plan A does not work.

iv. **Adaptable People Think Ahead:** Always open to opportunity, adaptable people are always on the lookout for improvement; minor tweaks that will turn ordinary into extra-ordinary because they are not married to the one-size-fits-all solution.

v.   **Adaptable People Do not Whine:** If they cannot change or influence a decision, they 'yup, you guessed it, adapt and move on.

vi. **Adaptable People Talk To Themselves:** But not in a weird way. When they feel their blood pressure rising, their teeth coming together and their fists clenching, they flip the "mental switch" through self-talk. Engaging in positive self-talk is the single greatest habit you can learn for yourself.

vii. **Adaptable People Do Not Blame:** They are not victims to external influences because they are proactive. To adapt to something new you must forego the old. Adaptable people do not hold grudges or apportion blame needlessly but instead absorb, understand and move on.

viii. **Adaptable People Do Not Claim Fame:** They do not care about the limelight because they know it will soon burn out. Rather than wasting effort on a temporary issue, they shift their focus to the next obstacle to get ahead of the game so that, when everybody else finally jumps on board, they have already moved on to the next challenge.

ix. **Adaptable People Are Curious:** Without curiosity, there is no adaptability. Adaptable people learn and keep learning. Curiosity enables growth; it pulls you along, as opposed to willpower, which pushes you forward. Willpower only lasts so long as you like being pushed. Does anybody like being pushed? Didn't think so.

x. **Adaptable People Adapt:** How is that for defining a concept using the concept?

xi. **Adaptable People Stay Current:** If you want to adapt to change, you must know what to adapt to, and why it is important. Communication is at the heart of everything we do, and adaptable people realize the impact their words, tone and body language have on others which is why they plug-and-play according to the personalities involved.

xii. **Adaptable People See and Cherish Systems:** Adaptable people see the entire forest rather than just a few trees. They have to, otherwise, they would lack the repertoire of context within which to base their decisions to adapt.

xiii. **Adaptable People Open Their Minds:** If you are not willing to listen to others' points of view, then you will be limited in your thinking, which means you will also be limited in your adaptability. The more context you have, the more choices that position you toward change.

xiv. **Adaptable People Know What They Stand For:** The choice to change is not an easy one; however, neither is the choice to remain the same. Choosing to adapt to something new and forego the old requires a strong understanding of personal values; knowing what is important to you—and what is not—that cajoles you along the pathway of adaptability. [121]

xv. **Adaptable People Speak the 'Team' Language:** Recognition is a key tool at work. Teams need recognition. They need to feel it. Team recognition varies from culture to culture. Recognizing their efforts out of the spotlight is one of the best ways to motivate your team. Ultimately, it is all about building a culture of recognition in the workplace. In a study in the United States, it was found that only 12% of employees leave their workplace for more money; 88% leave for reasons like not feeling trusted or valued. If you want to be one effective manager, employee recognition is important and more important is choosing the language to show appreciation. Appreciation, conversely, concentrates on execution plus the employee's value as a person. Recognition is about changing

---

121. Jeff Boss , 14 Signs Of An Adaptable Person   See also
https://www.forbes.com/sites/jeffboss/2015/09/03/14-signs-of-an-adaptable-person/#2966f4ce16ea

performance and focuses on what is good for the company. Appreciation highlights what is good for the company and what is good for the person. Most departments in an organization have a common language and a common process.

e. **Adversity Quotient (AQ):** AQ is about how you respond to life, especially the tough stuff. It is a gauge or measure of how you respond & deal with everything, from everyday hassles to the big adversities that life can spring on you. The meaning of the word adverse is hostile or critical situation. To Stoltz, adversity is like a mountain to climb. Three types attempt the climb: quitters, who either do not start, or who quit soon after starting; campers, who climb for a while and then pitch their tents hoping for conditions to change that they prefer, and just keep waiting; and climbers, who continue, no matter what, to the top. We all face some adversities in life; it is only during adversities that one really comes to know one's true friends and well-wishers. Like IQ, EQ, or SQ, there is an AQ (adversity quotient) which is a score that measures the ability of a person to deal with adversities in his or her life. One needs to increase resilience to overcome adversities in life. The term was coined by Paul Stoltz in 1997 in his book *Adversity Quotient: Turning Obstacles into Opportunities*[122]. To quantify adversity quotient, Stoltz developed an assessment method called the Adversity Response Profile (ARP). The AQ is one of the possible indicators of a person's success in life and is also primarily useful to predict attitude, mental stress, perseverance, longevity, learning, and style of responding to changes in the environment. The more resilient you are, the more constructively and effectively you can respond to and work through life's difficulties. Having this resilience, this ability to handle adversity also makes life more

---

[122]. Paul G. Stoltz, 1977, From Adversity Quotient: Turning Obstacles into Opportunities. John Wiley & Sons, Inc., New York

fulfilling. You are not so easily dragged down by tough situations. There are umpteen examples of people who fought adversities and have become successful. The richest person in the whole world could not make any money at the onset.

Bill Gates' first company, Traf-O-Data (a device which could read traffic tapes and process the data), failed miserably. When Gates and his partner, Paul Allen, tried to sell it, the product would not even work. Gates and Allen did not let that stop them from trying again to fix the problem. Traf-O-Data helped them prepare Microsoft's first product a couple of years later. As a young man, Abraham Lincoln went to war a captain and returned a private. Afterwards, he was a failure as a businessman. As a lawyer in Springfield, he was too impractical and temperamental to be a success. He turned to politics and was defeated in his first try for the legislature, again defeated in his first attempt to be nominated for congress, defeated in his application to be commissioner of the General Land Office, defeated in the senatorial election of 1854, defeated in his efforts for the vice-presidency in 1856, and defeated in the senatorial election of 1858. At about that time, he wrote in a letter to a friend, "I am now the most miserable man living. If what I feel were equally distributed to the whole human family, there would not be one cheerful face on the earth.' Robert Sternberg received a C in his first college introductory-psychology class. His teacher commented that "there was a famous Sternberg in psychology and it was obvious there would not be another." Three years later Sternberg graduated with honours from Stanford University with exceptional distinction in psychology, summa cum laude, and Phi Beta Kappa. In 2002, he became President of the American Psychological Association. Charles Darwin gave up a medical career and was told by his father, "You care for nothing but shooting, dogs and rat catching." In his autobiography, Darwin wrote, "I was considered by all my masters and my father, a very ordinary boy, rather below the common standard of intellect," but he clearly evolved.

According to Sumner Redstone, great success is built on failure, frustration, even on a catastrophe. Albert Einstein did not speak until he was 4-years-old and did not read until he was 7 years of age. His parents thought he was 'sub-normal,' and one of his teachers described him as 'mentally slow, unsociable, and adrift forever in foolish dreams.' Einstein was expelled from school and was refused admittance to the Zurich Polytechnic School. He did eventually learn to speak and read. Even to do a little mathematics. Micheal Jordan states that 'I have missed more than 9000 shots in my career. I have lost almost 300 games. 26 times I have been trusted to take the game winning shot ... and missed. I've failed over and over and over again in my life. That is why I succeed. English crime novelist John Creasey got 753 rejection slips before publishing 564 books. 18 publishers turned down Richard Bach's story about a "soaring eagle." Macmillan finally published Jonathan Livingston's *Seagull* in 1970. By 1975 it had sold more than 7 million copies in the U.S. alone. Thomas Edison's teachers said he was 'too stupid to learn anything." He was fired from his first two jobs for being "non-productive.' As an inventor, Edison made 1,000 unsuccessful attempts at inventing the light bulb. When a reporter asked, "How did it feel to fail 1,000 times?" Edison replied that he 'didn't fail 1,000 times but the light bulb was an invention with 1,000 steps.' Robert Langer, a professor at Massachusetts Institute of Technology (MIT) offers a course on failure. He does that because failure is a far more common experience than success. Robert Langer recalled humming along to the Rolling Stones hit "You Can't Always Get What You Want" in his MIT apartment, anxiously awaiting the results of his PhD qualifying exam. He recounts that it was a very hard test and really thought he had failed. However, in the end, the Faculty Review Board may have been kind to pass him. Since graduating from MIT in 1974 in chemical engineering, Langer has gone on to serve as an Institute Professor at MIT, the highest distinction awarded to an MIT faculty member; preside over the largest academic biomedical engineering laboratory in the world; conduct research in medicine and biotechnology that has improved the lives of over 2 billion people, become the most cited engineer in history; and garner countless awards and accolades for his work. Though it may seem easy to imagine Langer breezing through graduate school with a clear vision of his future accomplishments, he states that uncertainty and failure were very much a part of his college life. An interviewer once asked him if anybody ever failed the course on failure. He thought a moment and replied, "No, but there were two Incompletes."

Winston Churchill repeated a grade during elementary school, and, when he entered Harrow, was placed in the lowest division of the lowest class. Later, he twice failed the entrance exam to the Royal Military Academy at Sandhurst. He was defeated in his first effort to serve in Parliament. He became Prime Minister at the age of 62. He later wrote, "Never give in, never give in, never, never, never, never - in nothing, great or small, large or petty - never give in except to convictions of honour and good sense. Never, Never, Never, Never give up." I do not know the exact number of attempts and failures Edison had before he created the light bulb. It is, however, debated that he failed 10,000 times. Nevertheless, what a great man Edison was. His response to his repeated failures was "I have not failed; I've just found 10,000 ways that don't work". Socrates was called "an immoral corrupter of youth" and continued to corrupt even after a sentence of death was imposed on him. He drank the hemlock and died corrupting. Eric Hoffer stated among others that 'our achievements speak for themselves. What we have to keep track of are our failures, discouragements, and doubts. We tend to forget the past difficulties, the many false starts, and the painful groping. We see our past achievements as the end result of a clean forward thrust, and our present difficulties as signs of decline and decay.

Bob Marley (Robert Nesta Marley) had little formal education and was a reluctant interviewee in his lifetime. He felt uncomfortable being asked questions by journalists. There are aspects of his past on which he did not want to dwell, particularly his feelings about his white, absent father, Norval Marley, a man who claimed to have been a captain in the colonial Caribbean army, but was not. At the age of four, folks discovered that when Marley read palms, his predictions would come true. He stopped reading palms at age 7, however, when he decided to become a singer. He died tragically prematurely in 1981, aged only 36, and highly mythologized. Shortly before his death from cancer, Marley received the Order of Merit from Jamaica. This award can be given to "any citizen of Jamaica … who has achieved eminent international distinction in the field of science, the arts, literature or any other endeavour. In 1978, the United Nations awarded Marley a Peace Medal in recognition of his advocacy for "disenfranchised blacks around the world. In 2014 Forbes, listed him as the sixth highest-earning dead celebrities. In 2014, the Bob Marley and the Wailers greatest hits album "Legend" cracked the Billboard Top 10 list after Google Play made it available for 99 cents. His influence can be measured in many ways; for example, three decades after his death, Marley has over 30 million Facebook followers.

Organizations must avoid individuals who tend to be easily discouraged when confronted with even minimal adversity. Such people will infect and weaken others in a team. They will kill the overall morale and culture. On the contrary, candidates who stuck to a job in dire circumstances, even though the business subsequently closed deserve commendation. According to Daniel Jackson, an MIT professor of computer science, there is what I call 'little-f failure' and 'big-F failure, where Little-f failure is when you do something and you screw it up … Big-F failure is when your whole life comes to nothing.[123] Business leaders should strive to institute programmes to destigmatize failure and build resilience. It is scary to fail, as we will doubt your ability, our worthiness, and our intelligence in confronting it. Nevertheless, failure is no reason to stop trying. It may give you the opportunity and space to reflect upon the mistakes you made and learn a lesson from them. To fail is, therefore, expected to be seen as about being human.

Case Study: Albert Einstein's Doctoral Study Journey

Einstein's first PhD thesis advisor was one Dr. Weber. He found that Dr. Weber's lectures were very traditional, so he lost interest, and stopped attending after two weeks. As his PhD project, Einstein proposed measuring "c" using an interferometer, similar to the Michelson-Morley experiment, of which he did not know at the time. Weber rejected the proposal. Next, Einstein proposed investigating the effect of heat on the electrical conductance of a material, and that was rejected too. Then, Einstein did some standard work on heat conduction, and wrote up the results as a dissertation. Weber rejected it because it had been written on the wrong kind of paper. Einstein chose not to rewrite it on the required paper, and it is lost to history. Einstein's next advisor was Kleiner at Zurich Polytechnic in 1901. Einstein proposed the extension of intermolecular force theory from liquids to gases. He wrote a dissertation and submitted it to Kleiner. Kleiner delayed reading the thesis for several months, and then rejected it because it contained remarks critical of Boltzmann and others. Einstein withdrew the thesis. In 1905 Einstein approached Kleiner with a thesis on the electrodynamics of moving bodies. It was rejected because a)

---

123 http://news.mit.edu/2019/mit-students-organize-fail-conference-destigmatize-failure-build-resilience-0528

the professors who reviewed it did not really understand it; and, b) it was purely theoretical in nature.

Later in 1905 Einstein submitted another dissertation which presented his results on measuring the molecular dimensions of sugar molecules. It was rejected for being too short. He then added one sentence, and resubmitted it. It was reviewed by Kleiner and Burkhardt, and accepted. Einstein sent the thesis for publication in Annalen der Physik, but it was returned because better data was then available. Einstein added an addendum based on the new data. The thesis was published. Experiments by others showed a discrepancy in Einstein's conclusions but Einstein could find no error. He asked a friend to check his calculations, and the friend found an error. Einstein published a correction.

One of the reasons for Einstein's difficulties stemmed from the fact that atomistic ideas were not fully accepted by the academic world until about 1910. In 1905 and early 1906, he published five papers. It was after getting over all these hurdles that today Einstein is, generally, considered the most influential physicist of the 20th century. Among the many surprising things about the life of Albert Einstein was the trouble he had getting an academic job. Indeed, it would be an astonishing nine years after his graduation from the Zurich Polytechnic in 1900 — and four years after the miracle year in which he not only upended physics but also finally got a doctoral dissertation accepted — before he would be offered a job as a junior professor. [124] He did not shine as a student, and his job application letters came off pretty desperate yet he persevered to become the greatest physicist of the 20th century. Sometimes the 'bad' is actually good.

---

124. Peter L. Galison, Gerald Hilton and Sulvan S. Swerber, ed, 2008, Einstein for the 21ST Century; J=His Legacy in Science, Art and Modern Culture, Princeton University Press

f. Wisdom or Intelligence Quotient: Wisdom intelligence is having a deep understanding of the reality of people, things, events or situations, resulting in the ability to choose or act accordingly to produce optimum results. Wisdom can be gained by experience (the long road) or it can be imparted instantly from above (the short road). In terms of "long road" wisdom, young people have a limitation in this area due to their age, which limits their ability to think critically unless they learn how to tap into the wisdom given instantly from above. This makes sense since the Greeks viewed wisdom as being horizontal, an asset to be gained by experience, as well as a vertical asset, something acquired instantly from a higher source. Athena, for instance, was considered the god of wisdom for the Greeks. They believed Athena and other gods could impart wisdom. In the Christian doctrine, James 1:2, sums this up when he writes among others that 'if any of you lacks wisdom, he should ask God, who gives generously to all without finding fault, and it will be given to him. But when he asks, he must believe and not doubt, because he who doubts is like a wave of the sea, blown and tossed by the wind.' Wisdom is crucial to help people discern what is emerging in front of them, to uncover options and suspend them for a moment before making the crucial decision so they can navigate through life and social situations to gain personal advantages.

g. Character Intelligence: Character is pursuing and developing moral excellence, which leads to self-mastery. Character conveys the process of engraving or chiselling to give form to raw material. For instance, skilled workers using the hammer and chisel crafted ancient statues very methodically and patiently, shaping some of the most renowned pieces of art we admire today. Within time, an onlooker could see a face or an image emerge from granite. This process also happens with people. During our childhood, we are similar to a marble slab, which, over time, through choice, action and self-correction, you and I create the right actions and new outcomes, which form a new character. Virtue and character are fashioned into one's constitution by adopting the highest principles of conduct, and through determination to change and self-correct, a person begins to distinguish himself or herself as unique.

h. **Spiritual Intelligence**: In looking at spirituality through the lens of intelligence, Emmons (1999) opines that spiritual intelligence is a framework for identifying and organizing skills and abilities needed for the adaptive use of spirituality. Emmons (2000a) proposes four components for SI:

   i. Ability to utilize spiritual resources to solve problems;
   ii. Ability to enter heightened states of consciousness;
   iii. Ability to invest everyday activities and relationships with a sense of the sacred;
   iv. Capacity for transcendence of the physical and material; and

A somewhat different framework is offered by Vaughan (2002) who defines SI as a capacity for a deep understanding of existential questions and insight into multiple levels of consciousness; it implies awareness of our relationship to the transcendent, to each other, to the earth, and to all beings. When you have favour, people will relax their policy guidelines and protocol to accommodate you. The term, spiritual intelligence and spiritual quotient is mostly attributed to Danah Zohar and Ian Marshall based on their pioneering book, *SQ: Connecting With Our Spiritual Intelligence*. They describe SQ as 'our most fundamental intelligence. It is what we use to develop our capacity for meaning, vision and value. It allows us to dream and to strive. It underlies the things we believe in and the role our beliefs and values play in the actions that we take. Spiritual Intelligence explores how accessing our SQ helps us to live up to our potential for better, more satisfying lives. Spiritual intelligence is the ability to build and sustain a relationship with

God where you attract His unrelenting favour, to the point where it begins to overflow into your life. Favour can be defined in many ways. Cicero coined its original meaning; 'to show kindness to someone' or a 'gift given as a mark of favour.' Lance Wallnau [125] defines favour as the affection of God towards you that releases an influence through you so that other people are inclined to like, trust and cooperate with you. It is a measure of grace (God's nature) bestowed on someone, imparting genuine, endearing qualities, which enable you to attract and influence others. As a leader, you need the edge that God's favour can produce for you. Real intelligence is using a combination of these four intelligences at any given time in conjunction with your mental capacity intelligence. Aspects of spirituality include the following:

i.   **Responsibility:** You might have asked yourself what your purpose in life is, or whom you are responsible for. Thinking about these makes us realise that we should have a vision of how we are to spend our lives. After all, we are not here forever, and we should make some form of contribution to the next generation.

ii. **Humility**: When you think about it, we are just a speck in the universe. We are just one of the 7 billion people on Earth; just one among those 108 billion people who have ever lived. So, what makes us think that our existence is more important than that of others?

iii. **Happiness:** The world has progressed and it has offered us convenience. Nevertheless, can we truly say that we are a lot happier now? What exactly are the things that make us happy? We all want to be happy. But then, how, exactly, do we go about it?

---

125. http://lancewallnau.com/impact

iv. **Grace:** This implies living in alignment with the sacred (divine, a universal life force, nature) manifesting love for and trust in life. Also, it suggests loving, revering and cherishing life based on gratitude, beauty, vitality, and joy. Moreover, it means having an optimistic outlook based on faith or trust.

v. **Meaning:** Experiencing significance in daily activities through a sense of purpose and a call for service, including in the face of pain and suffering.

vi. **Transcendence:** This suggests going beyond the separate egoistic self into an interconnected wholeness. It involves nurturing relationships and community with acceptance, respect, empathy, compassion, loving-kindness, and generosity.

vii. **Thou Orientation and Holism:** This suggests the need to utilize a systems perspective, see wholeness, unity, and the interconnection among the diversity and differentiation.

viii. **Truth:** This implies to accept and forgive, embrace, and love. It involves openness; an open heart and mind, and open curiosity. It leads to a Peaceful surrender to Self (Truth, God, Absolute, true nature). It is self-acceptance, self-compassion, and inner-wholeness. It requires the persona to maintain humble receptivity, surrendering, and allowing wants and needs to happen.

Based on his study of some of the world's major spiritual traditions (Buddhism, Christianity, Confucianism, Islam, Judaism, Shamanism, and Taoism). Walsh [126] identifies and discusses 7 common practices that are universal across these spiritual

---

126. Walsh, Roger. (1999). Essential Spirituality: The 7 Central Practices to Awaken heart and mind. New York: John Wiley & Sons

traditions. Amram [127] on the other hand developed an ecumenically-grounded theory of SI based on interviews with 71 people of different traditions designated as spiritually intelligent by their associates. A minimum of 4 interviews was conducted within each of the following spiritual traditions: Buddhism, Christianity, Earth-Based (Shamanic & Pagan), Hindu, Islam/Sufism, Jewish, Non- Dual, Taoism, and Yoga. In addition to the well-defined traditions, the largest single group of participants (20) could be characterized as eclectic in their spiritual orientation, following their own unique personal integration of several traditions. Based on the 45 initial interviews with participants, 13 preliminary themes were identified. These initial themes were used by the authors of this paper to generate some of the items developed in this study. As interviews continued, Amram [128] later refined, expanded and clustered the themes into 7 major themes which emerged as nearly universal across the spiritual traditions and participants. These themes are:

a.   **Consciousness**: Development of refined awareness and self-knowledge, featuring intuitive trans-rational knowing, mindfulness, and spiritual practices.

b.   **Grace**: Living in alignment with the sacred, manifesting trust in and love for life that is based on gratitude, beauty and joy.

c.   **Meaning**: Experiencing significance in daily activities through a sense of purpose and a call for service, including in the face of pain and suffering.

---

127. Yosi Amram and D. Christopher Dryer, The Integrated Spiritual Intelligence Scale (ISIS): Development and Preliminary Validation, Institute of Transpersonal Psychology Palo Alto, CA

128. Amram, Yosi (2007). The Seven Dimensions of Spiritual Intelligence: An Ecumenical Grounded Theory. Paper Presented at the 115th Annual (August 2007) Conference of the American Psychological Association, San Francisco, CA.

d. **Transcendence**: Going beyond the separate egoistic self into an interconnected wholeness, including a holistic system's worldview and the nurturing of human relationships through empathy, compassion, loving-kindness and I-Thou orientation.

e. **Truth:** Living in open acceptance, forgiveness, curiosity and love for all that is (all creation), including respect for the wisdom of multiple spiritual traditions.

f. **Peaceful Surrender**: Peacefully surrendering to higher-self (God, Truth, Absolute, or true nature), including self-acceptance, inner-wholeness, equanimity, humility and 'egolessness.'

g. **Inner-Directedness**: Inner-freedom aligned in responsible wise action, including discernment, integrity, and freedom from conditioning, attachments and fears.

Spiritual quotient (SQ) is a measure that looks at a person's spiritual acumen; it is as important as intelligence quotient (IQ) and emotional quotient (EQ). While IQ looks at cognitive intelligence, EQ looks at emotional power of a person and spiritual quotient (SQ) looks at spiritual power of a person. Spirituality increases the ability of a person to be creative and to be aware and insightful. The power of intuition and awareness can be increased with the help of spirituality. Why is SQ even more important in today's time? It helps tremendously in coping up and doing away with modern problems of terrorism, inconsiderateness, and lack of humanness. The concept of Spiritual Quotient (SQ) is fast emerging as the next big aspect of scientific study as it directly correlates to a person's awareness and consciousness. Vidya Hattangadi posits that human beings have five senses: sight (eyes), hearing (ears), taste (tongue), smell (nose), and touch (sensatory). Spirituality is the ability to recognize that there is intelligence beyond our five senses. There is a universal power that creates and governs everything within and beyond the worlds we know, and that power is omnipresent. We can surrender to this supreme intelligence through our awareness. We call this universal power by different names as per our religious faith. Spirituality makes things easier for us to go through life's journey with all its ups and downs. It makes our lives happier [129].

The US Department of the Army sums up leadership traits into ten (10) categories, which are:

a. **Composure:** A leader must display composure especially in dangerous and life-threatening situations. Composure is a key component of leader presence; a leader who shows hesitation in dire circumstances can trigger a negative chain reaction among others.

b. **Confidence:** Confidence is the faith that leaders place in their own abilities to perform in any situation, especially when under stress and with little or no available information. Leaders who know their own capabilities and believe in themselves are confident and this confidence grows from professional competence. Adversely, too much confidence can be detrimental, truly confident leaders do not need to advertise their gift, their actions prove their abilities.

c. **Communication:** Competent and confident leaders that get results depend on effective communication. Although communication is usually viewed as a process of providing information, communication as a competency must ensure that there is more than the simple transmission of information. Communication needs to achieve a new understanding and must create new or better awareness; communicating critical information in a clear fashion is an important skill to reach a shared understanding.

---

129. Vidya Hattangadi, Importance of spirituality quotient, See http://drvidyahattangadi.com/importance-of-spirituality-quotient/

d. **Lead by Example:** This is essential to leading effectively over the course of time. Leaders   provide an example for others to follow, and this competency reminds us that every leader in the U.S. Army is a role model.

e. **Physical Fitness:** Physical fitness is absolutely critical for leaders in the U.S. Army and is defined as having sound health, strength, and endurance, which sustain emotional health and conceptual abilities under prolonged stress. Physical fitness is one of the few traits or behaviours that may not transcend from the military to civilian leadership model.

f. **Mental Agility:** Mental agility is a flexibility of mind, a tendency to anticipate or adapt to uncertain or changing situations. Agility assists thinking through second-and third-order effects when current decisions or actions are not producing the desired effects. It helps break from habitual thought patterns, to improvise when faced with conceptual impasses, and quickly apply multiple perspectives to consider new approaches.

g. **Achieves Success:** Ultimately, leaders exist to accomplish goals and objectives set forth by the U.S. Army. Getting results, accomplishing the mission, and fulfilling goals and objectives are why leaders exist; leaders get results through communication and influence.

h. **Have Courage:** Personal courage encompasses courage at all levels: emotional, mental, and physical courage are key to effective leadership in all organizations. Courage can be displayed in a multitude of different ways and not easily identifiable to the researcher. This will be a challenge to articulate in subsequent research.

i. **Technical and Tactical Proficiency:** This can be described as the ability to understand every technical aspect of you and your subordinate's weapons systems (U.S. Department of the Army, 2006). Tactical proficiency is the ability to manoeuvre you and your unit in a tactical manner given any situation in any part of the world. This would include operations in urban terrain, built up areas, and desolate areas in Africa. A leader must have both technical and tactical competence to lead effectively.

j. **Be Adaptive:** Adaptive leadership includes but is not limited to being an agent of change, helping other members of the organization, especially key leaders, to recognize that an environment is changing and building consensus as change is occurring. As this consensus is built, adaptive leaders can work to influence the course of the organization. Depending on the immediacy of the problem, adaptive leaders may use several different methods for influencing their organization. These can range from "crisis action meetings" (when time is very short) to publishing white papers or other "thought pieces" that convey the need for change.

It must be remembered that we should try to achieve a balance between all eight traits. One is probably not going to master all of them. We may have to tackle them as a team, and the organization can make progress in building a successful social strategy. Research suggested that social intelligence or quotient is essential for effective leadership and helps teams work better together. It is the investment you need to make in developing better working relationships so that others want to work with you. Strong relationships improve our immune system and help combat disease. Loneliness and weak relationships are one of the major sources of stress, health problems and depression. Our relationships affect every area of our lives—from colleagues to spouses to friends, and to kids.

Difference between IQ, EQ, SQ and AQ

There are grey difference between 1Q, EQ and SQ. These are:

IQ: Intelligence quotient is an attempt to gauge human intelligence. While people have different cognitive strengths and weaknesses, psychologists have found that there is a common component called 'general intelligence' or 'G'. General intelligence has been defined in various ways. However, I personally prefer this definition of Robert Feldman: 'the capacity to understand the world, think rationally, and use resources effectively when faced with challenges.'

EQ: Emotional quotient is the way of managing our own emotions in positive ways so that we could effectively deal with the vicissitudes of life. It was developed by Daniel Goleman in the mid-1990s. Studies reveal that those with high EQ scores find it easier to create interpersonal relationships and to fit into group situations. People with higher emotional intelligence are also better at understanding their own psychological state, which can include managing stress effectively and being less likely to suffer from depression.

SQ: Spiritual quotient is going beyond your cognitive and emotional skills. It is acknowledging your mortality and thinking of what you could offer humanity. It is living in humility; bearing in mind that you are just a tiny component compared to the vastness of the universe. A robust understanding of SQ motivates people to balance their work commitments, time with family and inner growth.

AQ: It is one's ability to adapt to change – or even embrace it – in order to continue growing and advancing one's career. A strong AQ allows one to recognize that changes are happening in customer demand or new modes of technology are reshaping one's business. It allows one to grab those opportunities when they come, rather than waiting until one's company or one falls behind. A healthy AQ can also tell one that one's way of interacting with one's peers is no longer serving one's best interests or helping one reach one's professional goals. Perhaps something has changed inside the company culture. Maybe there has been a creative shift in the company's strategy. Perhaps there has been a shakeup in the organizational structure. Whatever the cause, the one thing that remains certain is change. It is one's ability to recognize that changes are happening and to adapt to those changes in a timely manner.

Your IQ is often easiest to assess. It is evident from your professional qualifications and technical skills. You may demonstrate your IQ when you approach an unknown skill and start picking it up, or pass through training classes with flying colours. On the contrary, your EQ can be a little harder to pin down – at least in the beginning. Someone's EQ is often defined through their "soft skills," and those may take longer to show in a professional setting. You demonstrate your EQ when you effectively engage well with others, know how to communicate, and understand what it takes to contribute meaningfully to the company or team. Your EQ also shows when you are open to constructive criticism and are willing to work on those soft skills like leadership, resilience, and inclusiveness that have room for improvement.

Your AQ shows through your ability to handle challenges, and to handle setbacks and the "curveballs" that are thrown your way, and use them for information that will ultimately help you move forward. The best way to estimate your AQ may be to examine the way that you have adapted to past issues. These days, companies need to look for professionals who possess a blend of all three attributes – IQ, EQ, and AQ – in more or less equal measure. This can be difficult for anyone who has relied primarily on their IQ alone to move them forward in their career. Unfortunately, these days, technical knowledge has a short shelf-life, so your ability to continuously evaluate the atmosphere of a company (using your EQ) and then make changes as necessary (using your AQ) is an essential part of your value to your company and peers. Without AQ, EQ and IQ are like a two-legged stool, unstable, and likely to fall. In the near future, we will see AQ measures embedded and used as an indicator of future success in education and organisations. According to Alvin Toffler, 'the illiterate of the 21st Century will not be those who cannot read and write, but those who cannot learn, unlearn, and relearn.'

Despite the above, others have posited that the total 'intelligence' (or meta-intelligence) of an excellent leader is made up of five interdependent intelligence modes. These are:

a. Intra- and Interpersonal Intelligence: Leaders who have an authentic identity. Intra-and interpersonal intelligence – including emotional intelligence – centres around the degree to which my identity as a leader has crystallised and I have become a person in my own right. I know who and what I am as a leader; what my strengths and weaknesses are. I know what I stand for. I know my impact on others and their impact on me. This intelligence is the anchor and starting point for each of the others. However, more important than having a crystallised identity is that my identity is infused with authenticity. Having an authentic identity is the highest form of this intelligence. It relates to having a sense of being true to myself as a leader.

b. Systemic Intelligence: Leaders who have a big picture of how the world works in terms of real time, dynamic patterns. Systemic (including cognitive) intelligence entails leadership mastery at crafting a real time, integrated and dynamic understanding of how the emerging world works within the leader's operating arena. Put differently, it is a 'working theory' of the leader's operating arena against the backdrop of the emerging world order as sketched in the introduction. This theory is used by the leader as a 'Google map' to chart and travel in their operating arena. This understanding is expressed as a constructed dynamic pattern of how the world functions, whether as a vicious or virtuous cycle. The pattern in force is informed by a limited set of underlying governance rules that have been uncovered.

c. Ideation Intelligence: Leaders who can visualise inspiring new, boundary busting dreams and legacies as a means to bring desired futures into being. The crux of this intelligence is imagining. Ideation (including spiritual) intelligence encompasses the leadership mastery of having limitless dreams about what the world can, may, and should be. It is about idealising a better future and enriched sense of ultimate purpose for all people. This intelligence entails a leader becoming masterful at dreaming in their search to make the world a better place for current and upcoming generations. This can range from how to make the existing better, to how to add something new, through to how to change what exists into something different and better. Ultimately, it is about how to bring the completely new into being.

d. Action Intelligence: Leaders who can bring about lasting, meaningful change on a large scale. Intelligence is navigation into the future to make desired dreams a reality. Action intelligence encompasses the leadership mastery of bringing about lasting, meaningful change on a large scale. Desired futures resulting from imaging dreams must be turned into action through affecting real, genuine change. Traditional change management is premised on linearity and predictability. It is no longer good enough in the emerging world order. In the emerging world order, change takes on pervasive, radical, fundamental and chaotic features. It is non-linear in nature. It is highly unpredictable in its outcome. Under these conditions, the action intelligent leader needs to adopt a reflective, real time action learning process to create lasting, meaningful change. This process is made up of successive cycles of exploration, discovery, application, and learning/reflection. Mahatma Ghandi who pursued India's independence; Malala Yousafzai who stood up against the Taliban for women's rights; and Ché Guevara as instigator of the South American and Cuban revolutions, Kwame Nkrumah of Ghana are examples of leaders who characterise this type of intelligence.

e. Contextual Intelligence: Leaders are able at all times to be optimally matched to their context, using the right interpretive framework to engage with it. Contextual (including cultural) intelligence pertains to ensuring, on an ongoing basis, a dynamic, optimal match between the leader and his/ her context as delineated by the operating arena of their organisation. This requires, on the one hand, in depth insight into the leadership challenges and the demands of their operating arena, currently and going into the future. On the other hand, it requires matching a leader's requirements and profiles. Critical to this fit is the adoption of an appropriate interpretive framework. It requires a certain way of seeing and dealing with the world to have a constructive contextual engagement with the emerging world.

Summary

In leadership and management, intelligence plays central role in guiding choices or actions. Skill and cognitive intelligence of the manager or leader is therefore central to any success. Team member characteristics are generally divided into behavioural proclivities like conflict management style; proximal psychological states like beliefs, values and perceptual patterns; and more distal or deeper general psychological states like intelligence. The inner-core strengths include traits like character, positive emotions, positive beliefs, self-concept, and values. Outer-core leadership competencies are made up of a person's capabilities, commitment, and connectedness. The Chapter further looks at skills and types of intelligence in leadership. In particular, cognitive intelligence in leadership is comprehensively treated, and ends by emphasizing the adaptability quotient as the additional trait that every effective and resilient leader must have in our rippled and technologically endemic environment. With intelligent leadership, a leader not only has a focus on the here and now, but also put measures in place to ensure the good work outlives its tenure. Any organization that wants continuing success needs intelligent leadership. The type of intelligence that the individual must have at his disposal is covered in this chapter. This section also examines the grey difference between intelligence quotient (IQ), emotional quotient (EQ) and spiritual quotient (SQ) and what is referred to as 'total intelligence' or meta-intelligence. The case journey of Albert Einstein's doctoral study is also brought to the fore as an example of how, intelligence could be misconstrued.

Chapter Five

Selected Traits of Leadership

'Unless you have mastery over the totality of your own nature,
you will be prone to causing a lot of leadership damage'
Treasurer and Captain Havlik [130]

Humility Versus Hubris

There has been an increasing awareness of the importance of leadership and decision making. The book entitled the *Contrarian's Guide to Leadership*, by Sample[131] espouses the idea that 'the very concept of leadership is elusive and tricky.' Contrarian leaders think differently from other people. They maintain their intellectual independence by thinking gray, and enhance their intellectual creativity by thinking free. Contrarian wisdom holds that judgments should be arrived at slowly or not at all. Most people immediately categorize things as good or bad, true or false, friend or foe. Nevertheless, truly effective leaders see shades of grey. The essence of thinking grey, according to Sample, is not to form an opinion about an important matter until you have heard all the relevant facts and arguments, or until the circumstances force you to form an opinion. Resist the temptation to immediately classify everything you read or hear as either true or false, good or bad, right or wrong, useless or useful. Binary thinking can lead to

---

130 Bill Treasurer and Captain John Havlik, The Leadership Killer,

131 . Steven B. Sample, The Contrarian's Guide to Leadership, Jossey-Bass, 2002-03-09 192 pp

disaster. It is hard to define in a way that is satisfactory to everyone, although most people believe they know it when they see it.

While there is a plethora of literature available on factors which make a leader effective and how leaders influence and motivate their subordinates to achieve organizational goals, [132] there is scant literature available on negative aspects of leadership. Effective and ethical leadership are fundamental to the success in any organization – none more so than in a country's military. Organizations can succeed or fail because of good or bad leadership. As has been noted, by whom and how decisions are made can have serious implications across all levels of society. Several people have been successful in their life and have been inflicted by excessive pride and self-confidence. Hubris has been described as an occupational hazard for political, military and business leaders. The Hubris Syndrome – possibly an acquired personality disorder – develops when individuals find themselves in positions of substantial power, without any previous history of psychiatric illness. [133] There are times when the manifestations of such behaviours demonstrate noticeable signs of narcissism, and in extreme cases, hubris [134]. Leaders whose thinking are constrained within well-worn ruts, who are governed by their passions and prejudices, who cannot think either free or grey, who cannot even appreciate the creative imagination and fresh ideas of those around them, are as anachronistic and ineffective as the dinosaur.

---

[132]. Northouse, P.G. (2007). Leadership theory and practice (4th Ed.). Thousand Oaks, CA.

[133]. Owen D and Davidson J (2009) Hubris Syndrome: An Acquired Personality Disorder? A Study Of US Presidents And UK Prime Ministers Over The Last 100 Years. Brain 132: 1396–1406.

[134]. Eleftherios P Diamandis and Nick Bouras, Hubris and Sciences

Hubris in Leadership

Hubris, as an old concept, originated from the Greek mythology. Overall, hubris is associated with an absence of humility and a sense of being 'intoxicated by power'. [135] Hubris is 'exaggerated pride or self-confidence'. It inflates the ego and, thus, diminishes and eventually destroys moral character. Hubris pushes leaders to seek power and amass it for self-aggrandizement, not for the good of the people they lead or for the benefit of their organizations. Power, especially absolute and unchecked power, is intoxicating and is manifested behaviourally in a variety of ways, ranging from amplified cognitive functions to lack of inhibition, poor judgment, extreme narcissism, deviant behaviour, and even cruelty. The risk of hubris affects politicians, leaders in business, scientists, academia, the military, entertainers, athletes and doctors (among many others). Hubris, in business, political and military arenas has been characterized as excessive self-confidence, exaggerated self-belief and contempt for the advice and criticism of others. Hubristic behaviour of overconfidence, extreme pride together with an unwillingness to disregard advice makes powerful people in leadership positions to over-reach themselves with negative consequences for themselves and others. As the dangerous consequences of hubristic behaviours become more apparent and well described, it is imperative that individuals, organisations and governments act to prevent such phenomena. Responsible leaders, including acclaimed scientists should exercise greater humility to the complexity and inherent uncertainty of their activities and strive to seek out and challenge hubristic behaviours.

Hubris turns a leader's attention away from enriching the lives of others to enriching himself. With leadership comes power. This

---

[135]. Russell G (2011) Psychiatry and politicians: The 'Hubris Syndrome'. The Psychiatrist 35: 140–145.

breeds hubris, a malignant vice for leaders. It is corruptive and compromising; it strikes at a leader's integrity and effectiveness. It provokes leaders to abuse their power. Hubris ruins leaders and damages the people they lead. However, because of the leaders' exalted position, the threat of insidious hubris comes with the position. Hubris leads to rigidity, incompetency and complacency, plus a tendency to intimidate others and a lack of gratitude. Hubris turns otherwise good individuals into jerks, raging narcissists and all-around horrible people. Eventually, hubris robs leaders of their moral foundations. The consequences of the Hubris Syndrome for political leaders such as Tony Blair and Margaret Thatcher were seen widely as profound and ultimately self-destructive, as their terms of office were ended prematurely by their own members of Parliament. Similarly, business leaders' hubris has been shown to have deleterious consequences for individuals themselves; for example, it results in losing their jobs, as well as make their organizations lose market share. Hubris is one of a number of 'darker-side' leadership traits. Unfortunately, far too many bad, hubristic leaders operate in the business world.

Previous research on hubris tended to tackle the subject from a variety of different directions. Some researchers have focused their attention 'downstream' from leaders' hubris, exploring the ways in which hubris manifests in actions such as reckless risk taking, rash merger and acquisition behaviours, and the concomitant effects on firm performance. Others have attempted to explain various 'upstream' factors in an individual's history, context or personality that predispose them towards hubris. These factors include individuals' attributions of causes of previous organizational success, media praise, self-importance, narcissism and a sense of exemption from rules, socially constructed confidence, and inflated core self-evaluation rooted in the traits of self-esteem, emotional stability, generalized self-efficacy and locus of control [136]. Much of this previous 'upstream' work at the individual level of analysis has focused largely on leaders' and chief executive officers' (CEOs) personality traits and such related constructs. The cognitive and affective factors associated with leaders' hubris are less well documented or understood. Hubris is implicated heavily in the issues of leaders' judgment and decision making; there is also a pressing need to scrutinize the real-time psychological processes which may underpin the manifestation of hubris in leadership. The functioning of intuition is a central cognitive factor, and that when intuition becomes misunderstood, unchecked or unbridled within the 'cognitive economy' of a powerful individual hubristic behaviour is more likely to appear.

US former President, Nixon felt he was above the law, and that getting to his desired outcome of re-election justified taking whatever steps that he deemed are necessary. While the history is complex, it is hard not to see hubris as, at least, part of the problem. Consider Hollywood film mogul Harvey Weinstein, who for decades auditioned young female talent on his infamous casting couch. Or, remember United Airlines CEO Oscar Munoz, whose boorish insensitivity went viral after a "bloodied customer" was dragged off of a United flight. In one week, United lost more than half a billion dollars in market capitalization because of Munoz's behaviour. Then there is former Wells Fargo CEO John Stumpf, who tried to blame 'some 5,300 employees for gross corporate malfeasance that became public. During a US Senate Banking Committee hearing, one senator called Stumpf 'gutless.'

Points of Pressure in Leadership

Leaders often work under heavy pressure, in an environment where rippled intelligence abounds which takes the form of the 'Three Rs':

a. **Responsibility:** Because leaders have many duties and obligations, they often forget to take good care of themselves. They tend not to eat well, exercise or get enough rest.

b. **Results:** Since leaders must constantly meet goals, they may sacrifice the means for the ends, losing track of being a good leader and a good person.

c. **The 'Role' of a Leader:** Leaders must assume an elevated role, which 'comes with many demands, often leaving them facing unrealistic expectations that they can be unshakeable and invincible at all times.'

These pressure points mark the times that hubris can worm its way into a leader's heart. Think of hubris as a stealthy, pestilential entity that burrows deep inside you. Hubris exploits the moments when you feel the most pressure, so it can poison your thinking and cause you to act in selfish, shabby and dishonourable ways.

Hubristic Leadership Behaviour

Charisma, charm, the ability to inspire, persuasiveness, breadth of vision, willingness to take risks, grandiose aspirations and bold self-confidence; these qualities are often associated with successful leadership. Nevertheless, there is another side to this profile; for these very same qualities can be marked by impetuosity, a refusal to listen to or take advice and a particular form of incompetence when impulsivity, recklessness and frequent inattention to detail predominate. This can result in disastrous leadership, and cause damage on a large scale. The attendant loss of capacity to make rational decisions is perceived by the general public to be more than 'just making a mistake'. A common thread tying these elements together is hubris, or exaggerated pride, overwhelming self-confidence and contempt for others [137]. In ancient Greece, 'hubris' described behaviour in which a leader or other powerful individual who was intoxicated with excessive pride, unfaltering self-belief and overweening self-confidence treated others with disregard, disrespect and contempt. The classical narrative is moralistic in that power and unremitting self-regard eventually 'go to the head' of a hubristic leader to the extent that s/he misperceives, misinterprets and misjudges the realities of the situation and make serious and fatal errors of judgment (e.g. the Dædalus-Icarus episode in the *Metamorphosis*).

A fall from grace and retribution in the form of nemesis (after the Greek god Ne´mesis) follows, construed as punishment and revenge for the individual having had the temerity to assume 'god-like' powers and thereby attempting to usurp the authority of divine beings. In the ancient Greek world, hubris was considered to be one of the most dangerous traits one could exhibit. In the classical Greek myth, when Daedalus and Icarus escaped from the labyrinth in Crete, Daedalus advised his son not to fly too low, in order to avoid being too close to the moisture of the sea or, too high and close to the heat of the sun, as he had used thread and wax to make their wings. Despite this advice, an excessively exuberant Icarus flew too close to the sun and his wax wings melted causing him to fall into the sea. Icarus' hubris, his disobedience of his father in flying too high, is a cautionary tale about humility and restraint, the danger of audacity. Although hubris may be associated with leaders' personality traits such as narcissism, including grandiosity, which have been widely documented and researched in management and organization studies [138]. Owen specifically describes the Hubris Syndrome as unique, and an acquired disorder that develops only after a leader has held power for a period of time;

---

137. Owen D. Hubris and Nemesis in Heads of Government, J R Soc Med , 2006, vol. 99 (pg. 548-51)

138. Maccoby M (2004) Narcissistic leaders: The incredible pros, the inevitable cons. Harvard Business Review, January, 92–101.

moreover, it is only applicable if there is no history of psychiatric illness. The 14 symptoms of the Hubris Syndrome, proposed by Owen [139] after studying the illness in heads of government who held offices over a period spanning a hundred years, included a narcissistic propensity to see the world as an arena to exercise power and seek glory, exaggerated self-belief bordering on a sense of omnipotence and accountability only to a 'higher court' such as history or God.

These symptoms were mapped by Owen and Davidson [140] against the American Psychiatric Association Diagnostic and Statistical Manual for Mental Disorders 4th edition (DSM IV) criteria for narcissistic personality disorder (NPD), antisocial personality disorder and histrionic personality disorder and serves to distinguish the Hubris Syndrome from other seemingly related disorders. Owen [141] speculated on the psychiatric and neurobiological bases of the Hubris Syndrome. First, he noted that the Hubris Syndrome shares common elements with narcissistic and sociopathic personality disorders (e.g. poor decision-making, impulse control and modulation of aggression, and lack of appropriate empathy). Second, he hypothesized that deficiencies of serotonin (which is involved in the regulation of decision-making and punishment-related information) could be implicated in the Hubris Syndrome. Third, Owen suggested that the neurobiological effects of conscious expectation observed in laboratory studies mirror the conscious exhilaration and intoxication associated with the Hubris Syndrome. Finally, Owen noted that dopaminergic receptors facilitate the type of addictive behaviour which may be associated with the 'high' that accompanies the influence of power and also may underpin

---

[139]. Owen D (2008) In Sickness and in Power: Illness in Heads of Government During the Last 100 Years. London: Methuen; Westport, CT: Praeger (revised edition 2011, London: Methuen).

[140]. Owen D and Davidson J (2009) Hubris Syndrome: An acquired personality disorder? A study of US presidents and UK prime ministers over the last 100 years. Brain 132: 1396–1406.

[141]. Owen D (2011) Hubris and Neurosciences. Lord Owen Speaking at the Daedalus Trust Research Cafe´ in Collaboration with the Mind Brain Forum, Magdalen College Oxford, 7 October 2011.

tendencies towards grandiosity and associated impairments to risk appraisal and the ability to foresee undesirable outcomes. Unlike most personality disorders, which appear by early adulthood, we view hubris syndrome as developing only after power has been held for a period of time, and therefore manifesting at any age. The Hubris syndrome was formulated to reflect a pattern of behaviour in a person who:

  i.   Sees the world as a place for self-glorification through the use of power;
  ii.   Has a tendency to take action primarily to enhance personal image;
  iii. Shows disproportionate concern for image and presentation;
  iv.   Exhibits messianic zeal and exaltation in speech;
  v.   conflates self with nation or organization;
  vi.   Uses the royal 'we' in conversation;
  vii. Shows excessive self-confidence;
  viii. Manifestly has contempt for others;
  ix.   Shows accountability only to a higher court (history or God);
  x.   Displays unshakeable belief that they will be vindicated in that court;
  xi.   Loses contact with reality;
  xii. Resorts to restlessness, recklessness and impulsive actions;
  xiii. Allows moral rectitude to obviate consideration of practicality, cost or outcome; and
  xiv. Displays incompetence with disregard for nuts and bolts of policy making.

In the case of the hubris syndrome, a context of substantial power is necessary, as well as a certain period of time in power, although the length has not been specified, varying in the cases described from 1 to 9 years. The condition may have predisposing personality characteristics, but it is acquired; that is, its appearance post-dates the acquisition of power [142]. The proposed criteria for the hubris syndrome, and their correspondence to features of cluster B personality disorders are:

1. A narcissistic propensity to see their world primarily as an arena in which to exercise power and seek glory; NPD.6;
2. A predisposition to take actions which seem likely to cast the individual in a good light—i.e. in order to enhance image; NPD.1;
3. A disproportionate concern with image and presentation; NPD.3;
4. A messianic manner of talking about current activities and a tendency to exaltation; NPD.2;
5. An identification with the nation, or organization to the extent that the individual regards his/her outlook and interests as identical; (unique);
6. A tendency to speak in the third person or use the royal 'we'; (unique);
7. Excessive confidence in the individual's own judgement and contempt for the advice or criticism of others; NPD.9;
8. Exaggerated self-belief, bordering on a sense of omnipotence, in what they personally can achieve; NPD.1 and 2 combined;
9. A belief that rather than being accountable to the mundane court of colleagues or public opinion, the court to which they answer is: History or God; NPD.3;
10. An unshakable belief that in that court they will be vindicated; (unique);

---

142. David Owen and Jonathan Davidson, Hubris syndrome: An acquired personality disorder? A study of US Presidents and UK Prime Ministers over the last 100 years. A Journal Of Neurology Brain 2009: 132; 1396–1406

11. Loss of contact with reality; often associated with progressive isolation; APD 3 and 5;
12. Restlessness, recklessness and impulsiveness; (unique);
13. A tendency to allow their 'broad vision', about the moral rectitude of a proposed course, to obviate the need to consider practicality, cost or outcomes; (unique);
14. Hubristic incompetence, where things go wrong because too much self-confidence has led the leader not to worry about the nuts and bolts of policy; HPD.5.

Here:

> **APD** = Anti-Social Personality Disorder;
> **HPD** =Histrionic Personality Disorder;
> **NPD** =Narcissistic Personality Disorder.

The five remaining symptoms are unique, in the sense they have not been classified elsewhere. They are: (i) conflation of self with the nation or organization; (ii) use of the royal 'we'; (iii) an unshakable belief that a higher court (history or God) will provide vindication; (iv) restlessness, overrides practicalities, cost and outcome. In making the diagnosis of the hubris syndrome we suggest that (-+) 3 of the 14 defining symptoms should be present; of these, at least one must be amongst the five components identified as unique.

Hubris has been seen in all walks of life including politics, business, the military, science, academia, entertainment, sports and medicine, among many others. In aviation, investigations into fatal plane accidents identified erroneous decisions by the captain whose position of power in the flight deck dismissed concerns by other members of the crew. Moreover, the crew often failed to question or challenge the captain's decisions. [143] In medicine Atul Gawande [144] suggested that the behaviour of

---

[143]. Helmreich RL, Merritt AC, Wilhelm JA: The evolution of Crew Resource Management training in commercial aviation. Int J Aviat Psychol. 1999; 9(1): 19–32

[144]. Gawande A: Being Mortal: Medicine and what matters in the end. Metropolitan Books, 2014

doctors medicalizing old age and not accepting that life/death is not curable is a sign of hubris within the profession. He argues that doctors should move away from simply fighting for longer life, to things that make life meaningful. A leading medical school in UK decided that it is no longer enough to have high grades to become a medical student but would-be doctors must also display humility. [145]

Phenomena of hubristic behaviour were possibly present in investigators of some of the fraudster studies reported in recent years. Among numerous examples, three articles are cited here, one from the physics world and two from medicine. Jan Hendrik Schön rose to prominence after a series of breakthroughs in semiconductors, most of them published in Nature and Science, which were later discovered to be fraudulent. [146] Hwang-Woo-suk, until 2005, was considered one of the pioneering experts in the field of stem cells and was best known for two articles published in the journal *Science* in 2004 and 2005, where he reported that he had succeeded in creating human embryonic stem cells by cloning. [147] He was called the "Pride of Korea" in South Korea. These reports were later found to be fabricated. Another tragic example of possible hubris was the report in *Nature* of a new and simple way to produce inducible stem cells. The method was soon found to be irreproducible and was retracted, but in the meantime, one of the senior authors committed suicide. [148]

The "intellectual celebrity syndrome" was implied by Winkler [149] for writers and scholars who risk seeking to popularise serious

---

145. http://www.telegraph.co.uk/education/educationnews/4793869/Medical-students-must-now-have-humility-as-well-as-straight-As.html.

146. Service RF: Scientific misconduct. Bell Labs fires star physicist found guilty of forging data. Science. 2002; 298(5591): 30–1.

147. Hwang WS, Ryu YJ, Park JH, et al.: Evidence of a pluripotent human embryonic stem cell line derived from a cloned blastocyst. Science. 2004; 303(5664): 1669–74

148. Anonymous: STAP retracted. Nature. 2014; 511(7507): 5–6

149. Winkler JT: The intellectual celebrity syndrome. Lancet. 1987; 329

ideas or influence contemporary events by transmitting them to the general public in a distorted and unusable manner. Winkler suggested that this phenomenon resembles a disease characterised by the presence initially of a pleasant exhilaration, followed by celebration, eccentric indulgent and somnolent phantasies. Nobel Prize laureates who undertake projects or accept positions beyond their capabilities was described by Diamandis [150] as 'Nobelitis'. Diamandis claims that the Nobel Prize seems to provide laureates with reassurance that they hold some super-powers that they did not realise before and that the prize will assist them to go on to even greater achievements.

Research has yet to formally establish the incidence of the Hubris Syndrome amongst senior business leaders. However, it seems likely that the power and status associated with senior executive positions in organizations could be a fertile breeding ground for this condition to develop and proliferate, with damaging consequences on a scale similar to those seen in politics. From the perspective of behavioural decision theory, hubristic CEOs possess a degree of certainty about the accuracy of their judgments exceeding the accuracy of their predictions. CEO hubris amounts to one form, albeit with major real-world implications – of cognitive bias and is worthy of the attentions of decision researchers. In the business world, the 'hubris hypothesis' was first posited by Roll (1986) in a study of corporate mergers and acquisitions. Hayward *et al.* [151] argued that, even though many business founders are aware that most ventures fail, hubristic entrepreneurs are often quite unshakeable in their beliefs that they are the ones who can beat the odds to the extent that they seek out and underestimate risk. Hayward *et al.* attribute this risky behaviour to hubristic

---

[150]. Diamandis EP: Nobelitis: a common disease among Nobel laureates? Clin Chem Lab Med. 2013; 51(8): 1573

[151] Hayward, M.L.A., Shepherd, D.A., Griffin, D.W., 2006. A hubris theory of entrepreneurship. Management Science 52, 160–172.

entrepreneurs' overconfidence in, and overestimation of, their knowledge, predictive skills and personal abilities. Leaders, CEOs and entrepreneurs, by virtue of their position and power, do not have as many 'social correctives' as do other employees: they are, in their relative isolation, especially vulnerable to hubris. [152] When Fred Goodwin (formerly 'Sir Fred Goodwin'), ex-CEO of the Royal Bank of Scotland, proposed buying the Dutch Bank ABN-Amro (a deal which went ahead, but eventually back-fired disastrously) there were sceptics within the organization, but Goodwin choose hubristically to ignore them. A further example is to be found in Richard Fuld's leadership at Lehman Brothers. Corporate hubris can also operate at company level where leaders can 'infect' the organization in which they work. This notion has been developed by Owen [153] in his updated autobiography, drawing on his recent experience of international business and citing Enron, HBOS and BP. We will return to the issue of the social moderation of hubris in a later section. The speed of communication in contemporary times, combined with the widespread application of social media and easy access to large groups of people, might predispose leaders to both collective and individual hubristic decision making. The consequences of hubristic behaviour can be profound with dangerous consequences. [154] Acclaimed scientists should exercise greater humility at the complexity and inherent uncertainty of their activities and strive to seek out and challenge hubristic behaviours. Mentors are encouraged to discuss hubris and related behaviours with their mentees and stress the importance of humility in their future activities

---

152

[153] Owen, T. (2009a) Social Theory and Human Biotechnology. New York: Nova Science Publishers. With a
Foreword by Prof. Derek Layder (Univ. Leicester).

[154]. Garrard P: The Leadership Hubris Epidemic: Biological Roots and Strategies for Prevention. Palgrave Macmillan, 2017

Humility in Leadership

Humility is defined by the *Oxford Dictionary* as the 'quality of having a modest or low view of one's importance.' Humility is the element that prevents a sense of overconfidence and exaggerated self-importance, and it helps to avoid being 'infected' by hubris. The Greek philosopher, Socrates, was noted for proclaiming that, 'One thing I know is that I do not know anything", which epitomizes his sense of humility. It is rather surprising that humility is not formally taught at any level of education. Most of us are left to self-discover humility, and many, never discover it. The opposite may happen too. A number of objectively clever, creative and successful people may develop megalomania, which, when left unchecked, can reach the level of hubris. According to Forbes, the X-Factor in leadership is not responsibility or personality but humility. Staying humble means being aware of, and admitting, what you do not know. It means accepting that making mistakes and asking for help is a normal phenomenon. When you are humble you open yourself up to continuous growth and learning, and you prime yourself to handle the inevitable lows of start-up life with grace and dignity. Being humble as a leader makes you more relatable and approachable. In turn, it creates a more humanistic work environment where your employees will feel more comfortable being open, taking risks and showing vulnerability. Those that are well-versed at practising humility tend to see their position of leadership differently. Most humble leaders see themselves as servant leaders, which is a form of leadership, or a philosophy of leadership, in which CEOs view themselves as people offering service to those below them. Instead of viewing their perch as power or a way to control people and outcomes, servant leaders view their position as an opportunity to serve and grow their employees and organization. In 2017, both Glassdoor and Comparably reported Sameer Dholakia, CEO of SendGrid, as the most highly rated tech

CEO. Forbes subsequently brought attention to the CEO by writing about his servant leadership style: 'Being a servant CEO means inverting the traditional organizational chart and putting the CEO at the bottom. Dholakia acknowledges his job is difficult, "but the folks doing the hard rowing of the business are not the CEO and adds that, he does not have to take a phone call from a customer who's upset about a bug. I don't have a sales quota." Dholakia further thinks a leader's primary job is to empower others.' It's about questioning ourselves each day.'

The questioning of self and of the company helps one to remain humble. It opens the door to possibility and steers clear of ego, which can get in the way of true problem-solving. Such leaders radiate empathy instead of ego. Empathy, which is the ability to understand how others feel, can be a powerful tool in not only getting people motivated, but helping employees to attack challenges and strive for excellence. If others know that you can see the world from their perspective, it fosters a feeling of trust and support. Humility is necessary in science and technology since the remarkable contemporary advances and discoveries could encourage a feeling of acquired excessive power, with the consequence of developing hubris. Many successful people have frequently overestimated their own abilities, and believed that their performance is superior to the performance of others by displaying excessive pride and self-confidence. There are times when the manifestation of such behaviours demonstrates evident signs of narcissism, and in extreme cases, hubris.

Reality Checks

Good leaders can turn to these reality checks to remain humble:

a. **Ask Questions:** You do not know everything, so do not pretend you do. Others will appreciate that you know you do not have all the answers.

b. **Show Your Warts:** No one's perfect. Your mistakes demonstrate that you are human, just like everyone else.

c. **Surround Yourself With People Who Are Smarter Than You Are.** As Steve Jobs advised: It doesn't make sense to hire smart people and then tell them what to do; we hire smart people so they can tell us what to do.

d. **Spend Time With People You Outrank:** They are closer to the work than you are, and you can learn from them.

e. **Open Yourself Up To Feedback:** It is impossible to gauge your own leadership prowess objectively. Ask for 'honest, unfiltered feedback.'

f. **Give Someone 'Permission To Help You Check Yourself':** Identify a trusted confidant to look out for you when your ego works against you.

g. **Say 'Thank You' Sincerely and Often:** Being grateful is respectful and polite; being ungrateful is arrogant.

h. **Pick A Side:** As a leader, decide if you are there to help others or to help yourself. Choose whether you will "lead or rule.

i. **Develop the Art of Thinking:** Most people are terrible listeners because they think talking is more important than listening. But contrarian leaders know it is better to listen first and talk later. And when they listen, they do so artfully. A contrarian leader is an artful listener because artful listening is an excellent means of acquiring new ideas and gathering and assessing information. If leaders can listen attentively without rushing to judgment, they will often get a fresh perspective that will help them think independently. This kind of leader listens carefully to his or her inner circle and even the most obnoxious self-appointed advisers. Artful listening is important for maintaining the contrarian leader's intellectual independence. It enables them to see things through the eyes of their followers while at the same

j. **Listening Gray:** Just as thinking grey is important, so is listening gray. You must absorb stories, reports, complaints, accusations, extravagant claims and prejudices without immediately offering a definitive response. The contrarian leader acknowledges the communication without rendering judgment, but promises that the matter will be looked into. Refer the matter to the most senior officer who reports directly to you, and suggest that the matter be investigated and dealt with. Another important part of artful listening is to know when to stop listening. At some point, a leader must either make a decision or delegate it to someone else and move on. Listening carefully and intensively at the beginning can save the leader a lot of time in the end.

k. **Maintaining the Hierarchy:** Listening grey requires open communication at all levels of the organization. It requires that leaders avoid categorizing people into an "A" list and a "B" list, and means they should not dismiss ideas strictly because of who they come from. On the other hand, open communication can destroy the hierarchy in place and diminish the effectiveness of managers. For example, if the CEO speaks directly with a line manager, and acts on that contact, he or she makes it seem as if the higher-level manager is unimportant. His or her credibility is undermined. The way to avoid this trap is to make clear that everyone in the organization can communicate directly.

l. **Clarify Roles:** It helps to clarify the roles experts and leaders should play. Experts are deep specialists whose role is to offer leaders greater insight than they have in one small area; the leader's role should be to integrate the advice of several experts into a coherent course of action.

In dealing with experts, it is very important for leaders to know precisely what their goals are and how they think a particular expert can help them achieve those goals.

Bill Treasurer, [155] on the other hand, lists some "Ten Tips for Thriving Leadership" which is considered of great benefit in our environment driven by inordinate ego and pride. To remain humble, balanced and focused, some ten tips are recommended to the leader to follow:

a. **Lead Yourself First:** As a leader, you cannot lead others if you cannot govern yourself. Signs that you do not have a handle on your actions include: You are often angry. Your life is a disordered disaster. You miss deadlines. You are negative and judgmental. You complain all the time. If these traits define you, assess yourself objectively. Take the necessary steps to improve yourself and your life.

b. **Value Values:** Values are basic and fundamental beliefs that guide or motivate attitudes or actions. They help us to determine what is important to us. Values describe the personal qualities we choose to embody to guide our actions; the sort of person we want to be; the manner in which we treat ourselves and others; and our interaction with the world around us. They provide the general guidelines for conduct; great leaders live up to their principles and morality. They align their "goals, priorities and actions" with their core beliefs.

c. **Name Your Fear:** Often, fear rules hubristic leaders. They deal with their fears by making others fear them so they feel less vulnerable. They fear being disrespected or judged, not getting what they want, not being in charge and not being rewarded when they believe they are due.

---

155. Bill Treasurer and John R. Havlik (2018), The Leadership Killer Reclaiming Humility in an Age of Arrogance, Little Leaps Press

Face your fears; reject those that make you a lesser leader.

d. **Start and End Your Day With Two Questions:** At the start of each day, American scholar, inventor and politician Benjamin Franklin, for example would ask himself, "What good shall I do this day?" This helped him orient his actions toward being of service and offering a positive influence. Reflecting at the end of the day, he asked, "What good have I done today?"

e. **Respect Self And Others:** Some leaders disrespect others, yet assume others will respect them because of their position. Leaders must merit respect through their actions: treating others as being of equal importance, letting them speak about their concerns and listening with interest. When others make mistakes, leaders should be understanding.

f. **Play The Tape Forward:** The first part of the word "leadership" is "lead," which means, 'stay out in front.' Focus on the future, not the past. Plan for the skills the people you lead will need in the years to come. Be thoughtful about your firm and its future requirements. Forecast the goals you want to achieve and plan the necessary actions to attain them.

g. **Polish Your Conscience:** Would you be proud of how *USA Today* would tell your life story on its front page? Keep a clear conscience. Do things that enable you to feel good about yourself and the way others see you. Give time to a charity. Assist others. Become a mentor to newer employees.

h. **Be Grateful and Gracious:** Life is short. You are here, and then you are gone. Make your time on Earth positive. Be thankful to those around you, including those you lead.

Express your appreciation daily to those who share your journey through life.

i. **Earn Your Trident Every Day:** Leading others is a singular privilege. Nevertheless, leadership is difficult and arduous. You must deal with perplexing situations and capricious people, often with inconclusive information. All US Navy Seals aspire to earn the Trident – the Navy's Special Warfare breast insignia. As a leader, you must earn your trident every day. Accept leadership's formidable complexities, and work to lead others with respect and honour.

Summary

There is an increasing awareness of the importance of leadership and decision making. While there is a plethora of literature available on factors which make a leader effective and how leaders influence and motivate their subordinates to achieve organizational goals, there is scant literature available on negative aspects of leadership. Effective and ethical leadership are fundamental to the success in any organization – none more so than in a country's military. Organizations can succeed or fail because of good or bad leadership. This chapter considers some traits of leadership with special focus on humility and hubris. The chapter delves into the effect and impact of these traits in team behaviour and organisational health.

Chapter Six

Contaminated Choices in Leadership

'Different kinds of contaminants, diffusion, volatilisation, sorption, chemical (abiotic) degradation and Biodegradation, have different concentration limits at which they start to affect us or the environment'

Toxic and Destructive Leadership

Recent abuses of authority in business, politics, and religion have revived interest in destructive leadership. Although philosophers such as Plato, Hobbes and Russell have analysed leadership, modern social science has tended to take a one-sided view of the topic, emphasizing its positive and constructive aspects while avoiding its darker side.[156,157,158] Contaminants are defined as 'substances (i.e. chemical elements and compounds) or groups of substances that are toxic, persistent and liable to bio-accumulate, and other substances or groups of substances which give rise to an equivalent level of concern. Contamination is the presence of a constituent, impurity, or some other undesirable element that soils, corrupts, infects,

---

156. Hogan, R., & Kaiser, R. (2005). What we know about leadership. Review of General Psychology, 9, 169–180

157. Kellerman, B. (2004). Bad leadership: What it is, how it happens, why it matters. Boston, MA: Harvard Business School Press.

158. Yukl, G. A. (1999). An evaluation of conceptual weaknesses in transformational and charismatic leadership theories. Leadership Quarterly, 10, 285–305.

makes unfit, or makes inferior a material, physical body, natural environment, workplace. If the additional reactions are detrimental, other terms are often applied such as 'toxin,' 'poison,' or pollutant, depending on the type of molecule involved. [159] The *Mariam Webster Dictionary* defines contamination as 'to make unfit for use by the introduction of unwholesome or undesirable elements.' In medicine, it is the presence of an infectious agent on a body surface or on or in clothes, bedding, toys, surgical instruments or dressings, or other inanimate articles or substances including water, milk, and food, or that infectious agent itself. In environmental chemistry, the term "contamination" is, in some cases, virtually equivalent to pollution, where the main interest is the harm done on a large scale to humans, organisms, or environments. An environmental contaminant may be chemical in nature, though it may also be a biological (pathogenic bacteria, virus, invasive species) or physical (energy) agent. [160]

Destructive leadership can also be defined with reference to its principal direction or target: toward oneself (personal destructiveness) or toward the organization and its internal members and external stakeholders. Personal destructiveness can be seen as the undesirable things that leaders bring upon themselves, reprimands, criminal records, or tarnished reputations. Personal destructiveness involves harmful consequences experienced by the self; the most common form might be derailment, being fired, demoted, or otherwise failing to progress in one's career. [161,162,163] Organizational

---

159. Alters, S. (2000). Biology: Understanding Life. Jones & Bartlett Learning. p. 828.

160.

161. Bentz, V. (1985, August). A view from the top: A thirty year perspective of research devoted to the discovery, description, and prediction of executive behavior. Paper presented at the 93rd annual convention of the american psychological association, Los Angeles, CA

162. Leslie, J., & Van Velsor, E. (1996). A look at derailment today. Greensboro, NC: Center for Creative Leadership

destructiveness occurs when leaders bring misfortune to their followers, including internal and external stakeholders, and to social institutions. This could be a demoralized work force, environmental disasters, and countries driven to poverty. Organizational destructiveness is different from personal destructiveness. It might actually enhance a leader's power and longevity, as when dictators control the media, weaken countervailing social institutions, use the military to suppress dissidence, or usurp national resources for personal gain. However, organizational destructiveness also affects the quality of life for employees and citizens and jeopardizes an organization's purposes. [164,165] Destructive leadership distinguishes between occupying a leadership role and being effective in that role. Leadership is to be viewed as a functional resource for group performance; it involves influencing individuals to forego, for a limited time, their selfish, short-term interests and contribute to long-term group goals within an environmental or situational context. All significant human achievement requires leadership to unite people, channel their efforts, and encourage their contribution toward the goals of the collective enterprise. Thus, leadership effectiveness concerns how well a group is able to accomplish its purpose. In this view, leadership is a value-neutral term; it connotes social influence vis-à-vis group performance regardless of the context.

Deciding whether leadership is constructive or destructive is a matter of long-term group performance: how well did the team perform relative to its competition in achieving its goals? The test of toxic leadership, from this perspective, is a matter of outcomes; the essence of destructive leadership concerns

---

163. McCall,W.,&Lombardo, M. (1983). Off the track: Why and how successful executives get derailed. Greensboro, NC: Center for Creative Leadership

164. Kaiser, R., & Hogan, R. (submitted for publication). Leadership and the fate of organizations: On the measurement of effectiveness. Manuscript

165. Hogan, R., & Kaiser, R. (2005). What we know about leadership. Review of General Psychology, 9, 169–180.

negative organizational outcomes, and certain processes are more likely than others to lead to such outcomes. Based on the foregoing discussion, we define destructive leadership in terms of five features, summarized below. These five elements describe what destructive leadership is; the toxic triangle identifies the leader, follower, and environmental factors that make it possible.

Our first point is that destructive leadership is seldom absolutely or entirely destructive: most leadership results in both desirable and undesirable outcomes. Leaders, in concert with followers and environmental contexts, contribute to outcomes distributed across a destructive–constructive continuum. Outcomes associated with destructive leadership are largely located at the spectrum's constructive end. Emphasizing outcomes highlights the distinction between destructive leadership as a process and its consequences.

Secondly, destructive leadership involves control and coercion rather than persuasion and commitment, and these are found, primarily, at the negative end of that spectrum. Constructive leadership can sometimes yield bad results, but their outcomes are largely located at the spectrum's constructive end. Emphasizing outcomes highlights the distinction between destructive leadership as a process and its consequences. Tyranny and dominance are a negative prototype in implicit leadership theory; most working adults consider despotic control to be the antithesis of desirable leadership.

Thirdly, destructive leadership has a selfish orientation. It focuses on a leader's objectives and goals, as opposed to the needs of constituents and the larger social organization. Efforts to maintain a destructive leader's regime, thus, often preclude developing, empowering, and involving followers.

Moreover, the effects of destructive leadership are seen in organizational outcomes that compromise the quality of life for constituents (whether internal or external to the organization) and detract from their main purposes. Negative organizational outcomes are the product of dysfunctional leader behaviours and susceptible followers interacting in the context of a contributing environment. Followers must consent to, or be unable to resist, a destructive leader. In such cases, leadership results in bad consequences for the group; hence, destructive leadership.

Finally, destructive organizational outcomes also depend on susceptible followers and conducive environments. Most research on destructive leadership, like leadership, more broadly, is "leader-centric" [166,167] and the roles of followers and environmental contexts have not received adequate attention. We now attempt to remedy this focus.

The term 'environmental contaminant' is another name for pollution. A contaminant is a substance that is where it should not be, and is at high enough levels to have a negative effect on our health or on the health of animals or plants. A contaminant is any potentially undesirable substance (physical, chemical or biological). [168] Toxicity is the degree to which a chemical substance or a particular mixture of substances can damage an organism. Toxicity can refer to the effect on a whole organism, such as an animal, bacterium, or plant, as well as the effect on a substructure of the organism, such as a cell. By extension, the word may be metaphorically used to describe toxic effects on larger and more complex groups, such as the family unit or society at large. Sometimes the word is more or less synonymous with poisoning in everyday usage. There is a growing incidence of toxic leadership in organisations across the

---

166. Kellerman, B. (2004). Bad leadership: What it is, how it happens, why it matters. Boston, MA: Harvard Business School Press

167. Hollander, E. P., & Offermann, L. (1990). Power and leadership in organizations: Relationships in transition. American Psychologist, 45, 179–189

168. http://www.nativeknowledge.org/db/files/aboutcon.htm

world. This is clear from anecdotal evidence as well as research, which suggests that one out of every five leaders is toxic. Research shows that closer to three out of every ten leaders are toxic. This cancer of toxicity threatens the wellbeing of both individuals and organisations. It also affects the performance of a society and country. Toxic leaders' destructive behaviours and characteristics can make individuals, groups, organizations, communities seriously and permanently damaged. Toxic, poisonous leaders are the leaders who lead and harm the employees, the business environment and the organizational climate. It is necessary to differentiate the toxic leader from the boss or manager who is bad and oppressive. Such leaders do not care much about what is outside them. Destructive leadership entails the negative consequences that result from a confluence of destructive leaders, susceptible followers, and conducive environments[169]. It is an approach that harms people by poisoning activities that generate enthusiasm, creativity, autonomy, and innovation.

Toxic leaders spread this poison with an excessive control mechanism. Padilla *et al.* have discovered that, with the exception of a few discussions of charisma, social scientists have avoided the dark side of leadership. Although this seems to be changing, careful reading of the literature shows that destructive leadership is not explicitly defined. Some writers regard destructive leadership as an oxymoron and maintain that leadership is, by definition, a positive force. As an example of a bad leader, as Burns [170] puts it, Hitler ruled the German people, but he did not lead them, because he failed to create "lasting, meaningful opportunities for the pursuit of happiness." Another perspective might regard Hitler and Mother Teresa as leaders

---

169. Art Padilla a, Robert Hogan and Robert B. Kaiser, The toxic triangle: Destructive leaders, susceptible followers, and conducive environments, The Leadership Quarterly · June 2007
170. Burns, J. (2003). Transformational leadership. New York: Atlantic Monthly Press

because they both built constituencies and influenced others to pursue objectives. The definition is further complicated because non-destructive leaders are not, invariably, good. Mother Teresa, a Nobel Peace Prize winner who worked for the world's poor and was beatified by the Catholic Church, also accepted over US$1.25 million and the frequent use of a private jet from Charles Keating, the principal figure in the U.S. savings and loan scandal of the 1980s. [171,172,173] Although Keating was convicted of stealing millions of dollars from investors, Mother Teresa wrote to the court urging leniency, and refused a district attorney's request to return the money.

Mother Teresa worked hard to improve the lives of the less fortunate, but some might question whether her ends justified her means. Some authors focus on destructive leadership as a process. They emphasize syndromes such as narcissism and psychopathy that are associated with alienation and betrayal. If leaders, in combination with followers and contexts, harm constituents or damage organizations, then destructive leadership has occurred. This is consistent with the dictionary definition of 'destructive' as causing destruction or designed... to destroy. With reference to disastrous outcomes, the study of organizational destruction, gives indication of concern that narcissistic leaders damage followers' psychological well-being. If destructive leadership is defined in terms of harmful outcomes, then it is possible for 'good' leaders to produce bad outcomes, and "bad" leaders to produce desirable outcomes. The worst political and business leaders, Hitler, Stalin, Charles Keating, Dennis Kozlowski, brought some value to their constituents. [174]

---

[171] Joly, E. (1983). Mother Teresa of Calcutta: A biography. San Francisco: Harper & Row

[172] Kwilecki, S., & Wilson, L. (1998). Was Mother Teresa maximizing her utility? An idiographic application of rational choice theory. Journal for the Scientific Study of Religion, 37, 205–221.
173

[174]. Kellerman, B. (2004). Bad leadership: What it is, how it happens, why it matters. Boston,

A review of military history and current headlines provide proof that examples of toxic leadership continue to this day. The US Army recently released a study reporting that 80 percent of the officers and NCOs polled had observed toxic leaders in action and that 20 percent had worked for a toxic leader. Many researchers have defined toxic leadership in their context, but defining "toxic leadership" remains an exasperating task primarily due to differences in perceptions about how leadership is viewed, since one subordinate might view a leader as toxic and another might view the same person as a hero. [175] Toxic leadership is not a new phenomenon. In the book, *Surviving Toxic Leaders*, Gangel identifies toxic leadership characteristics in the great biblical patriarch Jacob, who was deceptive and stole his brother's birth right. Biblical David was a great military leader and king, but also with the following significant toxic leadership behaviours: ethical failure, poor judgment, and murder. [176] At all levels of an organization, strong leadership is required to maximize productivity, create a positive environment, and ensure relevance. Good leadership is imperative because organizations often emulate the personality of their leaders. In addition to this, a toxic leader need not necessarily display toxic behaviours in all situations. To add to the complexity, different toxic leaders demonstrate varying levels, and types of toxicity and the impact of their toxic decisions and actions also vary to a large extent (Walton, 2007).

Based on the research in military organizations, Reed stated that leaders who exhibited negative and destructive leadership tendencies in using their position tended to propel their organizations towards destruction. [177] While Reed's paper dealt

---

MA: Harvard Business School Press.

175. Lipman-Blumen J, (2005). The Allure of Toxic Leaders, Why We Follow Destructive Bosses and Corrupt Politicians--and How We Can Survive Them, Oxford University Press, Oxford, New York.

176

with the problem of destructive leadership existing in the armed forces, this issue was found to exist in the corporate sector as well. Toxic leadership has existed in organizations, societies and nations, and history is witness to all those leaders who have displayed toxic behaviours to fulfil personal needs. Some of the definitions from the academic and management literature include destructive, degrading, disrespectful, dysfunctional, and abusive leadership and/ or supervision. Toxic leadership is a style of leadership in which leaders, due to their negative behaviour and detrimental personal characteristics inflict long lasting and serious harm directly on their followers and indirectly to their organizations. Goldman, (2009) defines toxic leadership as "being destructive, disturbing, and dysfunctional acts of supervision that spread among members of the workforce." Flynn (1999) provides a clear and pragmatic characterization of toxic leadership to align the leader's behaviours and actions with the effects that they have on the workplace environment. "A manager who bullies, threatens, yells. The manager whose mood swings determines the climate of the office on any given workday. Who forces employees to whisper in sympathy in cubicles and hallways." The competence of toxic leaders cannot be underestimated as many times they are influential leaders who have 'the right stuff', but just in the wrong intensity, and with an objective guided by an agenda based on self-interest (Williams, 2005).

According to Mehta and Maheshwari, toxic leadership could thus be described as, 'a series of purposeful and deliberate behaviours and acts of a leader that disrupt the effective functioning of the organization and are intended to manoeuvre, deceive, intimidate, and humiliate others with the objective of personal gains. [178] Some leaders put themselves, career, and

---

[177]. Reed, George. E. (2004). Toxic leadership. Military Review, (July-August 2004) 84, 67-71.

[178]. Sunita Mehta and, G.C.Maheshwari, Toxic Leadership: Tracing The Destructive Trail, International Journal of Management (IJM), Volume 5, Issue 10, October (2014), pp. 18-24

mission focus solely as the only priority; there is little to no regard for the impact on subordinates. When leaders place their own well-being and power above their supporters' needs, "followers suffer poisonous effects. As was noted by Chetwode, if the leader always puts his own ease, comfort and safety first and every time over the honour, welfare and comfort of the men he commands, then he has become toxic. Lipman – Blumen see it in leaders who engage in numerous destructive behaviours and who exhibit certain dysfunctional personal characteristics. To count as toxic, these behaviours and qualities of character must inflict some reasonably serious and enduring harm on their followers and their organization. Williams also identifies it as leaders who take part in destructive behaviours and show signs of dysfunctional personal characteristics. To count as toxic, these behaviours and qualities of character must inflict some reasonably serious and enduring harm on their followers and their organization. Inwardly motivated, inherently destructive, and violate the legitimate interests of the organization.

Bad leadership that is left unchecked compromises the organization's values and norms, and promotes noncompliant behaviours. According to Frost [179], toxic feelings in the work environment are an emotional state where negative feelings are more intensified and include psychological repetition, rupture, and depletion phases. In the psychologically repetitive phase, the individuals are unable to psychologically analyse a severe experience that affects them, and they cannot predict the negative results of repeating experiences. When the transition phase is passed, the individuals are moving away from their social environment and colleagues. In the depletion phase, the mental and physical energy of the individuals are depleted due

---

[179] Peter J. Frost , Toxic Emotions at Work: How Compassionate Managers Handle Pain and Conflict .Harvard Business School Press, 2003

to those negative experiences. Recent studies show that a toxic leader's poison could spread to individuals, teams and the whole organization in a stealthy manner. [180]

Those who abuse the power they wield, particularly over subordinates, to serve and satisfy personal ends focus on visible short-term mission accomplishments. They provide superiors with impressive, articulate presentations and enthusiastic responses to missions. However, they are unconcerned about, or oblivious to, staff or troop morale, and climate. They are seen by the majority of subordinates as arrogant, self-serving, inflexible, and petty; normal by-products of organizational life that can have serious negative effects on individuals and their organizations. [181] Leaders who take part in destructive behaviours, show signs of dysfunctional personal characteristics. Commanders, who put their own needs first, micro-manage subordinates, behave in a mean-spirited manner, or display poor decision-making. The definitional differences provide valuable insight into the dynamics of toxic leadership and provide a reason why toxic leaders can go undetected. This work supports three main parts to defining toxic leadership: destructive behaviour, dysfunctional personality characteristics, and a negative impact on the organization.

The interpersonal style of the leader, thus, has implications in formulating the organizational culture, both when it is positive and when it is negative. Recent research has also shown that toxic leaders had an evident lack of concern for the welfare of subordinates, a personality that negatively affected organizational culture, and a belief by subordinates who felt that their superior's actions were driven primarily by selfish motives

---

[180]. LUBİT,R. Coping with Toxic Managers, Subordinates,and Other Difficult People. Prentice Hall, 2004.

[181]. Lemmergaard, J., & Muhr, S. L. (2013). Introduction to Part II: Leadership Behaviour in Practice. I J. Lemmergaard, & S. L. Muhr (red.), Critical Perspectives On Leadership: Emotion, Toxicity, and Dysfunction (s. 29-32). Cheltenham: Edward Elgar Publishing. New Horizons in Leadership Studies series

and self-interest. Quite effectively, Reed [182] points out that from the follower's perspective, toxic leadership can best be defined as 'I'll know it when I see it'. Toxic leadership is thus seen as an approach that creates an environment wherein employees are rewarded for agreeing with the leader and reprimanded for challenging his/her authority. In this type of environment, enthusiasm, creativity, autonomy, and innovativeness of the people are curtailed and the leader's interest assumes paramount importance. This kind of destructive leadership has today emerged as a silent killer that tends to position leaders who have a capability to hurt and eliminate those subordinates who question their authority and decisions. Toxic leadership not only impacts performance at the organizational level but also at the individual level. Reed highlights that people and organizations suffer and often perform at less than their best as a result of toxic leadership. Toxic leaders sap the cognitive and emotional strength out of most people, even hard-charging and highly motivated individuals. Humans can only be beaten down and beat up for so long. Practically, there is abundance of leaders who are perceived to be detrimental to the organization and who cause severe physical and psychological damage to their subordinates.

Lower psychological safety in employees most often results in less trust, which results in decreased efficiency and effectiveness. Morale drops, the climate in the organization sags, and workers start feeling uninvited. Although an understanding of effective leadership is imperative for developing managers and supervisors, it is equally important to identify the behaviours of leaders who knowingly or unintentionally inflict enduring harm on their subordinates. The other side of leadership, which includes the negative aspects

---

182. George E. Reed, Tarnished : Toxic Leadership in the US Military, Lincoln, University of Nebraska Press/ Washington, DC, Potomac Books, 2015, 175 pp.

such as subordinate harassment, ridicule, physical hardships, mental torture, and an increasing work place stress and unhappiness, has been ignored in leadership research and very few studies exist on these aspects. Reed even cites the appropriately-titled book *The No Asshole Rule*, whose content fits nicely in describing the toxic leader construct, especially from the perspective of the average employee. It is important to note that this type of leadership is a pattern of behaviour as opposed to a one-time event or an occasional and rare occurrence. Reed addresses this point by noting that being upset and perhaps even yelling at a subordinate does not make one a toxic leader. Very often, that may be exactly what the subordinate needs at that moment. However, a leader who consistently treats his/ her subordinates rudely, disrespectfully, and only as a means to an end, is in all likelihood a toxic leader. Recent spate of corporate scandals and catastrophic failures at mega corporations such as those at Enron, WorldCom, Bear Sterns and Lehman Brothers and others have been attributed, to some extent, to leadership behaviours. Emerging economies face many problems like poverty, unemployment, population explosion, epidemics, etc., and such failures of corporations and scandals in government projects further add distress to the economy, individuals, employees, investors and government. Some business scandals have called to question various leadership models that have been proposed by researchers in last three decades. Recent scams, scandals, and failures have been ascribed to the actions of toxic leaders who develop toxic instruments to create toxic assets without due consideration to the potential catastrophic damages to others. In all these cases, the leaders were found to be blame-worthy for allowing such damaging behaviour, and to make matters worse, by being party to deceit. The failure to curb such destructive and toxic behaviour allows ruthless and unscrupulous leaders to fulfil their illicit goals and damage the organizations.

According to Lipman-Blumen [183] the repertoire of toxic leaders covers a broad spectrum; it includes leaders with mild, unintended toxicity to leaders who are seen as being absolutely evil, and includes tendencies such as dishonesty, hypocrisy, sabotage, manipulation, fraud and unethical behaviour. History has also thrown up leaders whose leadership can be identified as toxic; one of them, Adolf Hitler, is a prime example of being a destructive leader. A look into the past of toxic leaders shows that they do not develop toxic tendencies in a day; in fact, their style evolved over a period of time. It became highly toxic, when it was left unquestioned by superiors or peers. When these leaders take higher-level positions in the organization, the impact of their behaviour is even greater. Leadership toxicity also stems from a perceived threat to the status, power and control, which elicits toxic behaviour in leaders who are vulnerable. Minor changes in an executive's authority and accomplishments, which are generally attained after a lot of hard work and effort, can be perceived as a threat and cause psychological insecurity and generate fierce defensive reactions. These executives become more vulnerable and sensitive, and they feel that their identity and reputation is at stake.

Ludeman and Erlandson [184] explained how successful leaders failed to use their emotional intelligence to such an extent that 'the more executive authority people achieved, the more pressure they felt and the more prominent their faults became' which in turn intensified their sense of vulnerability and generally triggered toxic behaviour. The drive to acquire power and authority could also become an addiction for some leaders. It is also possible that this insatiable desire could become so strong that a leader might focus all his energy to protect or enhance his status and authority. This innate desire explains why

---

[183]. Op sit

[184] Kate Ludeman, Eddie Erlandson (2004), Tappiing the full power of the Alpha Leader, 2006 Forum on Emerging Issues, April 26-27, 2006

successful leaders find themselves in difficult situations when asked to relinquish power and authority resulting in an increased risk of leadership toxicity.

Organizations could also become an incubator of toxic or dysfunctional behaviour by providing their own toxins, through counterproductive policies and practices, including unreasonable goals, excessive internal competition, and cultures that encourage blame game. Leaders who uncompromisingly pursued unreasonable profits from quarter to quarter could also be a major source of this kind of leadership. Another source of toxicity is when average performance is given more weightage over merit-based output. These types of organizational practices tend to suffocate the above average performers who feel disillusioned and dejected.

Another reason for the emergence of toxic leadership is when personal agendas of leaders take precedence over the long-term well-being of the organization. [185] When dysfunctional behaviour of leaders in senior positions are modelled by the subordinates, then the focus is more on individual interests than on organizational objectives resulting in an ineffective organization. When the followers avoid disagreements with leaders for fear of reprisal, an opportunity arises for workplace toxicity to emerge.

Leaders who usurp their position and authority in such situations tend to take control of the workplace and become quite rigid and adamant in their approach blinded to new ideas or suggestions from subordinates. Impatient and short-tempered leaders who are constantly on the edge at the place of work could also be the cause for emergence of toxicity. These leaders develop a habit of throwing temper tantrums, shout, make unreasonable demands, use abusive language and belittle employees openly. When subordinates are treated as financial

---

[185] Sally Atkinson, David Butcher, Trust in managerial relationships,

liabilities by the senior leadership instead of assets, it could create a culture of toxicity and could lead to a decay of the morale and self-esteem of the employees. As toxicity emerges in leaders, hardworking and sincere subordinates tend to move away from the toxic atmosphere and there would be higher employee turnover. According to the Padilla *et al.* [186], 'negative organizational outcomes are not only the product of dysfunctional leader behaviours but also susceptible followers and the contributing environment in which they interact.'

These three components form the 'toxic triangle'. The three components of the toxic triangle, their characteristics and their interactions with each other determine the level of intensity of toxicity existing in organizations. To take the topic to a higher level, Reed highlights the uniqueness of the military as a profession (similar to medicine, law, and law enforcement) and how it is a reflection of society, whether made up of conscripts or volunteers. Reed argues that the military, as one of the most respected professions, has a responsibility to weed out toxic leaders and ensure that the quality of leadership in the military is the best it can be. Often, Reed notes, the very nature of military service, with its culture and ethic of mission accomplishment, a can-do attitude, and a 24/7 work ethic, contributes to micromanagement and toxic leadership. Toxic leaders might think "I don't have time to worry about anything but accomplishing the mission" which easily can default to psychological and emotional abuse of subordinates. I do not think Reed is making excuses for toxic leadership as much as he is explaining that organizational culture can, and will contribute to how leaders lead.

---

[186] A. Padilla et al. / The Leadership Quarterly 18 (2007) 176–194

Signs and Characteristics of Toxic Leadership

Looking at organizations where toxicity exists, things might appear to be normal from outside, but there would be serious trouble within the organization. Feeling of helplessness, reduced autonomy, lack of opportunity for participation, erratic job situation, reduced efficiency and innovation, lower job satisfaction, psychic and psychosomatic problems such as anxiety, depression, frustration, and stomach problems, are all known symptoms of toxic a leader's effect. [187] Some other characteristics that have been linked to toxic behaviours are aggression, abusive behaviours, egotism, greed, selfishness, and lack of integrity. Toxic leadership behaviours fall on a continuum ranging from insignificant gestures to physical abuse of others, and from petty pilfering to fraud and cheating and distortion of facts against the organization. Toxic leaders are not interested in mentoring and developing subordinates. They enjoy controlling and subjugating, and are seen insulting and abusing others. All those who come into contact with these leaders are affected by the toxic leaders' behaviours and decisions. However, toxic leaders are generally indecisive unless there is a crisis. When a decision is made, it is often quick and appears to lack rationale. An important way to look at toxicity in an organization is to look at the impact of such leadership on the culture of the organization. All these behaviours and characteristics of toxic leaders result in a culture, which is ambiguous and results in stressful employees.

Studies have also shown that abusive leadership has a positive relationship with turnover intentions and employee stress, and negative relationship with organizational commitment and job satisfaction. Outcomes at individual's levels include lack of motivation, sexual harassment [188], and decreased job

---

187. Ashforth, B. E. (1997). Petty tyranny in organizations: A preliminary examination of antecedents and consequences. Canadian Journal of Administrative Sciences, 14, 126-140.

188. Chan, D. K. S., Lam, C. B., Chow, S. Y., & Cheung, S. F. (2008). Examining the job-related,

satisfaction. [189] In addition to this, employees who face attack on self-esteem display low self-confidence and a reduced sense of self-efficacy leading to deterioration in individual performance. [190] When working with toxic leaders, employees are left with two options; namely, conform or leave. Leaving would lead to higher turnover resulting in increased cost of recruitment and a possible economic consequence for the organization. Those who remain will have reduced commitment and loyalty for the organization. Some people, however, may view toxic leadership as good and follow willingly. These employees would possibly be groomed to become the next generation of toxic leaders. In military settings, toxic leadership is considered to be even more damaging as the impact of toxic leaders on their subordinates' performance is greater for those who find their jobs meaningful and have a strong sense of commitment. [191] Reed [192] stated that in a military organization, toxic leaders erode unit cohesion and reduce team spirit, and, under worst case scenarios, toxic leadership could even lead to mutiny and death. Other less serious outcomes include loss of trust, reduced effectiveness and commitment, misinterpretation of communication, and diminished follower well-being. [193] In short, toxic leadership affects a soldier's mindset, loyalty, and mission accomplishment. Toxic leadership is a very sensitive issue. Toxic leaders themselves do not think they are toxic, and if questioned on the issue, they would more than likely say, they were acting with the best of intentions.

---

psychological, and physical outcomes of workplace sexual harassment: A meta-analytic review. Psychology of Women Quarterly, 32, 362-376.

[189]. Tate, B. W. (2009). Bad to the bone: Empirically defining and measuring negative leadership. (Doctoral dissertation). Retrieved from ProQuest (Accession 3381024).

[190]. Kusy, M., & Holloway, E. (2009). Toxic workplace: Managing toxic personalities and their systems of power. Jossey-Bass, San Francisco.

[191] Harris, K. J., Kacmar, K. M., Zivnuska, S., & Shaw, J. D. (2007). The impact of political skill on impression management effectiveness. Journal of Applied Psychology, 92, 278-285.

[192]. Reed, Op sit

[193]. Ashford, Op sit

Subordinates' opinions on the same leader depend on their individual interactions and results in being loved by some and hated by others. Every leader at one time or another has been labelled openly or in private as toxic. The most evident implication is that as toxic leadership is related to decreased employee performance, commitment, and job satisfaction, strong efforts should be made to reduce the likelihood of such destructive behaviours.

A typology of typical, potentially toxic leadership conduct

Type	Examples
Lack of Integrity	Deception; Bending rules to get results; Blaming others for own mistakes; Covering up own mistakes; Opportunism; Ethics and conduct unconnected
Demeaning/ Devaluing	Personal attacks; Ridiculing; Mocking; Belittling; Disrespect; Inconsiderate; Character assassination
Punitive/ Coercive	Rule by fear; Rule by insecurity; Favouritism; Selective distribution of rewards/recognition; Unreasonable, unrealistic personal/ work demands; Ruthless elimination of all opposition: real or imagined
Manipulative/ Exploitative	Distortion of facts/reality to serve own ends; Backstabbing; Setting up persons against each other; Rumour mongering; Non-disclosure and/or selective release of vital information
Egocentric/ Self-serving	Centre of universe; God's fit to mankind; Claimed sole source of credit/success; Self-promotion; Personal need satisfaction takes precedence; Own and organisational interests completely fused; Consummate self promoter
Divisive/ Elitist	Ostracising; In-Out group; Scape-goating; Marginalisation; Collusion
Abrasive/ Abusive	Intimidation; Excessive/ Misplaced anger; (Physical) acts of aggression; Harassment; Rudeness
Aloof/ Distant	Disengaged; Disinterested; (Deliberate) Ignoring of concerns/ideas/suggestions; Underestimation of the demands posed by challenges/ set backs on persons
Excessive control	Stifling of dissent; Suppressing (or downplaying) of criticism/concerns; Micro-management; Over rigid; Suspicious; Lack of trust; Source of all answers; Blind adherence to past success recipes
Unpredictability/ Inconsistency	Mixed messages; Knee-jerk, hasty decisions; Quick fixes; (Frequent) directional changes without proper justification; Emotional volatility; Constant mood swings; Indecision; On-going crisis management

Toxic leadership often causes employee dissatisfaction, low productivity, interdepartmental conflict, stagnant innovation, and a high turnover rate. Unfortunately, in many organizations toxic leaders are a painful, but undeniable reality. With their destructive behaviour patterns and dysfunctional interactions, they create a disillusioned and demotivated workforce. Here are some of their additional, common characteristics.

a. **Arrogance:** Toxic leaders are very boastful and arrogant. They think that they are always right, and expect others to accept their word as gospel truth. They extend no help to others, and they hate it when someone else dares to correct them, especially if that someone is a subordinate.

b. **Autocracy:** A toxic boss does not want any opinion other than their own to be heard. They expect others to quietly follow their every direction, without ever questioning the direction. A toxic boss often fancies themselves as the top dog or a self-styled king, and their behaviour is often reflective of that. Employees are minions, lesser beings who exist only to do the leader's bidding.

c. **Irritability:** Perhaps not surprisingly, toxic leaders also come across as highly irritable. They do not want to be bothered for anything. Since they are not open to other ideas from anyone else, they despise being asked questions and avoid it as much as possible. Under a toxic leader, the organization becomes stunted because of the lack of innovative and free-flowing ideas.

d. **Maladjusted:** Beneath the tough and arrogant veneer of a toxic boss is an ill-tempered child who is mortified of change. They are highly inflexible, and take changes very hard. The toxic boss is likely to be the most vehement opponent of any changes in the organization.

e. **Lack of Confidence:** Though they act supremely confident, a toxic leader has no confidence in themselves. Consequently, they also find it extremely difficult to trust team members. Because of this lack of confidence, tough problems are often ignored or swept under the carpet.

f. **Incompetence:** A toxic leader may think that they are the best, but they are incompetent and may often struggle to make even the most commonsensical decisions, or do the simplest of tasks. Their sense of importance and usefulness only comes from criticizing others, and making them out to be less than they really are.

g. **Hierarchical:** Without the rigid structure of hierarchy, toxic leadership will   wither and die. If you are under a toxic leader, you will often feel the pressure of the corporate power structure above you. A toxic leader is adept at controlling team members using hierarchy and seniority.

h. **Unrealistic Expectations:** Toxic leaders are notorious for setting objectives that are unfair and unrealistic. Team members struggle with unachievable goals, and get demoralized. Workload piles up, and the company becomes set up to fail.

i. **Symbols of Personal Authority:** These symbols include, first, right to common parking spaces, complete access to everything, and perhaps even studding the entire workplace with their own portraits and stories of accomplishments.

j. **Discriminatory:** Not surprisingly, toxic leaders are often discriminatory. Their biases and prejudices often appear in the guise of sexism, racism, ageism, and other discriminatory behaviour.

If you recognize any of these signs in yourself, you could possibly be a toxic leader who leads a group of dissatisfied and demotivated employees. If so, take the necessary steps for a sincere change to improve yourself as a leader and as a person.

The military invokes many images of professionalism, and this is known throughout the world. This is accomplished through outstanding leadership. Strong leadership is a value that we must consciously protect. Toxic leadership in the military is often seen in the form of bad command climate and/or inefficient mission execution and is contrary to the military's core identity of strong leadership. The military should use time and resources to study the effects of toxic leadership because they are in the business of developing leaders, and the price of poor leadership is devastating. Interestingly, a research paper entitled "Antecedents & Consequences of Toxic Leadership in the U.S. Army" by John P. Steele highlights a positive aspect within by highlighting that 'results confirm that leaders who were classified as toxic got their intended results more than any other leadership type," however only by a small margin. Yet, the results rarely outweigh the negative impacts of toxic leaders. Toxic leaders "provide superiors with impressive, articulate presentations and enthusiastic responses to missions." In other words, it acknowledges that toxic leaders are good performers; particularly, they are good at providing the necessary care and feeding up the chain, which provides them space and a cover to create a toxic atmosphere down their respective chains. "Simply put, they produce results. Although it can be argued that these results are short-lived and ultimately damaging to the organization. In an effort to achieve a desired result, organizations and followers may tolerate a toxic leader and the effect he or she may have on the organization. Toxic leadership is not an anomaly, but to be expected. Even leaders who are widely applauded as exemplary are not necessarily without their occasional toxic chinks.

Jean Lipman–Blumen provides the most descriptive and inclusive definition of toxic leadership. "Leaders who engage in numerous destructive behaviours and who exhibit certain dysfunctional personal characteristics. To count as toxic, these behaviours and qualities of character must inflict some reasonably serious and enduring harm on their followers and their organization. Aside the above characteristics, the following sums up expanded characteristics of the toxic leader: [194]

Toxic Leader Characteristics

Destructive behaviour… Results In Negative Impact	Dysfunctional Personality	Positive Aspects of Personality
Deceptive, Incompetent Ignorant , Cruel, Evil, Greed Mistrust, Lack of restraint Manipulate people, Malevolent, Abusive, Bad leadership, Bullies Corrosive leadership, Harassing leaders, Jerks, Assholes, Tyrannical, Incompetence, Irresponsible, Avarice And Greed, Deception, Malicious Malfeasance, Malevolent Failure to understand and to act competently and effectively in leadership situations. Reckless disregard for the costs of their actions to others as well as to themselves	Lack Of Integrity, Avarice , Cowardice, Cynicism, Narcissism, Paranoia, Megalomania, Moral Blind spots, Demanding, Autocratic, Unrelenting, Lacks empathy, Personal inadequacy, Maladjusted, Malcontent, Egotistic, Malfunctioning, Maladjusted, Sense Of Inadequacy, Malcontent, Amoral, Cowardice, Insatiable Ambition, Egotism, Arrogance, Selfish Values, Lack Of Integrity, Insatiable Ambition prompts leaders to put their own sustained power, glory, and fortunes above followers' well-being, Enormous Ego that blinds leaders to the shortcomings of their own character and thus limit their capacity for self-renewal, Arrogance, Amorality prevents acknowledging their mistakes and instead leads to blaming	Charming, Forge, quick relationships, Ability to charm supervisors, Self-confidence, Magnetic enthusiasm

Source: Quincy L. Davis [195]

Nine other characteristics supported by other literature include insatiable ambition, arrogance, cowardice, egotism,

---

194. Lipman Blumen, Allure of Toxic Leadership, pg. 21.

195. Quincy L. Davis, A Comprehensive Review Of Toxic Leadership

incompetence, lack of integrity, maladjusted, malcontent, and malevolence. The following characteristics were mentioned in three of the studies: maladjusted, malcontent, malevolent, egotistic, and ambitious. "Toxic leaders are defined as leaders who take part in destructive behaviours and show signs of dysfunctional personal characteristics." Most of the repeated characteristics fall within the classification of dysfunctional personality traits. Most publications reviewed overwhelmingly described toxic leaders with negative characteristics. However, Colonel Box in his publication titled "Toxic Leadership in the Military Profession" states that the "toxic leader's self-confidence, magnetic enthusiasm and unrelenting drive to attain prestige and power enable them to climb the rungs of power and to be effective in some aspects of leadership." This idea is supported by Lipman-Blumen's reminder that it is unlikely that we will find saints in the military. "Do not look for saints among formal leaders. Saints rarely seek elected or appointed office. They seldom enter the rough-and-tumble of politics or the corporate world. Nor are we likely to encounter saintly leaders in the spit and polish of the traditional military. Consequently, the potential for toxic leadership exists in each leader because even beloved icons of leadership can display frailties. Consequently, the potential for toxic leadership exists in each leader because even beloved icons of leadership can display frailties.

According to Kusy and Halloway, negative behaviour triggers an adverse response and "soon the triggers and reactions begin to damage the team or individuals, who may react in ways that reinforce the toxic behaviours. Emulation is a significant danger of toxic leadership. Emulation may be invisible at first but soon crop up, threatening every dynamic of the organization. Like an invisible toxin in drinking water, its accumulation and inherent dangers soon begin to cause harm. Abubrey states the following:

"Organizational corruption extends beyond the behaviours and traits of individuals and encompasses the effect that corrupt acts have on the group, unit, or organization. Left unchecked these actions can spread to others of the organization and amplify the scope of the problem in ways that threaten the culture and climate of the organization. Steel emphasizes that toxic leadership may be even more damaging in a military setting than in civilian corporations because the impact that toxic leaders have on their subordinates' performance is greater for those who identify a strong sense of value and meaning in their jobs (as attributed to individuals that serve in the military). In other words, the best soldiers are the ones who are most likely to be affected by toxic leaders.

Causes of Toxic Leadership

John P. Steele's "Antecedents & Consequences of Toxic Leadership in the U.S. Army," provides a very useful leadership model based on three factors: leaders, followers, and the environment. Davis proposes to add a fourth factor; nature. Nature may also contribute to toxic leadership in that some of the toxic leaders' behaviour may be inherent to being human. The following may be causes of toxic Leadership:

Leaders	Followers	Environment	System Causes of Toxic Leadership	Nature
Power	Low maturity	Instability	Attraction	Leaders are human – with both negative and positive tendencies
Personality	Ethics/Values	Perceived Threats	Selection	Sin
Ideology	Similar View	Cultural Values	Attrition	Emotions; Being Human.

Enormous Ego that blinds leaders to the shortcomings of their own character and thus limit their capacity for self-renewal.	Psychological needs of followers.	Lacks of Checks	Inherent paradoxical nature of leadership. Some of the toxic leadership types reflect some desired qualities of military leadership	
Their deep-seated sense of inadequacy has arrested their personal development.		Migration-changes in structure or work assignments designed to accommodate a toxic person.	Inadequate development (i.e. Mentors… positive role model to emulate)	
Failure to personally achieve Maslow's level four dealing with esteem or level five dealing with self-actualization and giving.		The Disbursement of knowledge and power within an organization	Failure to place limits on power or to recognize toxic behaviour in subordinates.	
Enabling or overlooking negative behaviours to retain a productive toxic person. (allows emulation				
Lack of accountability				

Personality also plays a role in causing toxic leadership. In *Toxic Leaders – When Organizations Go Bad*', Marcia Lynn Whicker explains that toxic leaders fail to personally achieve Maslow's 'level four' dealing with esteem, or 'level five' dealing with self-actualization and giving. Instead, toxic leaders find themselves stuck on "level two," security needs. "Maslow categorized human needs into a five-level pyramid and suggested that people move upward as needs at a particular level are met. The levels start with basic physiological needs forming the base and then ascend through safety, love and belonging, esteem, and finally, self-actualization. Until needs and desires are met at any given level, the individual cannot progress to the next level. While 'trustworthy leaders usually operate at level four or five,' destructive leaders are still concerned with meeting their safety needs at level two or possibly their love and belonging needs at level three." Nevertheless, implementation of a systemic solution set that addresses causal factors found in the leadership, follower, environment, and nature dimensions should ensure that the toxicity level within the organization remains insignificant. When people are treated as 'less than human,' 'less than capable' or as 'pawns in a game" some extremely negative things happen in the organization that derail its success. Attempts to control what people do and say makes them feel inadequate and unappreciated. Withholding information to preserve power creates an environment of suspicion. The effects of these behaviours over time is numbing. The downward effect on morale and productivity is easily visible in the fear, frustration and uncertainty on people's faces.

Side Effects of Toxic Leadership on Organizational Culture:

    a. Low productivity
    b. Low morale
    c. Rampant fear
    d. High stress
    e. Decreased learning
    f. Employees becoming detached and insulated to protect themselves
    g. Detached employees help each other less and do not communicate as proactively
    h. Lack of proactive communication and teamwork leads to diminished company reputation
    i. Employees fail to find meaning in their work
    j. People dread what each day may bring
    k. Trust in each other and in the organization is lost

l. People leave, generating high turnover
m. The ripple effect from #1-12 above leads to deteriorating organizational results.

Toxic leadership is unethical. It harms people, groups and organizations. The side effects are crippling. We must carefully prevent this kind of un-leadership from happening in our organizations. The literature in the field of innovation management suggests that, first, organisational culture has a link with performance if it is capable of adapting to changes in the environment. Moreover, organisational culture has long been believed to be an important means for organisations to integrate internal processes and adapt to external conditions. Leadership, which is one of the essential factors continuously proposed to influence innovation, inspires and directs an organisational culture that promotes innovation, can foster product champions or epic innovators who assist in the innovation implementation process, and can create the organisational structure necessary to encourage innovativeness. In addition, effective leadership can result in the development of innovation, productivity and sustained competitive advantage for organisational leadership growth. Organisational innovation can be affected by the dimensions of organisational culture, such as education and growth, participative decision making, assistance and participation, power sharing, status differentials, communication and acceptance of conflict and risk. [196]

Solutions to Toxic Leadership

Shalley and Gilson propose that managers should facilitate and support employees besides fostering relationships with them. The following solutions for toxic leadership are recommended:

---

[196] Hurley, R.F. and Hult, G.M. (1998) 'Innovation, market orientation, and organizational learning: an integration and empirical examination', Journal of Marketing, Vol. 62, No. 3, pp.42–54.

Leaders	Followers	Environment	System	Nature
Evidence of emulation	Lack of emulation	Restructuring the organization	Selection	Religion/ Relationship with God
Training	Direct feedback	Expanding the organizational resource base	Evaluation	
Unbiased feedback (surveys)	Resilience training	Abolish the organization	Education	
360 Evaluation	Positive affectivity	Accountability	Assignment	
Coaching-trained facilitators	Ingratiation	Leadership	Improve methods of organizational governance (possibly prevents emulation)	
Regulate moderating behaviours	Undermine		Create a committee to coach, teach and mentor all future brigade and battalion commanders	
Publically admit any behaviour which has caused your people hurt or discouragement	Overthrow		Multi-Rater Assessments (360-degree multi-source assessment)	
Ask for forgiveness and prayer and make someone you trust a monitor of your public behaviour	Leave the organization		Academic institution reform (improve leadership training/ education).	
Be patient.			Counsel	
Developing self-insight/ awareness			Impose term limits	
Maintaining self-control			Removing toxic leaders	
Accountability				
Positive Leadership				
Confront				
Tolerate				

In fact, if leaders have a supportive style, it is possible for creativity to happen; it is also seen as essential that leaders understand staff. Leadership is recognised as one of the most important factors influencing organisational innovation, especially transformational leadership in empowering subordinates and creating an appropriate climate for innovation. Some unethical leadership relationships involve destructive leaders, combined with susceptible followers and conducive environments. Destructive leadership entails the negative consequences that result from a confluence of destructive leaders, susceptible followers, and conducive environments. The figure below illustrates the situation where leaders, followers, and environments reinforce unethical situations. The elements illustrated in the "Toxic Triangle" perpetuate the "Dark Side of Leadership" and are characterized by the leader's lack of ethics and selfish aims.

The toxic triangle: elements in three domains related to destructive leadership.

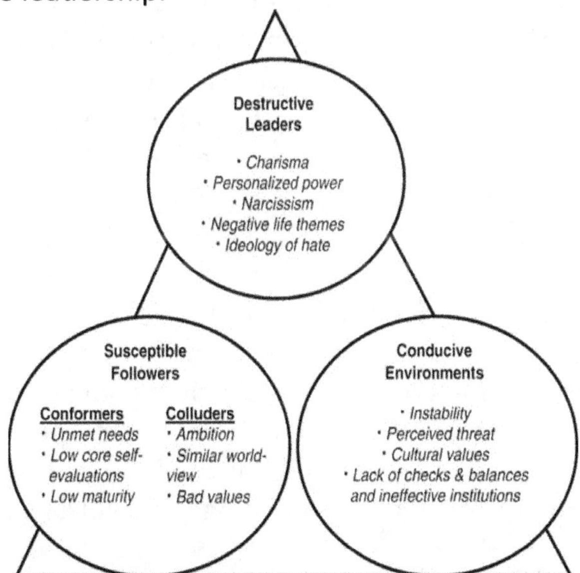

Source: Padilla et al. (2007)

In the book titled *Surviving Toxic Leaders: How to Work for Flawed People in Churches, Schools, and Christian Organizations*, Gangel [197] states that the first step is for the leader or manager to admit that they have the disease, and once that happens they are well on their way to a cure. Gangel also reports that 'Stanford Graduate School of Business has an advisory council made up of 75 distinguished people. Each of them was asked to recommend the most important capability for leaders to develop. They unanimously selected self-awareness. [198] Self-awareness can be improved through a variety of methods. Some of these are 360° evaluations, unbiased feedback, mentorship, counsel, training/education and confronting the issues at stake. A 360-degree leadership assessment is a form of feedback for leaders in which their skills, effectiveness and influence as an executive, leader or manager are evaluated. With this sort of evaluation, the leadership in a company receives feedback from a set of colleagues. It is a process in which employees receive confidential and anonymous feedback from the people who work around them. This typically includes the employee's manager, peers, and direct reports. Managers and leaders within organizations use 360° feedback surveys to get a better understanding of their strengths and weaknesses. 360° Feedback can also be a useful development tool for people who are not in a management role. 360° feedback measures behaviours and competencies and provide feedback on how others perceive an employee. It also addresses skills such as listening, planning, and goal-setting and focuses on subjective areas such as teamwork, character, and leadership effectiveness. Data suggest that positive leaders see a strong majority of their subordinates emulating them and sharing the leader's vision versus just the opposite for toxic leaders. Once the toxic behaviour is identified, a range of solutions exists. One

---

197. Gangel, Surviving Toxic Leaders: How to Work for Flawed People in Churches, Schools, and Christian Organizations
198. Gangel, Ibid

immediate solution is training. Training is implemented to fill a knowledge, skill, or attitude gap. As indicated above, the ideas will help to prevent the negative impacts of toxic leadership: unbiased feedback, 360° evaluations, education, improve methods of organizational governance, term limits, accountability and positive leadership. Implementing solutions may bring greater self-awareness and ultimately self-correction of individuals with toxic tendencies, but also remind organizational leaders of their responsibility to hold subordinates accountable for actions contrary to the organization's core values.

Narcissism as a Factor of Toxic Pathway

As has been noted, narcissism is the pursuit of self-gratification from vanity or egotistic admiration of one's idealised self-image and attributes. The fifth edition (2013) of the *Diagnostic and Statistical Manual of Mental Disorder*s (DSM), defines the concept in terms of the personality traits of grandiosity and attention-seeking and in terms of significant impairments in personality functioning as looking excessively to others for the regulation of self-esteem, viewing oneself as exceptional, having impaired empathy, and having mostly superficial relationships. Persons who display either narcissistic personality disorder, or the narcissistic personality type are preoccupied with maintaining excessively positive self-concepts. They become overly concerned with obtaining positive, aggrandizing feedback from others and react with extreme positive or negative emotions when they succeed or fail to receive confirmation that others hold them in high regard. The Merriam-*Webster Dictionary* defines a narcissist as extremely self-centred with an exaggerated sense of self-importance; marked by or characteristic of excessive admiration of or infatuation with oneself. Most, if not all, toxic leaders have a high level of narcissism.

Notable behaviours such as being a poor listener, hoarding the credit, excessive bravado, and showing disdain for subordinates, are all classic signs of a leader being both toxic and narcissistic. Reed discusses seven bad habits that unsuccessful and narcissistic leaders practise with recurring themes being that the leader is smarter than everyone in the room, they can do no wrong, they ruthlessly stifle any dissenting opinions, and it is their way or the highway. The business of the military is dangerous and lethal. Unwavering trust in the character and competence of the leader and obedience to lawful orders from superiors are the bedrock to the professional military ethic. Arguments that the strict hierarchical nature of the military having anything to do with producing or protecting toxic leaders, as mentioned by Reed, hold some merit. Leading by example and mentoring are two fundamental techniques of developing others and it is certainly not a stretch of the imagination to suggest that passing on toxic leadership techniques to others occurs in the military, and essentially in any organization. Additionally, the intensely loyal bonds that are built in military units often result in the covering up, hiding, or just surviving of toxic leaders. A huge advantage that toxic leaders have is that they normally are very good at hiding their abusive behaviours from their superiors.

The Repercussions of Bad Leadership

Bad leadership undermines several important factors of a leader's impact:

    a. **Mission**: Strong leaders purposely pursue worthy goals. Hubristic leaders subvert their organizations' goals to their own personal goals.

    b. **Morale**: In any organization, success depends on high morale among the workforce. Hubristic leaders destroy morale. They make their followers feel as if they are cogs in machines that exist to extol their leaders' virtues.

c. **Performance**: People do not work hard for leaders they dislike.

d. **Loyalty**: The only loyalty hubristic leaders feel is toward themselves. It is no surprise that their followers are not loyal to them.

e. **Ethics**: Strong leaders are ethical. Hubristic leaders are the opposite. Eventually, they exude "moral decay" and cause others to compromise their   ethics as well.

f. **Reputation**: Leadership should be a noble activity dedicated to the firm and   to   people   you   lead. Hubristic leaders care only about themselves and develop contemptible   reputations   within   their organizations.

According to an old Ghanaian myth, two wolves live inside every person. One is aggressive, manipulative and angry. That is your bad wolf. The other is generous and trustworthy and strives to do what is right. That is your good wolf. These two wolves struggle within you for dominance. It is your job as a leader – and as a responsible human being – to choose the good wolf over the bad wolf. So, "feed the good wolf" – but do not ignore the bad wolf. That only makes it more vicious. Redirect its energies; provide a reasonable outlet for your aggressive wolf – perhaps through exercise or a martial arts class. "Rather than starve one, guide both." Leaders must be introspective and vigilant to ward off hubris. To avoid a swelling ego and its bad effects, raise your consciousness.   It is important for the individual to be on guard when success is bestowed. At your peak, hubris may go into overdrive to convince you that success makes you special, the rules do not apply to you and as a big winner you can do whatever you want. This faulty mind-set accounts for the shameful fall of many formerly respected leaders. Catering to your ego is a negative dynamic. "Thriving leadership" is a positive dynamic built on leading "with virtue, integrity and humility." Use your "leadership power" on behalf of your firm and those you lead. Help them get ahead. When leaders lead properly, optimism becomes their defining characteristic. Effective leaders are enthusiastic, energetic, happy about the present and confident about the future. Moreover, the people they lead feel the same way. They will look forward to going to work in an environment where employees and leaders thrive together.

Good Leadership as a Choice

Good leaders are exemplary, decisive people with discipline, integrity, good judgment and high ideals. They work to improve themselves as leaders – and as human beings. They focus on others, not themselves. Good leaders respect the people around them and work to ensure their success. Nothing in life is guaranteed. Good leaders may do everything right and still fail miserably. Because of their character, they do not let failure undermine them. They understand that it has a saving grace: It keeps people humble. Good leaders are experts at "ego management." They are confident, but not arrogant. To stay grounded, they remind themselves that, in the larger scheme of things, they are insignificant. As has been noted by Brain Tracy, good leaders have some seven qualities.

These qualities are as depicted below:

Great leaders find the balance between business foresight, performance, and character. They have vision, courage, integrity, humility and focus along with the ability to plan strategically and catalyse cooperation amongst their team.

a. **Vision**: According to Jack Welch, 'good business leaders create a vision, articulate the vision, passionately own the vision, and relentlessly drive it to completion.' Great leaders have a vision… They can see into the future. They have a clear, exciting idea of where they are going and what they are trying to accomplish and are excellent at strategic planning. This quality separates them from managers. Having a clear vision turns the individual into a special type of person. This quality of vision changes a "transactional manager" into a "transformational leader.' While a manager gets the job done, great leaders tap into the emotions of their employees.

b. **Courage**: Winston Churchill observes that 'courage is rightly considered the foremost of the virtues, for upon it, all others depend. One of the more important qualities of a good leader is courage. Having the quality of courage means that you are willing to take risks in the achievement of your goals with no assurance of success. Because there is no certainty in life or business, every commitment you make and every action you take entails a risk of some kind. Among the seven leadership qualities, courage is the most identifiable outward trait.

c. **Integrity**: Zig Ziglar claims that, 'with integrity, you have nothing to fear, since you have nothing to hide. With integrity, you will do the right thing, so you will have no guilt.' In every strategic planning session that I have conducted for large and small corporations, the first value that all the gathered executives agree upon for their company is integrity. They all agree on the importance of complete honesty in everything they do, both internally and externally. The core of integrity is truthfulness. Integrity requires that you always tell the truth, to all people, in every situation. Truthfulness is the foundation quality of the trust that is necessary for the success of any business.

d. **Humility**: Humility gets results. Larry Bossidy, a former CEO of Honeywell and author of the book *Execution*, explained why leadership characteristics, such as humility, make you a more effective leader. He states that the more you can contain your ego, the more realistic you are about your problems. You learn how to listen, and admit that you do not know all the answers. You exhibit the attitude that you can learn from anyone at any time. Your pride does not get in the way of gathering the information you need to achieve the best results. It does not keep you from sharing the credit that needs to be shared. Humility allows you to acknowledge your mistakes.' Great leaders are those who are strong and decisive but also humble. Humility does not mean that you are weak or unsure of yourself. It means that you have the self-confidence and self-awareness to recognize the value of others without feeling threatened. This is one of the rarer attributes – or traits – of good leaders because it requires containment of one's ego. It means that you are willing to admit you could be wrong, you recognize you may not have all the answers. Moreover, it means that you give credit where credit is due – which many people struggle to do.

e. **Strategic Planning**:   Henry Minzberg has emphasized that 'strategy is not the consequence of planning, but the opposite: it's the starting point.' Great leaders are outstanding at strategic planning. It is another one of the more important leadership strengths. They have the ability to look ahead, to anticipate with some accuracy where the industry and the markets are going. Leaders have the ability to anticipate trends, well in advance of their competitors. They continually ask, "Based on what is happening today, where is the market going? Where is it likely to be in three months, six months, one year, and two years?" They do this through thoughtful strategic planning. Because of increasing competitiveness, only the leaders and organizations that can accurately anticipate future markets can possibly survive. Only leaders with foresight can gain the "first mover advantage.'

f. **Focus**: Successful people maintain a positive focus in life no matter what is going on around them. They stay focused on their past successes rather than their past failures, and on the next action steps they need to take to get them closer to the fulfilment of their goals rather than all the other distractions that life presents to them,' so says Jack Canfield. Leaders always focus on the needs of the company and the situation. Leaders focus on results, on what must be achieved by themselves, by others, and by the company. Great leaders focus on strengths, in themselves and in others. They focus on the strengths of the organization, on the things that the company does best in satisfying demanding customers in a competitive marketplace. Your ability as a leader to call the shots and make sure that everyone is focused and concentrated on the most valuable use of their time is essential to the excellent performance of the enterprise.

g. **Cooperation**: Napoleon Hill emphasizes that, 'if your imagination leads you to understand how quickly people grant your requests when those requests appeal to their self-interest, you can have practically anything you go after.' Your ability to get everyone working and pulling together is essential to your success. Leadership is the ability to get people to work for you because they want to. Good leaders believe in the 80-20 rule, which is that, twenty percent of your people contribute 80 percent of your results. Your ability to select these people and then to work well with them on a daily basis is essential to the smooth functioning of the organization. Gain the cooperation of others by making a commitment to get along well with each key person every single day. You always have a choice when it comes to a task: You can do it yourself, or you can get someone else to do it for you.

h. **Communication**: Effective leaders are also strong communicators. Another important trait that the best leaders strive to perfect is the ability to speak effectively and persuasively. In fact, many tend to practice public speaking within their own businesses until they are ready to branch out into professional paid speaking gigs. Although talking in front of crowds is a top fear for the majority of us, conquering this fear is what makes a good leader become a great leader. Communication is the cornerstone of team interaction, without which teams would not be able to share information and knowledge, discuss and debate issues, or strategies or develop solutions to problems.

i. **Leading by Example**: Most of the time, leaders think about good leadership qualities and how to apply them on a daily basis. They also know that they must lead by example to truly earn the will of their followers. The ability to commit to this principle is another huge characteristic of good and great leaders. It should be remembered that, the most important contribution you can make to your company is to be a leader, accept responsibility for results, and dare to go forward. [199]

Institutionalizing more emphasis on emotional intelligence and other interpersonal skills will go a long way in decreasing the number of toxic leaders. Finally, Reed acknowledges that the military needs to look more closely at its leadership development schools, human resources practices (for example, evaluations and promotions systems), and other organizational systems and processes that might encourage or create toxic leaders, to find ways to stamp out such abusive leaders in the ranks. There are numerous leadership styles and situational leadership calls for the effective leader to be able to adjust their style to the situation. Power dynamics are inherited in every leader/ follower situation, but that leader power should be used to maximize the capabilities of followers and for the betterment of the organization. Toxic leaders do just the opposite. Do not measure leadership by how much you succeed; measure it by how much you improve your firm and the lives of those you lead. The sole, avid pursuit of success often ends in disgrace.

---

199. https://www.briantracy.com/blog/leadership-success/the-seven-leadership-qualities-of-great-leaders-strategic-planning/

The behaviour and performance of leaders need to be monitored and assessed to ensure that they engage in interactions with followers, which result in a healthy work environment. Executive mentors who work with leaders should evaluate the leader's interactions with subordinates, and educate and train the leader about the nature of dysfunctional behaviours and provide a feedback when they exhibit these potentially toxic behaviours. Organizations also need to formulate checks and controls for early identification of toxic leadership behaviours within the organization as it allows the organization the opportunity to intervene and assist in re-educating aberrant leaders. Identification in the early part of a leader's career also decreases the possibility of building strong toxic behaviours. Once toxic leadership behaviours have been exposed, recognized and appropriate action taken within the organization, such lessons learned can become an integral part of the selection or promotion process for future leaders. With this mechanism, the growth of toxic leadership may be curbed in an organization, and the same can be a lesson to curb their toxic tendencies. In case organizations do not have mechanisms to monitor toxic leadership behaviours, they can seek the professional intervention of external counsellors for helping the victims and also re-educating the deviant leaders. The last option available with an organization is to offer a safe exit for leaders who engage in toxic behaviour and rhetoric. Toxic leadership is extremely dangerous to individuals, and also to the sustainability of the organization. Individuals having toxic traits and potentiality of toxic and dysfunctional behaviours should not be allowed to operate and grow in an organization under any circumstance.

Machiavellian Principles for Today's Leader

Few historical figures are as divisive and polarizing as Niccolo Machiavelli. The fact that this Renaissance philosopher's works date back 500 years has not blunted its impact or controversy one bit. Some view him as the father of modern materialism, inspiring people to do or say anything to achieve personal gain, i.e. the ends justify the means. Others, however, see him as the world's first great realist and a positive influence on modern politics and capitalism. Some even think Machiavelli was the first to apply empirical scientific methods to human behaviour by making innovative generalizations based on experience, observation, and history. Machiavelli put forth the following principles for effective leadership. In any case, he predates us all by a few centuries, which makes these 10 Business and Leadership Lessons from Machiavelli remarkable, to say the least:

a. Whosoever desires constant success must change his conduct with the times. 'Leaders must learn to adapt in a fast-changing world to avoid corporate or political disaster.' That is, after all, why most companies fail.

b. Entrepreneurs are simply those who understand that there is 'little difference between obstacle and opportunity and are able to turn both to their advantage'. An entrepreneur's first and most important goal is to find a unique and innovative solution that solves a big customer or market problem. Without obstacles, there are no opportunities. And those same obstacles provide barriers to competitors, down the road.

c. Never was anything great achieved without danger. The willingness to take risks is a critical success factor. In Irreverent Career Advice for Up-and-Comers, I encourage young folks to, "Take big risks -- now!" since, "It gets much harder as you get older and begin to 'acquire' things you don't want to risk losing.

d. Where the willingness is great, the difficulties cannot be great. Finding your passion is not only the key to happiness, but also the key to business success. As Apple CEO Steve Jobs once said, "Your time is limited, so don't waste it living someone else's life. The only way to do great work is to love what you do." Amen.

e. I am not interested in preserving the status quo; I want to overthrow it. Most of you know that I abhor the status quo. In *Why Skeptics Make Great Leaders*, Steve Tobak wrote, that, 'cynics question common wisdom and those in authority. Theyare not just okay with the status quo. They seek a better way to do things and by so doing break rules and break moulds.' [200] Cynics question common wisdom and those in authority. Skeptics call out the boss, even if he is a scary a-hole. These are the folks who are not just okay with the status quo. These are the folks who seek a better way to do things. Management consultants refer these group of persons as 'great leaders.' Every manager, executive, or board director I have ever known has been a skeptic.

f. The first method for estimating the intelligence of a ruler is to look at the men he has around him. Weak leaders surround themselves with weak lieutenants. Strong leaders always hire the best at what they do ... assuming they can afford it.

g. Let passion be the foundation of your business: Perhaps one of the most critical ideas put forward in *The Prince* can be summed up as 'where the willingness is great the difficulties cannot be great.' This cardinal rule is true in many areas of life but none more than in the cut-throat world of business. Creating a marketplace out of

---

200. Steve Tobak, Why Skeptics Make Great Leaders, 2010 CBS Interactive Inc See also https://www.cbsnews.com/news/why-skeptics-make-great-leaders/

something you already love means that your life's work will be meaningful and fruitful. Creating a marketplace out of something you already love means that your life's work will be meaningful and fruitful. In the UAE, there is a wealth of united, passionate entrepreneurs. Just last year, the Global Competitiveness Report named UAE as one of the top 20 economies in the world. This has been so because they consider themselves as passionate business people.

h. Deal with business threats swiftly: When something threatens the stability of your business, the sooner you defend it, the better. Machiavelli gave this example: 'The Romans, foreseeing troubles, dealt with them at once, and, even to avoid a war, would not let them come to a head, for they knew that war is not to be avoided, but

is only put off to the advantage of others. When something threatens the stability of your business, the sooner you defend it, the better. So, how should a leading entrepreneur respond when their business meets a threat? Well, research published in the *Harvard Business Review* identifies three essential action points. First of all, you need to practise teamwork within your business; then, you also have to inquire inwardly about the problem at hand; finally, you need to experiment with various solutions. The more you practise these three small actions, the tougher your barrier against threats will be.

i. Take Decisive Action: The wise man does at once what the fool does finally. Favour decisive action instead of over-planning, which, in dysfunctional organizations, often results in analysis paralysis. In many environments where time is of essence and the condition keeps changing, decisive action is very essential. In every situation, our decisions may have lasting consequences, affecting ourselves   and others in the short and long term. In this context, an effective decision-making process can help us reflect and weigh the alternatives and finally choose the option that is the most appropriate for each situation. Taking decisive action moves an issue forward and is positive and action oriented. It is linked to resilience because taking decisive action is empowering, positive and allows a person to take control of   a situation instead of it controlling them. Life is uncertain, and yet, in business, you   must take decisive action in order to be successful. We have all had extremely difficult choices that we have had to make and feel the pressure to make a decision without all the facts. The worst thing you can do in these situations is to freeze up like a deer in the headlights. [201]

j. Learn from the greats: According to Machiavelli, 'a wise man ought always to follow the paths beaten by great men, and to imitate those who have been supreme'. It is a message that should be at the heart of every entrepreneur's ideals. Learning from the great businessmen that have come before you is a sign of strength. One way to do this is by enlisting the help of a mentor. Beware of 'yes' men: 'The servant thinking more of his own interests than of yours, and seeking inwardly his own profit in everything; such a man will never make a good servant,' stated Machiavelli, and in this instance, anyone below you can take the place of that figurative servant. Needless to say, you can easily transform your employees into 'yes' men, but that doesn't mean that you should believe them when they tell you that you are in the right. After all, perhaps they have their own motives for doing so. The quality of your life is

---

201. Jocko Willink and Leif Babin, Extreme Ownership: How U.S. Navy SEALs Lead and Win

determined by the amount of uncertainty you can comfortably live with.

k. Make friends in High Places: Above all else, business is about connections. This was a topic on which Machiavelli was crystal clear. One of his principles was that you should 'endeavour with the utmost diligence to avoid the hatred of the most powerful'. So, what is the next step for avoiding bad relationships with senior figures? Building good ones. Positioning this in a modern context, social media is your greatest tool. You now have access to entrepreneurs all around the globe at your fingertips. A colossal 80% of LinkedIn members believe that networking is essential to their success. They are not wrong. Creating bonds with people who can help you further down the line is a wise business move.

l. Don't micromanage, but focus on one goal: Micromanagement is the bane of many a would-be successful business. Do not be mistaken; business is war. If you take your eyes off the battlefield, you will be ruined. As Machiavelli put it, one 'ought to have no other aim or thought, nor select anything else for his study, than war.' In terms of business, this can be translated into the notion that your entire focus should be on your core goal. Trust those below you to do their jobs and focus only on your role in the company.

m. Encourage criticism and frankness: Overlooking the significance of employee feedback is a mistake, but a far worse one is neglecting to ask for upward criticism. It is just as crucial for managers to understand their own weaknesses as it is for employees. 'There is no other way of guarding oneself from flatterers except letting men understand that to tell you the truth does not offend you,' writes Machiavelli.

To excel in any field, you have to expect criticism and, once you have it, use it to your advantage. One five-year long study into upward feedback found that it is how managers use this information that is crucial. Those who met their employees to discuss the feedback after receiving it were far more likely to improve their working style than other managers.

Despite some progress in instilling ethics into business practice, businesses continue to make decisions that result in incredible harms to people and the environment around the world. Academics, the public, and the media have often singled out business leaders as unethical and responsible for the vast harms that their companies have done. Leaders have a reputation for being ill-intentioned and evil. They are known for their deceptive and manipulative behaviours and are comfortable with gaining at the expense of others. They will follow the explicit rules, or laws, but will ignore behavioural norms, including common expectations for reciprocity and ethical conduct. In the context of business, Machiavellian leaders are singularly focused on making profit. They will lie, deceive, and find loopholes in laws and regulations for the sake of the company's bottom line. Notably, the Machiavellian business leader aligns well with the classic shareholder theory of business, which states that a company's only responsibility is to make profit.

In stark contrast, transformational leadership shows promise for an effective, yet ethical, style of leadership. Transformational leaders are motivated by the interests of others and are willing to put their own interests aside. They hold nearly universal moral values such as justice and equality and inspire their followers to do the same. Together, transformational leaders and their followers engage in socially responsible business practices. Impressively, evidence shows that this ethical focus does not compromise profits and that transformational leaders are highly effective. Their followers are more satisfied, committed, and high-performing compared to followers under other leadership styles. So, not only are transformational leaders highly ethical, they also benefit a company's bottom line. Machiavellian leaders in business may seem like some of the worst offenders in making ethically-questionable decisions, while transformational leaders are an ideal that Machiavellian leaders should strive toward. Machiavellian leadership seems like such a natural fit for business leadership, since it encourages business leaders to focus only on profit-making.

Summary

Contaminants are defined as 'substances or groups of substances that are toxic, persistent and liable to bio-accumulate, and other substances or groups of substances which give rise to an equivalent level of concern. 'Contaminated' choices in leadership therefore lead to the creation of toxic environments at all workplaces. Recent abuses of authority in business, politics, and religion have revived interest in destructive leadership. Although philosophers such as Plato, Hobbes and Russell have analysed leadership, modern social science has tended to take a one-sided view of the topic, emphasizing its positive and constructive aspects while avoiding its darker side. Negative organizational outcomes are the product of dysfunctional leader behaviours and susceptible followers interacting in the context of a contributing environment. Great leaders find the balance between business foresight, performance, and character. They have vision, courage, integrity, humility and focus along with the ability to plan strategically and catalyse cooperation amongst their team. The chapter delves into all the above as a caution to the emerging leader.

Chapter Seven

The Concept of Battle Space and Management Decision

'Designing a winning strategy is the art of asking questions, experimenting and then constantly renewing the thinking process by questioning the answers. No matter how good today's strategy is, you must always keep reinventing it.'
Constantinos Markides

From Battle Field to Battle Space

In any warfare, the enemy and nature get a vote in any scenario. However, the information age has certainly changed the ways in which the military will fight the battles of the future. In multinational and multi-agency operations, the contributions of other participating nations and non-military actors is also harmonised wherever feasible, to achieve desired objectives. Broadly stated, strategy is the planning, coordination, and general direction of military operations to meet overall political and military objectives. Tactics implement strategy by short-term decisions on the movement of troops and employment of weapons on the field of battle. The great military theorist Carl von Clausewitz put it another way; he opines that tactics is the art of using troops in battle; strategy is the art of using battles to win the war. Strategy and tactics, however, have been viewed differently in almost every era of history.

Military strategy and tactics are essential to the conduct of warfare. Military forces, whether large-scale or small-scale, must have a clear objective that is followed despite possible distractions. Only offensive operations, seizing and exploiting the initiative, however, will allow the choice of objectives; the offense also greatly increases the possibility of surprise (stealth and deception) and security (protection against being surprised or losing the possibility of surprising the enemy). Unity of command, or cooperation, is essential to the pursuit of objectives, the ability to use all forces effectively (economy of force), and the concentration of superior force at a critical point (mass). Manoeuvre consists of the various ways in which troops can be deployed and moved to obtain offensive, mass, and surprise. To achieve success, the resources available to the commander should be harnessed in a manner that will fit into the following:

a. **Coordination:** Coordination brings together different Joint force capabilities and activities into an efficient and effective relationship. Complementary aspects are united, to promote mutual support, whilst potentially incompatible aspects are de-conflicted, to preserve and make best use of available fighting power.

b. **Synchronisation:** Coordination is enhanced by synchronisation, which sequences capabilities and activities, at appropriate tempo, in time and space. The dependency between events, and the availability of necessary resources, determines the degree of concurrent, sequential or independent activity that is possible or necessary.

c. **Prioritisation:** Coordination and synchronisation highlight competing demands for time, space and finite resources; prioritisation determines their allocation, in accordance with prevailing concept of operations. As circumstances change, the joint operational team should keep priorities under review to ensure that risks are analysed and managed appropriately, and that opportunities are exploited as they arise.

Battlespace is the area of air, sea, and land that is directly involved in war, often taken to include any technological, environmental, infrastructural, or temporal factors, which may be relevant to the success of a mission. In the military, battlespace encompasses 'all aspects of a joint operational area within which military activities take place'. It signifies a unified military strategy to integrate and combine armed forces for the military theatre of operations, including air, information, land, sea, cyber and space to achieve military goals. It includes the environment, factors, and conditions that must be understood to successfully apply combat power, protect the force, or complete the mission. This includes enemy and friendly armed forces, infrastructure, weather, terrain, and the electromagnetic spectrum within the operational areas and areas of interest. [202]

This new way of thinking about combat is called battle space, and is defined as:

> ... a physical volume that expands or contracts in relation to the ability to acquire and engage the enemy. It includes the breadth, depth, and height in which the commander positions and moves assets over time. Battle space is not assigned by a higher commander and extends beyond the commander's area of operation. It is based on the notion that commanders expand their thinking to develop a vision for dominating the enemy and protecting the force before any mental constraints are emplaced, such as overlays depicting phase lines, boundaries, and arrows.

Battle space provides a framework for commanders to view potential missions, forcing their thoughts from physical restrictions and allowing them to consider the mission, enemy, terrain, time and tactics (METT-T) uninhibited by externally imposed graphics. A tool for all levels of command, from squad leader to corps commander, battle space offers a holistic look at fighting an effective fight. It is a way to think about fighting - a

---

202. Military Jargon Database

visualization by commanders at every level of the entire battlefield and all phases of the campaign and operation. One such tool that is contained within the notion of battlespace is outlined by Lind, where he explains the Boyd Theory of maneuver warfare. Each party to a conflict begins by observing. [203] He observes himself, his physical surroundings and his enemy. On the basis of his observation, he orients, that is to say, he makes a mental image or 'snapshot' of his situation. On the basis of this orientation, he makes a decision. He puts the decision into effect. [204] The battle space has seven (7) dimensions, which include Maritime, Land, Air, Space, Information, Electromagnetic, and Time – none of which can be considered in isolation, as activity in one may have implications for the others.

a. **Maritime:** Covering 70% of the Earth's surface and reaching down to the seabed, the sea constitutes a significant proportion of the battlespace. It provides direct access to 150 coastal states and indirect access, via over-flight, to most of those without a seaboard. 70% of the world's population live within 100 miles of the sea and 80% of the world's cities are within 200 miles of the sea. Battlespace is likely to include sea and/or littoral regions.

b. **Land:** Land covers 30% of the Earth's surface and comprises diverse surroundings from flat desert, through jungle and heavy forestation to high mountains and sheet ice. Given the growing percentage of the world's population living in towns and cities, battlespace is highly likely to include urban areas. Variables such as climate, as well as deliberate alterations to aid or impede mobility; for example, can affect activities on land.

---

203. K. E. Hamburger, Leadership In Combat: An Historical Appraisal (United States Military Academy, Dept. of History, 1985).

204. Martin Blumenson and James L. Stokesbury, Masters of the Art of Command (Boston: Houghton-Mifflin, 1975), p. 603

Moreover, it is not just   land forces that operate on land; maritime (including amphibious), air, Special Forces (SF) and logistic elements all require access to land, or at least the effects of some of their activities are likely to be realised there.

c. **Air:** Air covers the entire surface of the Earth, extending to a finite upper limit. All components require access to the air, whether to fly aircraft or Unmanned Aerial Vehicles (UAVs) within it or to deliver weapons through it; there is considerable potential for friction between users.

d. **Space**: Anything in orbit or beyond can be regarded as being in outer space. Despite the potential requirement for any, or all components to use space, for intelligence, communications, navigation or meteorology, none yet has the capability to operate directly within it. National arrangements for space control and management are currently under development.

e. **Information:** The information dimension of the battlespace, including cyberspace, requires particularly agile management in order to exploit emerging information technology. Information management enables information flow and exploitation in support of effective decision-making.

f. **Electromagnetism:** The electromagnetic dimension, or Electromagnetic Spectrum (EMS), is finite and under ever-increasing pressure due to the proliferation of electromagnetic activity. It pervades the other physical environments, providing both potential benefit (a significant source of intelligence for example) but also potential vulnerability (in being comparatively easy to disrupt or deny). While bounded by the laws of physics, it is not constrained by terrestrial borders and is freely available to any individual who attempts to exploit it.

Moreover, it not only pervades the other dimensions of battlespace, but also extends beyond the confines of the joint operational area.

g. **Time:** While other dimensions describe where activity takes place, time is an additional dimension indicating when or for how long. Time is also used as a tool to orchestrate activities in other dimensions, through synchronisation or sequencing. Management of the timing and duration of activities, using a common or reference time zone throughout the joint operational area underpins effective battle management. [205]

Knowledge and understanding of the operational area's environment, factors, and conditions, to include the status of friendly and adversary forces, neutrals and non-combatants, weather and terrain that enables timely, relevant, comprehensive, and accurate assessments, in order to successfully apply combat power, protect the force, and/ or complete the mission. [206] Over the last 25 years, the understanding of the military operational environment has transformed from primarily a time and space-driven linear understanding (a 'battlefield') to a multi-dimensional system of systems understanding (a battlespace). This system of systems understanding implies that managing the battlespace has become more complex, primarily because of the increased importance of the cognitive domain, a direct result of the information age. Today, militaries are expected to understand the effects of their actions on the operational environment as a whole, and not just in the military domain of their operational environment. The same applies to civil organisations but many have failed to grasp the change let alone understand its implications.

---

[205]. Joint Doctrine Publication 3-70, Battle Space Management, June 2008

[206]. JP 2-01, (US DoD)

Summary

Broadly stated, defence strategy is the planning, coordination, and general direction of military operations to meet overall political and military objectives. The chapter exposes the reader to the concept of the battle space and management decision. In any warfare, the enemy and nature get a vote in any scenario. However, the information age has certainly changed the ways in which the military will fight the battles of the future. In multinational and multi-agency operations, the contributions of other participating nations and non-military actors is also harmonised wherever feasible, to achieve desired objectives. In this chapter some ideas from the military are borrowed for the good of the civil manager. The chapter concludes that, knowledge and understanding of the operational area's environment, factors, and conditions, to include the status of friendly and adversary forces, neutrals and non-combatants, weather and terrain that enables timely, relevant, comprehensive, and accurate assessments, in order to successfully apply combat power, protect the force, and/ or complete the mission.

Chapter Eight

Managing Millennials for Organisational Growth

The people who work for you aren't building a company for you, they are building it for themselves - they are the center of their own universe.
Just because you are the CEO, doesn't mean they are coming to work every day to make you happy. They want to be happy and it's your job to keep them that way."
Ben Lerer, Thrillist

Rethinking Human Resource Risks

Generational cut-off points may be viewed as a tool that allows for human resource analyses. Generations are often considered by their span, and research shows that each generation has some unique characteristics. In Africa, these general cohorts may cover periods before colonial adventurism, period of colonial domination, period after independence, the coup d'état era, and periods after constitutional rule. Embedded in these periods may be the influence of internet technology communication. Many life choices, future earnings and entrance to adulthood (rites of passage) have all been shaped by unstable global events in a way that may not be the case for their prior and younger counterparts. Beyond politics, most millennials have come of age and now form the bulk of the workforce facing the height of the prevailing social and corporate resource mobilization challenge. Technology, education and the rapid evolution of social media is another generational cohort-shaping consideration. This new wave presents a new security dilemma as the generation has undergone a large cultural and social shift. Now, the millennials are adults, so how do they compare with those who were their age in the generations prior? This write up seeks to compare generational cohorts with focus on the millennials. Overall, the assessment situates their choices and motivations in the context of security as a subject for consideration by the human resource practitioner. Managing people has been very difficult over the years. This is because generational theory explains that the era in which a person is born affects the development of their view of the world.

Our value systems are shaped in the first decade or so of our lives - by our families, our friends, our communities, significant disruptive events and the general era in which we are born. As time and environmental factors merge, every issue becomes evolving. In the past century, global forces, combined with the effects of international media and news channels, communication technologies and the increasing interconnectedness of the world have meant that increasing numbers of people around the world are impacted by defining events. Generations provide the opportunity to look at people by their place in the life cycle, whether a young adult, a middle-aged parent or a retiree – and by their membership in a cohort of individuals who were born at a similar time. According to the Pew Research Center, generational cohorts give researchers and human resource practitioners a tool to analyse changes in views over time. They can provide a way to understand how different formative experiences (such as COVID-19) and technological, economic and social shifts) interact with the life-cycle and aging process to shape people's views of the world.

A generation has collective attitudes about family life, sex roles, institutions, politics, religion, lifestyle, and the future. It can be safe or reckless, calm or aggressive, self-absorbed or outer-driven, generous or selfish, spiritual or secular, interested in culture or interested in politics. This, therefore, calls for constant re-tooling and re-engineering in the social field. On this score, it has been recommended that companies must not leverage the same blanket techniques to attract, engage and retain them because each generation has distinct characteristics. It is no wonder that these generations are struggling to coexist. Recognizing that one size does not fit all is critical, and the time to act is now. Companies need to better tailor their efforts towards specific cohorts, and understanding the generational cohorts, and the millennials in particular, may just be the best place to start. Targeting of some age brackets in the Human Resource process and security function has been recommended to deal with the fluid behaviour patterns being witnessed. This write up is an attempt to bring to the fore the lingering characteristics of the current crop of emerging workforce to precipitate discussion and engender change. In essence, it attempts to look at the whole gamut of the Human Resource function of attracting, hiring, engaging and retaining staff under the prevailing circumstance with security in focus.

Classification of Generational Cohorts

A number of studies have been conducted on the subject of general cohorts. In spite of the studies, there has been no consensus about the exact dates for each of the age cohorts. The social generations are mostly based on Western history and tied closely with the social fabric of those cultures. Close to 70 per cent of Africa's population now comprise of millennials. Many of them have grown up seeing mobile devices as a normal part of everyday life. As the region's future decision-makers, customers, and constituents, these millennials will be major stakeholders in the success of both Africa-based businesses and governments; from hiring top talent to ensuring satisfaction with public services. [207] Technology has also come to play a role in drawing lines between generations. This study will consider the mid-points of consensus for analysis.

Interestingly, around the world, there is no shortage of descriptive epithets for those born between 1980 and the mid-1990s. In Poland, the millennials are referred to as *Generation John Paul II* [208], and are referred to as *Generation Serious* in Norway. In Sweden they are called *Generation Curling*, while China refers to them as 'ken lao zu; *'the generation that eats the old'*, and in Japan they are referred to as 'nagar zoku'; *people who always do two things at time'*.[209] In the US, UK and Australia they go by *Generation Y*. In China, they are characterized as optimistic and entrepreneurial, with a historic role in transforming modern China into an economic power Another broader classification is the 'one child generation' said to be those born between the introduction of the one-child policy in 1980, and its softening to the two-child policy in 2013. In all, the four main generations that form the basis of the discussion are the GI Generation, (WWII Generation or The Greatest Generation) born between 1900 - 19120, Silent Generation born between 1920s – 1945, the Baby Boomer (1946-1964), Generation X (Thirteenth Generation) born between 1965- 1979 and Generation Y (Millennials) who were born between 1980-2000. [210] A summary of the cohorts is as shown in the graph below.

---

207. http://venturesafrica.com/millennials-growing-africas-mobile-economy/undefined

208. Colleen Carroll Campbell, The John Paul II Generation Grows Up: A Register series on the beatification of Pope John Paul II. Apr. 26, 2011. See also http://www.ncregister.com/daily-news/the-john-paul-ii-generation-grows-up

209. Kate Lyons, Generation Y, Curling or Maybe: what the world calls millennials. See https://www.theguardian.com/world/2016/mar/08/generation-y-curling-or-maybe-what-the-world-calls-millennials

210. Michael Dimock , Defining generations: Where Millennials end and Generation Z begins, January 17, 2019 Pew Research Centre, See also http://www.pewresearch.org/fact-tank/2019/01/17/where-millennials-end-and-generation-z-begins/

The generations defined

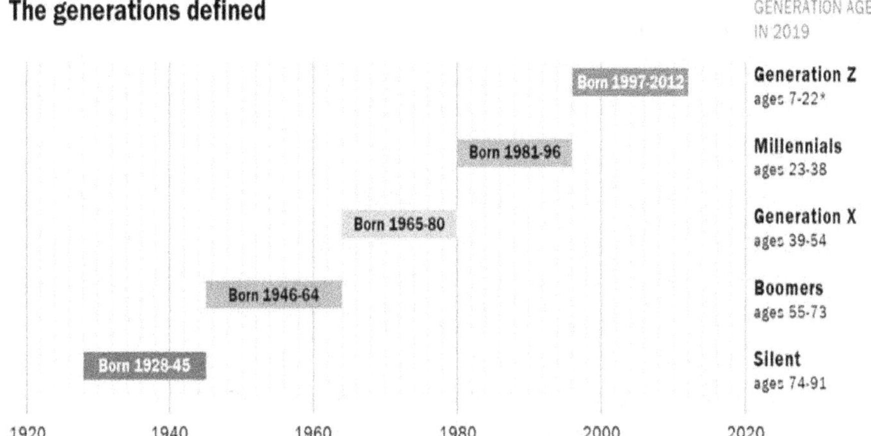

Source: Pew Research Centre

a. **GI Generation (1900s – 1920):** This generation may variously be called 'Government Issue' or 'General Issue'. The generation were born into the world prior to the discovery and introduction of drugs and other materials such as antibiotics, insulin, penicillin, nylon and many other things we would consider essential today. At their time, marijuana, heroin and morphine were all available over the counter in pharmacies. GI generation were credited with their civic mindedness. Society determined early on that this new generation of youth would grow up clever and develop the cooperative spirit in groups such as scouts, youth groups; even the word 'teenager' itself, was created for them, and they were driven together to rebuild the world. They formed the manpower component of the engine that beat the combined crises of World War 2 and the Great Depression. They worked as teams, obeyed hierarchal chains of command, and stuck to their task without complaint. No wonder they believe that it is 'good' and 'normal' for people to all agree, to work the same way and even to all look the same. Their guiding value system include never to give up, cultivating civic mindedness, conformity, stability and predictability, gallantry, hierarchical chains of command, and frugality with defined roles for males and females.

b. **Silent Generation: (1920s – 1945):** They are the generation who experienced the great depression and the Second World War. The silent generation is composed of persons born between the mid-1920s and the early 1940s. Due to the effects of the Great Depression and World War II on the birth rate, this generation had a much smaller population than those that followed. The term 'Silent Generation' first appeared in a 1951 essay in *Time* magazine, with reference to their silence during the McCarthy era and their willingness to assimilate into the social order. They were the first generation to enter college in big numbers. Hard work, delayed gratification, and automatic respect for authority were common. They often spent their entire career at one company. They are conservative, and structured, preferring rules, order and formal hierarchies. They have a 'waste not, want not" mentality, and hate getting into debt. Their idea of progress is slow, incremental advancement, while minimizing risk. They also believe that it is 'good' and 'normal' to work hard. They believe they can achieve anything by sheer hard work. They are suspicious of those who make money by luck or by gambling. Their defining and guiding values include dedication, duty before pleasure, adherence to rules, hard work, law and order, respect for position, cautiousness, self-sufficiency, delayed reward, sacrifice, conformity, modesty, patience, are reticent to express emotion, and have the 'waste not, want not' attitude.

c. **Baby Boomers** [211] **(1946-1964):** This group refers to the generation born during the 'baby boom' following World War II, usually in the period between 1945 and 1960. The term 'baby boom', referring to a conspicuous rise in childbirth since the late 19th century. They grew up with the eras of the Vietnam War, the Cold War, the Civil Rights Movement and Women's Liberation. Baby Boomers belong to the post-war generation of the drugs, sex, and grew up during a time of grand visions. They grew up with television and rock and roll and were the first with common access to recreational drugs. The moon landing gave them confidence that they could do what they set their minds to. Technology expanded, but they used it mostly to do more work. Baby Boomers are passionately concerned about participation in the workplace, motivated by vision, mission and strategy, and care about creating a fair and level playing field for all who agree with them. They have no difficulty legislating against the excesses of their own youth and their rallying cry is a greater sense of morality and social standards. Their defining and guiding values included, image, optimism, team orientation, personal growth, personal gratification, group together by similarity of belief, self-expressive, media savvy, excellence, big talkers, work involvement, health / wellness and nostalgia.

d. **Generation X** [212] **or Thirteenth Generation:** This generation can be traced back to as early as the 1950s, when it was used more broadly to refer to a 'generation of young people about whose future there is uncertainty'. The generation experienced a tripling of the divorce rate and both parents working. MTV [213], video games, and computers all made their mark. They used technology for a work-life balance and grew accustomed to moving around with autonomy. They grew up as "latchkey kids", children of divorce, experiencing an era of crises – from

---

[211] Charles Hamblett and Jane Deverson, Generation X" (Gold Medal d1582) (What's behind the rebellious anger of Britain's untamed youth?.Fawcett. 1964

[212] Douglas Coupland; Generation X: Tales for an Accelerated Culture

[213] MTV (originally an initialism of Music Television) is an American pay television channel owned by Viacom Media Networks (a division of Viacom) and headquartered in New York City. It is a pay television channel.

Watergate and Vietnam, to the energy crisis and the collapse of communism. They were the first children in history that mothers could take a pill not to have. As young adults, manoeuvring through a sexual minefield of AIDS and blighted courtship rituals as the legacy of the 60s revolution and feminism lives on. Their defining and guiding values include change, choice, global awareness, techno-literacy, individualism, lifelong learning, immediate gratification, diversity, survivors, informality, whiners, thrill seekers, not scared of failure, self-reliance, flexibility, fairness and tolerance.

e. **Generation Y –The Millennials: (1980-2000).** According to the Pew Research Centre [214], they make up more than 25% of the population and have been shaped by terrorism, cell phones, and social networking. Technology is an integral part of their life and they crave instant feedback. They are used to parents who praise them and tend to abstain from sex and drugs more than Gen X. They work well in teams and like diversity. One study showed that the quality of one's relationship with one's immediate supervisor accounts for 50% of job satisfaction. Growing up after the Cold War and in the new era of globalization, communication technology and wireless connectivity. They are living in an age of unprecedented diversity and exposure to other cultures and they grow up quickly.

Characteristics of Millennials

Seen as some of the most protected children in history, this generation is near arrogantly confident. More than any other young generation, they possess the ability to 'filter out every command, every request and every instruction that is not bundled with acceptable rationale. They tend to demand reasons and rationale, so the traditional 'because I said so' does not sit well with them. With unlimited access to information, they tend to be assertive with strong views. With this backdrop, they envision the world as a 24/7 place and

---

[214] The Pew Research Center is a nonpartisan American fact tank based in Washington, D.C. It provides information on social issues, public opinion, and demographic trends shaping the United States and the world

want fast and immediate processing of issues and demands. Because they have been told to be special over and over, they expect the world to treat them as such. They do not live to work as they prefer a more relaxed work environment with a lot of hand holding and accolades. Their defining and guiding values include, optimism, confidence, high self-esteem, media and entertainment overloaded, street smartness, diversity, conservative, networkers, civic duty, ethical consumption, achievement, morality, naiveté, change, techno-savvy and dependent. They are global citizens, with a multi-everything view.

The parents of millennials have cleared any obstacles from their children's paths, allege their critics, refusing to set boundaries, defending them to teachers who try to discipline them, even going with them to job interviews. We pad their world in every possible way, we pamper them from the beginning. In the estimation of Eberhard [215] , the parental sweeping has led to a generation of mollycoddled sub-adults who are psychologically knocked out by relatively minor blows such as the death of a dog or a boss telling them off. Using an analogy, he argues that, Sweden's liberal approach to parenting has bred a nation of ill-mannered brats, to the extent that, parents are now unwilling to discipline their children in any way. He adds that, we live in a culture where so-called experts say that children are 'competent' and the conclusion is that children should decide what to eat, what to wear, and when to go to bed. If you have a dinner party, they never sit quietly. They interrupt. They are always in the centre, and the problem is that when they become young adults, they take with them the expectation that everything is centred around them, which makes them very disappointed. They hesitate to say thank you. They do not open doors. If you see them on the subway, they do not stand up for elderly people or pregnant women. Stricter parenting has become a taboo for the millennial.

Security-Driven Human Resource Engagement with Millennials

The staff of every company is selected by the Human Resource (HR) team. This means that even before a member of staff is engaged, the HR department is responsible for making sure that company policies

---

[215] David Eberhard, How Children Took Power

are followed. The HR team ensures that all employees are aware of the rules, security policies, procedures, as well as disciplinary codes and measures to be taken in the event of a violation. It also means that if an incident happens, the HR department would be responsible for working with management to investigate and deal with any violations. These violations and breaches include cyber security, physical security, data security, employee conduct, workplace policy and system breach. A member of staff's entry and security engagement strategy, therefore, begins when the HR department is recruiting potential employees and continues for as long as they are employed. These requirements have been confirmed by empirical studies. In a survey by INSEAD Emerging Markets Institute, Universum, and the HEAD Foundation on 18,000 professionals and students across three generations from 19 countries, some important differences were found in the aspirations and values of these cohort generations.[216]
The team was optimistic that employers will consider employees' needs and expectations which often evolve over the course of their careers.

It must be borne in mind that workplace security risks vary depending on an organization's business, its location, its hours of operation, and the composition of its workforce. The security and safety function deals with both enterprise and employee safety and security. It includes the organization's efforts to prevent and/or mitigate loss, risks to or from personnel, threats to its physical assets, damage to its technology and intellectual property, or risks of any other kind arising from all elements surrounding the work environment. It also includes matters that focus on careers, communications, legal and regulatory issues, technology, metrics and outsourcing in the safety and security field, as well as effective safety and security practices and global safety and security issues.[217] Workplace safety and security is effective only when programmes, policies and procedures achieve their stated objectives. These are mainly aimed to prevent harm to people, property and the environment. Best practices vary depending on the

---

216. INSEAD Emerging Markets Institute, Universum, and the HEAD Foundation

217. Introduction to the Human Resource Discipline of Safety and Security, November 13, 2017, Society for Human Resource
See also https://www.shrm.org/resourcesandtools/tools-and-samples/toolkits/pages/introsafetyandsecurity.aspx

scope of the specific safety and security measures and relations with the HR function. The HR department is responsible for making sure the prospective employee meets the company's standards, not only in education and employment history but also in criminal and financial areas. The HR department should conduct background checks that include criminal histories and credit reports. These are especially important if the position being filled involves working with cash, cheques, invoices, bookkeeping, sensitive data or proprietary information. Security begins with recruitment and continues through the entire employment journey. In sum, the following are some of the issues which a security conscious HR function should consider in millennial environment where the issues are volatile, uncertain, complex, and ambiguous. These issues may include the following:

a. **Leadership:** The INSEAD report found that across the globe, becoming a leader was important to 61% of Gen Y, 61% of Gen Z, and 57% of Gen X respondents. However, responses varied by country: For example, in the Nordic countries, [218] respondents were significantly less likely to covet leadership roles than those in countries in South America. Among Gen Y respondents, 76% of Mexicans said attaining a leadership role is important, but only 47% of Norwegians said the same. 77% of American Gen Y professionals said that gaining a leadership position was important to them. Organizations should therefore keep these preferences in mind. Those in markets lacking enthusiasm for leadership, including Denmark, Sweden, and France, across which only 56% of Gen Y professionals said becoming a leader was important to them, will find their talent pipelines harder to fill; those in countries like Mexico, the U.S., and India will have to find ways to manage expectations and provide leadership experience or other motivation for ambitious workers. Men across all generations were more interested in future earnings and high levels of responsibility. The research also found that women, across both geographies and generations, were more likely to be put off by stress, more

---

218. The Nordic countries or the Nordics are a geographical and cultural region in Northern Europe and the North Atlantic. They include Denmark, Finland, Iceland, Norway, and Sweden, as well as Greenland and the Faroe Islands

likely to feel they lack the confidence to lead, and more likely to fear failing than their male colleagues.

b. **Entrepreneurial Ambitions:** The research also found a strong interest in entrepreneurship across all three generations. The results show that one in four students (Gen Z) is interested in starting their own business. In addition, among those already in the workforce (Gen Y and Gen X professionals), one in three yearned to be entrepreneurs. Gen Y professionals in Mexico (57%) and the UAE (56%) were the most interested in starting their own businesses. When asked whether they would want to work for an international company or start their own business, respondents in Gen Z favoured working for an international company, while Gen Y and Gen X professionals preferred starting their own business. To keep those interested in entrepreneurship close to the firm, leaders might want to consider 'intrapreneurship', [219] giving employees the ability to work on start-up projects within the firm. An intrapreneur may be an employee who is given financial support and autonomy to create new products, services and systems for the benefit of the company.

c. **Relying on Technology:** Unpredictable events happening outside an organization can be negative or positive, which makes it more difficult for leaders to make decisions. Gen Y professionals most likely to revolutionize their work in the coming decade, putting it ahead of wearable technology, project management, and audio/video conferencing. Companies may want to consider virtual reality as a tool for recruiting these cohorts. Gen X, on the other hand, believed virtual reality technologies would have a low impact on their work. They have the most enthusiasm for project management tools, with certain countries, such as Germany, Japan, and Russia, also expressing excitement about cloud computing and

---

[219]. According Financial Times, intrapreneurship involves creating or discovering new ideas or opportunities for the purpose of creating value, where this activity involves creating a new and self-financing organisation within or under the auspices of an existing company Entrepreneurial creativity and innovation within large, established organizations. Intrapreneurs are supposed to be rebels, breaking the rules and swimming against the corporate tide. Intrapreneurs are employees who do for corporate innovation what an entrepreneur does for his or her start-up

e-learning tools. When asked whether they saw technology as helpful to or hindering their work lives, older professionals considered technology a hindrance in Britain, Sweden, and Norway. Technology was mostly viewed as helpful by Gen Xers in Denmark, Sweden, and Mexico. Among Gen Y, respondents in Mexico, Sweden, and Germany perceived technology more favourably. Over 70% of Gen Y and Gen X professionals thought their employers' digital capabilities are important, but only around 40% of both generations said their companies' digital capabilities are high.

Finally, more than 70% of respondents across all generations said flexible working arrangements represent an important opportunity for their work lives in the next 10 years. In all these, we might be guided by the abuse of technology against corporate interest. In 2017, Russian soldiers were banned from sharing information online, including selfies. A new and revised law approved this month, now ban military personnel from posting about themselves or colleagues online, or using devices that can distribute audio, photo, video, or geolocation data via the internet. The law also forbids active-duty servicemen and reservists during training from sharing on the internet or with the media any information which might disclose their location, which units they serve with, information about fellow soldiers, and so on. Apart from that, servicemen are banned from even having on themselves devices that can store and/or transmit photos, videos, and geolocation data through the internet. The move is intended to stop sensitive information from appearing on social media. The sponsors of the Russian Bill explained that military members present a special interest for foreign intelligence services and terrorist groups. Therefore, sharing personal data while on duty might be dangerous for both soldier and the entire nation alike. The state had noted that the security personnel and journalists have been able to use social-media posts by Russian troops to, for example, gain insight into the country's military involvement in Syria and Ukraine.

d. **Training:** Respondents differed in their preferences for work training. When asked if they would take an online course if offered one by their employer, 70% of Gen Z respondents said yes, while 77% of Gen Y and 78% of Gen X professionals said they would take it. Given the choice between an online course and an in-person one, 69% of Gen Z chose an in-person programme, compared with only 13% choosing an online one. It was the Gen Xers who gravitated most toward online training, with 25% of respondents choosing this option. But 21% of Gen Y professionals also said they preferred online training over in-person teaching.

e. **Fitting In:** All generations were concerned about whether their personalities fit with where they work (50% of both Gen Y and Z respondents and 40% of Gen Xers). Japanese Millennials (66%) and Spanish Millennials (57%) were most concerned about fit; this was observed among Japanese Gen Zers (60%) and French Gen Zers (64%), too. However, what most bothered Gen X in general was not being able to enjoy retirement, getting stuck with no opportunities, or losing job security.

f. **Coaching and Mentoring:** In general, Gen Y and Gen X professionals are more enthusiastic about the coaching and mentoring that comes with management jobs than the higher responsibility. However, Gen Z cites higher levels of responsibility and more freedom as attractive attributes of leadership. Geographically, Gen X respondents in Spain put coaching and mentoring others as what is most attractive about leadership, but this was a lower priority for respondents from Germany, Norway, Denmark, Britain, and the U.S., who all put challenging tasks as the most attractive aspect. Men and women's leadership preferences also differed across generational cohorts. For Gen X, 63% of men and 52% of women said becoming a leader was important to them. Among Gen Y and Gen Z professionals, it was 63% of male respondents and 61% of women.

g. **Confidence:** The research identified four positive truths about Generation Y, including describing Generation Y as "a generation of new confidence, upbeat and full of self-esteem, the most educated-minded generation in history, a generation paving the way to a more open, tolerant society" and as "a generation leading a new wave of volunteerism". [220] It is important to acknowledge that, Neil Howe and William Strauss, who are credited with coining the term Millennial in their 1991 book *Generations*, define the group as those born between 1982 and 2000. [221,222] In his book, *Not Everyone Gets a Trophy: How to Manage the Millennials*, Bruce Tulgan defines two "waves" of Millennials: first wave (Generation Y) born 1978 to 1989, and second wave (Generation Z) born 1990 to 2000. And author David Stillman defines Millennials as people born between 1980 and 1994.

Workplace Generational Dynamics

Baby Boomers, Generation X, and Generation Y are the three generations currently in the workplace [223] As Baby Boomers retire, new workers from the millennial generation will enter and reshape the workforce. It is thus imperative to integrate these workers into the healthcare environment. As has been exposed above, the millennials are the group of people born between mid-1980s to year 2000. They have a differing value attachment; career paths and technology styles make them unknown to some employers. Currently, Millennials make up 33 percent of the U.S., and 35 of the UK work force, and estimated to form about 50% of the work force of both countries by 2020. They will also make up 75% of the global workforce. [224] As Leigh Buchanon writes in *Meet the Millennials*, "one of the characteristics of Millennials, besides the fact that they are masters of digital communication, is that they are primed to do well by doing good. Almost 70 percent say that giving back and being civically engaged are their highest priorities." The debate among some managers over Generation Y is their "being labelled lazy and filled with a sense of

---

220 Tulgan, B., & Martin, C. (2001). Managing Generation Y: Global citizens born in the late seventies and early eighties. Amherst, Massachusetts: HRD Press, Inc.

221 Neil Howe and William Strauss, Generations: The History of America's Future, 1584 to 2069, 1992

222 Neil Howe and William Strauss Millennials Rising; The Next Great Generation., 2000

223 Tapscott, D. (2009). Grown up digital, how the Net Generation is changing your world. New York, NY: McGraw-Hill Professional.

224. Jay Gilbert The Millennials: A new generation of employees, a new set of engagement policies. Issues: September / October 2011

entitlement. [225] Parallel generational differences were noted by these managers, including differences in education, salary expectations, autonomy preferences, management techniques, communication, workplace styles, and work-life balances. [226] However, the key to managerial success is the acceptance of the new generation. Managers should not ignore these differences, but should embrace them in order to get the most out of this new generation in the workplace.

Work–Life Balance and Employer Loyalty

Unlike past generations, Millennials value leisure over money, prioritizing flexible working hours over cash bonuses. They also expect to change jobs and career paths more frequently than previous generations. A survey conducted by PwC revealed that a quarter of Millennials expected to have six or more employers during their career. [227] Some researchers attribute this tendency to coming of age during a long recession, watching their parents struggle with a lack of job and retirement security. [228] Having grown up in a digital world, it comes as no surprise that 41 percent of Millennials in the PwC survey prefer to communicate electronically at work instead of face-to-face or over the phone. They are also comfortable using their own tech devices at work, and more than 75 percent of respondents said technology increases their effectiveness in the office. Comfort with technology, and multitasking, also has another upside for employers: Millennials are likely to be more collaborative, more comfortable working in teams, and potentially more productive. [229]

It is a well-established fact that employees more often leave managers and not organizations. Millennials value what they value - not what you value! Before you reward them, be sure to ask them what they want. You need to make sure that your expected outcomes are clearly

---

225 Gelbart, N., & Komninos, J. (2012). Who? where? Y? Charter Journal, 84(7), 20-23.

226. Jennifer Kilber, Allen Barclay and Douglas Ohmer, Seven Tips for Managing Generation Y

227. PwC. "Millennials at Work: Reshaping the Workplace." PWC.com. No date listed. Web.

228. Hartman, Mitchell. "Millennials at Work: Young and Callow, Like Their Parents."
NYTimes.com.
See also http://www.nytimes.com/2014/03/25/your-money/millennials-at-work-young-and-callow-like-theirparents. html?_r=0

229. Hartman, Mitchell. "Millennials at Work."

communicated. Do not hesitate to use their preferred method of communication. You need to offer praise in a variety of forms, but avoid cookie cutter employee-of-the-month programmes. Pull them into the design of incentive programmes. People tend to support what they help create. The Millennials have been nurtured by boomer parents who have been more nurturing than their parents. They have thus created a challenge for society by wanting to make their children suffer no negative consequences, from the environment or from their own actions. Millennials, therefore, expect special attention because they believe that they are special. Their parents have told them so. You need to develop relationships and take an interest in them. Empathy and genuine caring count a lot. However, do not make the mistake of trying to be like them. Telling them about your own mistakes will help build trust. If you must criticize, do it in a manner that lets them know you care?

Millennials tend to be myopic. The job of the human resource leader is to broaden their awareness. Prioritize time to participate in their learning. Share the information you get about the organization. It is a great way to build trust and a sense of partnership. Share the organization's culture by becoming a storyteller. Consequential thinking is another skill you need to foster. When you face a decision, have them come up with multiple possible outcomes for each possible solution to a problem. They hate ambiguity more than being micromanaged. With insufficient direction, they often exhibit a lack of focus, indecisiveness, and insecurity. Just do not be condescending. Millennials are not apathetic; they are just indifferent until they find a reason to care about something. In this respect, they are easy to motivate. They want to know why before what. Try to make them see that the organization's goals are an extension of their personal goals

Millennials in the African Context

Africa is by far the youngest continent in the world. Interestingly, is has been wrongly assumed that the African millennials are young and form the majority. However, unlike everything we have heard before, millennials in Africa are not the youngest, and neither are they in the majority. The oldest millennial is around 38 years of age with the youngest being about 23 years old. Out of a population of 1.2 billion in the continent, those aged 19 years and below are at 51%. Millennials make up less than 30% of the continent's population. A new generation which is the majority in Africa is here; Generation Z or the iGen cohort, of those between 15-20 years, are younger and they form the majority. The following are some of the characteristics of the African millennials:

a. **They Are All Mobile and Connected:** Although Africa has the highest growth rate in mobile phone penetration, there are only 420M unique mobile subscribers and a penetration rate of 43% against the global rate of 63%. Internet penetration remains significantly lower. There are only 300 million internet users, a majority of whom access the internet via their mobile phones. Currently, 75% of people in Africa are still offline. This is attributed to lack of basic infrastructures such as grid electricity; high data costs, and household income levels among other factors. Despite this, internet access, especially that via mobile phone subscription, is growing and predicted to reach 41 percent of Africa's population by 2020. The millennials consider the mobile first and thus have a higher phone usage. A defining characteristic of millennials globally is their usage and dependence on mobile phones. According to a recent GeoPoll rapid survey carried out among youth between the ages of 18-35in five Sub-Sahara African countries, there is an increased dependency on technology and a mobile first approach is being driven by African Millennials. The majority of them as are thus 'technosexuals.

b. **They Are All On Social Media:** There are currently only 170 million active social media users in Africa, equalling a penetration rate of only 14%, according to the 2017 Digital in Africa report by Hootsuite and We are Social. Whereas the percentage of the African population that uses social media is quite low, these numbers vary from country to country. Like their global counterparts, African millennials are increasingly using social media sites as tools for communication and a source of news and information. Social network platforms such as Facebook, WhatsApp and Twitter have become an integral part of everyday life, and over 60% millennials who have access to the internet say they use these platforms.

c. **That Millennials Are Killing TV, Radio, And Print:** Although social media has become the first point of breaking news in many regions, as seen in the percentage of those online and those on social media, in Africa, radio and TV are still king. Sub-Saharan African consumers watch TV or listen to the radio twice per day on average, while they access the internet only every second day. However, African millennials have a different view on ownership in media and this is driving the diminished importance of live TV as the dominant communications channel. This is a generation that has become a 'prosumer'-creating and consuming their own content on blogs, YouTube, and various other social channels.

d. **They Do Not Care About Serious Matters:** The assumption that millennials do not care about matters to do with political participation, civic engagement or public affairs has been attributed to their 'short attention span'. This is a myth as has been demonstrated by various research studies carried out on this demographic. A study in 2014/2015 by the Africa Barometer among a survey sample of respondents aged between 17-35 in 7 African countries shows strong evidence of interest in civic engagement, public affairs and politics among African youth. A more recent straw poll by GeoPoll in 2017 among a similar demographic in 5 African countries assessing their interest in public affairs shows concerns in levels of corruption, youth unemployment and distribution of national resources. Social media has become an important tool through which the connected Millennials voice their concerns and engage in the things that matter to them.

e. **Career Security:** In a survey conducted by Delliote in South Africa, diversity and flexibility were found to be key to loyalty. 43% of millennials envision leaving their jobs within two years with only 28 percent seeking to stay beyond five years. Employed Gen Z respondents express even less loyalty, with 61 percent indicating of leaving within two years if given the choice. [230]

f. **Rewards and Motivation:** Attracting and retaining millennials and Gen Z begin with financial rewards and workplace culture. Their choices are enhanced when businesses and their senior management teams are diverse, and when the workplace offers higher degrees of flexibility. Those who are less than satisfied with their pay and work flexibility are increasingly attracted to the gig economy, especially in emerging markets. Today, those born between 1980 and 2000 are now of working age, and they are changing the operation of the workplace as they go. As a socio-economic group, Millennials are growing in power and investment potential. In addition to reshaping the workplace, they are also influencing marketing and advertising strategies across the African continent. Learning how to work with Millennials has become increasingly important over the past few years, as studies have noted. This requires a shift in communication messaging, integrated communication through online and offline channels as well as having an understanding that the decision-making unit for Millennials has evolved. [231] African millennials are tech savvy and are increasingly choosing to shop online and with a mobile-first approach.

Improved access to the internet, greater mobile penetration and increasingly easy-to-use and navigate online experiences make consumers, especially African millennials, more likely to shop online. According to the PayPal and Ipsos third annual cross-border commerce report, South Africa's online expenditure is forecasted to grow to over R53 billion in 2018. In 2016, 43% of adults in South Africa shopped cross-border. The US is the most popular cross-border online shopping destination for South African online shoppers, followed by China and the UK. Within that landscape, the mobile phone is playing an increasingly critical role across the whole continent. Sub-Saharan Africa accounts for nearly a tenth of the current global mobile phone

---

[230] https://www2.deloitte.com/za/en/pages/about-deloitte/articles/millennialsurvey.html

[231] https://www.geopoll.com/blog/african-millennials-myths-reality/

subscriber base and is forecast to grow faster than every other region over the next five years. Businesses that want to remain competitive will therefore need to invest in their online – and mobile – commerce offerings in order to attract (and keep) millennial customers.

g.   **Brand Attachment:** African millennials communicate with brands mainly through social media. Social media has completely changed how young Africans interact with companies. Immediate access to information and brands has changed the relationship between businesses and customers, as well as the way customers approach buying products. The continued growth of social media – with 191 million active social media users across the continent (172 million of whom access social media through their mobile) – has meant that peer reviews and referrals online carry more weight than traditional advertising; peer-written content is millennials' most trusted source of information. Because millennials have more information at their fingertips than ever before, they demand the highest levels of service from the companies they support, so brands they desire.

h.   **Personalized Customer Service:** African millennials expect a personalised customer experience. In fact, they demand it and if they are not getting it, they will move their business elsewhere. With the wealth of information that they make available about themselves, their values and preferences online and through social media, they expect brands and businesses to not only know what they want, but also to provide it. Moreover, the results of a bespoke approach speak for themselves: brands that create personalised experiences see revenue increase by six to 10 percent. Small businesses have an advantage in this area, as there is more opportunity to get to know and build more meaningful relationships with customers than, where the same can be difficult in big businesses. Clever small business owners leverage this knowledge to provide customers with a personalised experience that makes them feel that they are more than just another customer.

i. **Expectations on Be-spoke Products:** African millennials want to co-create bespoke products to meet their unique needs. In the same way that they want to feel personally important to the business they are supporting, African millennials prefer to buy from brands that emphasise unique offerings that allow them to express themselves over mass-market alternatives. Co-creation is more than just a buzzword; 40 percent of millennials want to have a say or play an active role in co-creating the products that they spend their money on. By involving them in the decision process, businesses can drive both customer satisfaction and loyalty.

j. **Demand for Earned Loyalty:** African millennials are loyal – but you have to earn it. Research by Accenture indicates that millennials differ significantly from other generations when it comes to the concept of loyalty – and South African and other African customers differ even further. For instance, 88 percent of South Africans are loyal to brands that protect their private information, 67 percent are loyal to those that give them personalised discounts or special offers, and 52 percent are loyal to brands that support a cause that they value. If small businesses are able to capture the trust of their millennial customers, they will most likely remain loyal, an important trait to this generation. Companies that are able, for instance, to provide a one-stop shop for their needs will reap the rewards. [232]

Conclusion

Given these diverse expectation and choice characteristic, the human resource team needs to balance their output and demand. Human Resource departments face a major problem when it comes to millennials that work in their organization. Most of them do not stick around for very long. In a 2014 study conducted by Bayt, 46% of

---

[232] FedEx Express Sub-Saharan Africa Understanding the African Millennials 18 Jul 2018 http://www.hrpulse.co.za/editors-pick/236166-understanding-the-african-millennial-advice-for-small-business-owners-to-cater-to-todays-consumers

millennials indicated that they saw themselves working in their current job for the next two years or less. Workplace culture is an important factor in keeping millennials engaged and excited about their work. Millennials perform best in a workplace with a rich and inclusive culture. Because of where they sit within the organization, Human Resource departments can play a critical role in helping create the type of culture that brings out the best of Millennials in their workforce. The HR lead should endeavour to provide opportunities for millennials to connect with business leaders and senior management. If there is one thing millennials crave in the workplace, it is intentional mentoring. The HR lead has the unique opportunity to create this kind of culture within the organization by developing programmes and systems that support it. The Human resource partners should educate bosses or team leads on the best way to provide feedback and criticism. When employees are faced with a decision-making difficulty, they are often seeking an outside perspective to validate their thinking. Helping leaders and managers by teaching them how to provide criticism and feedback to millennials will go a long way in making both parties more successful in the long run.

Additionally, the team lead must create opportunities for millennials to feel heard. Whether it is a formal 360° performance review process or an informal lunch for employees to share their challenges and ideas, allowing millennials to feel like their voices are being heard is a great way to earn their trust and respect. The traditional and transactional role HR has played is on the verge of extinction as employees are looking for the companies, they work for to be more proactive in their professional development. A modern-day approach to human resources requires creating a culture where millennials feel like they have a voice and are being invested in by the people above them. In all our efforts, we should be able to diagnose their swing moods in order to risk-appraise them to be of benefit to the organisation. The human resource lead needs to develop the character in a consistent manner in order to engender collaboration from the millennials. Understanding their value may be the easy part, and the challenge would be how we would take the time to develop their leadership philosophy and then use it for the common good of the organisation.

Summary

Our value systems are shaped in the first decade or so of our lives. That is by our families, our friends, our communities, significant disruptive events and the general era in which we are born. As time and environmental factors merge, every issue becomes evolving. Generations are often considered by their span, and research shows that each generation has some unique characteristics. Generational cut-off points may be viewed as a tool that allows for human resource analyses. This section looks at generational cohorts and examines how millennials, in particular, are impacting organisation growth.

Chapter Nine

The Concept of Morale

'In war, the morale is to the physical as three is to one'
Napoléon Bonaparte, (1769–1821)

Tapping the Latent Potential of Man

Human resource is considered to be the most valuable asset of any organization. It is the sum of inherent abilities, acquired knowledge and skills represented by the talents and aptitudes of the employed persons who comprise executives, supervisors, and employees. It may be noted here that human resources should be utilized to the maximum possible extent in order to achieve individual and organizational goals. The attitudes, feelings and emotions of employees play a vital role in determining their performance and behaviour. These, in turn, determine the success and growth of the organisation. Morale, therefore, is the description of the emotions, attitude, satisfaction, and overall outlook of employees during their time in a workplace environment. It, generally, also refers to the esprit de corps, a feeling of enthusiasm, zeal, confidence in individuals or groups that they will be able to cope with the tasks assigned to them. A person's enthusiasm for his job reflects his attitude to work, environment and to his employer, and his willingness to strive for the goals set for him by the organization in which he is employed. [233] When employees are

---

233. A.Venkatachalam and P.Sakunthala, Concept of Employee Morale, Indian Journal; of

positive about their work environment and believe that they can meet their most important career and vocational needs, employee morale is positive or high. Part of effective productivity is thought to be directly related to the morale of the employees. Employees that are happy and positive at work are said to have positive or high employee morale.

Morale is the term usually applied to armed forces during wartime and to sports and athletic teams. It refers to team spirit and co-operation of people for a common purpose. Its importance has been realized by management only in recent years. It is felt by management that if the morale of the employees is high, production would be higher and vice-versa. Morale thus represents the attitudes of individuals and groups in an organisation towards their work environment. A person's enthusiasm for his job reflects his attitude of mind to work, environment and to his employer, and his willingness to strive for the goals set for him by the organization in which he is employed. Morale is a synthesis of superiors, his organization, his fellow-employees, his pay and so on. Feelings, emotions, sentiments, attitudes, and motives — all these combine and lead to a particular type of behaviour on the part of an individual or his group; and this is what is referred to as employee morale. It represents the attitudes of individuals and groups in an organisation towards their work environment and towards voluntary cooperation to the full extent of their capabilities for the fulfillment of organisational goals.

Evolution of Morale Study in the Military

Napoleon claimed that 'in war, three-quarters of victory is down to morale, only one quarter to the balance of military forces.' Indeed, success in a military undertaking does not depend solely on the number and skill of the soldiers, the brilliance of the strategists, or the quality of technical performance. Something extra is needed, something intangible, invisible, contingent, and volatile: that something is good troop morale. Morale is very important in asymmetric warfare. Maintaining a high level of morale is considered critical to military effectiveness and readiness for deployment. This implies that the operational capacity of military units is not only defined by tactical, logistical, and technological capacities, but also by the psychological readiness of soldiers, often referred to as morale. A high morale shields soldiers from the development of (battle) stress during military operations, [234,235] increases their level of performance [236, 237] and reduces the risk of posttraumatic stress symptoms. [238] Soldiers rely on unit leadership to define the mission and set the conditions for achieving mission goals. In exchange for their commitment to the mission, military personnel expect leaders to watch out for their best interests. If military personnel understand the mission and feel professionally and personally supported by their leaders, they will be willing to withstand the rigours of deployment. The main reason for the interest in morale is the presumed relationship of high levels of morale with superior performance under stress, adaptive responding to operational demands and positive job attitudes. [239]

---

234. Manning, F. J. (1991). Morale, Cohesion, and Esprit de Corps. In Gal, R. en Mangelsdorff, A. D. (Eds.), Handbook of Military Psychology (pp. 453-470). Chichester: John Wiley & Sons Ltd.

235. NATO Task Group HFM 081/RTG (2007, in press). A Leader's Guide to Psychological Support Across the Deployment Cycle, Belgium: Brussels

236. Britt, T. W., Dickinson, J. M., Moore, D., Castro, C. A., & Adler, A. B. (2007). Correlates and Consequences of Morale Versus Depression Under Stressful Conditions. Journal of Occupational Health Psychology 12(1), 34-47.

237. Gal, R., & Manning, F. J. (1987). Morale and its Components: A Cross-National Comparison. Journal of Applied Social Psychology, 17(4), 369-391.

238. Iverson, A. C., Fear, N. T., Ehlers, A., Hacker Hughes, J., Hull, L., Earnshaw, M., Greenberg, N., Rona, R., Wessely, S., & Hotopf, M. (2008). Risk factors for post-traumatic stress disorder among UK Armed Forces personnel. Psychological Medicine, 1-12.

239. Britt, T. W., & Dickinson, J. M. (2006). Morale during Military Operations: A Positive Psychology Approach. In T. W. Britt. C. A. Castro, & A. B. Adler (Eds.), Military life: The

Prior to the twentieth century, commanders attentive to their soldiers' morale mainly attended to their physical well-being. As long as an army was reasonably well fed, had adequate clothing and shelter, and could expect to be paid more or less regularly, its morale might be considered adequate to the task at hand. Belief in a 'cause' was thought less important than strong affection for a leader, or the promise of glory or loot. During eras when armies faced each other across open fields, the outcome of battles often hung on the state of morale. An intuitive desire for safety or instinct for survival could lead soldiers to abandon their duty and dissolve into rabble, while those suddenly inspired might snatch victory from defeat. Modern notions of troop morale arose out of the horrific casualties generated by the trench warfare of World War I. Some military historians suggest that stress-related casualties were almost unknown earlier. Evolution of weapons technology, mass armies, and general staff leadership increased the scale and magnified the intensity of warfare, levying terrific burdens on a soldier's mental fitness. Accordingly, troop morale attracted the detailed attention of military and medical authorities. In general terms, researchers understood that men subjected to severe combat conditions for prolonged periods would have to be relieved at regular intervals. Nevertheless, men unable to continue in combat were either deemed cowards or thought to be victims of a debilitating physical condition, 'shell shock.' Lord Charles Moran, a former World War I medical officer, wrote the first systematic explanation of troop morale.

Anatomy of Courage, [240] first published in 1945, postulated an explanation for troop morale and explained how it might be managed. Moran argued that courage had measurable limits and could be expended as easily as water can be poured from a

psychology of serving in peace and combat: Vol. 1. Military performance (pp. 157-184). Westport, CT:
Praeger Security International
240. Lord Charles Moran , Anatomy of Courage, 1945; repr. 1987.

beaker. Commanders had to determine how much bravery soldiers possessed and not allow them to exceed those limits without replenishment. Moran also believed courage was largely a function of a man's character. Cowards simply lacked moral strength. Events of World War II only partially supported Moran's notions. By then, psychiatrists and psychologists had more fully investigated the components of morale, and come to recognize that all troops, not just the weak or morally flawed, were subject to the effects of unrelenting fear and anxiety. Only a sense of duty allowed men to overcome their fears; thus, duty, devotion to a cause or to comrades joined the traditional factors (food, clothing, training, discipline, and leadership) as a defining component of morale.

Research conducted during the war especially that of S. L. A. Marshall, argued that troop morale rose and fell principally as a result of a shared sense of danger. According to Marshall's book, *Men Against Fire*, small group dynamics were more important to success in battle than any other factor. [241] Subsequent research, carried out by experts such as Samuel Stouffer, E. A. Shils, and Morris Janowitz, clearly demonstrated the connection between small unit cohesion, morale, and combat capability. [242] By investigating the German army of the Nazi era, Shils and Janowitz showed that the Wehrmacht's ability to fight so effectively, and survive for so long, resulted partly from the German focus on group leadership, human dynamics, and troop morale. Later research by Trevor Dupuy and Martin van Creveld underscored these conclusions. Moreover, Dupuy argued that German effectiveness at the tactical and operational level exceeded that of its opponents. Even when in retreat or significantly outnumbered, the Wehrmacht managed more

---

241. L. A. Marshall , Men Against Fire: The Problem of Battle Command in Future War, 1947; repr. 1978

242. E. A. Shils and and Morris Janowitz , Cohesion and Disintegration in the Wehrmacht in World War II, Public Opinion Quarterly, 12 (1948), pp. 280–315.

tactical victories and inflicted more casualties man-for-man than did its enemies. [243] Small professional armies, even when extraordinarily well led, trained, and disciplined, will nevertheless be subject to the same rigors as their ancestors; indeed, the exponential advances in military weapons technology, the increasing impact of artificial intelligence, and the exploitation of the electromagnetic spectrum will only increase the scope and lethality of battle, and magnify the pressure on combatants to survive and function effectively. It will also mandate the continued efforts of senior leadership and medical officers to understand and sustain morale, which is sure to remain crucial to measuring the critical interval between victory and defeat. [244]

Morale is an indicator of the attitude of employees towards their jobs, superiors and their organisational environment. It is a collection of the employees' attitude, feelings and sentiments. Flippo has described morale 'as a mental condition or attitude of individuals and groups which determines their willingness to co-operate.' Good morale is evidenced by employee enthusiasm, voluntary adherence to regulations and orders, and a willingness to co-operate with others in the accomplishment of an organization's objectives. Poor morale is demonstrated through surliness, insubordination, a feeling of discouragement and dislike of the job, company and associates. In the words of Yoder, "morale is a feeling, somewhat related to esprit de corps, enthusiasm or zeal. For group of workers, morale, according to a popular usage of the word, refers to the over-all tone, climate or atmosphere of work, perhaps vaguely sensed by the members.' According to William Spriegel, 'morale is the co-operative

---

243. Trevor N. Dupuy , A Genius for War: The German Army and General Staff, 1807–1945, 1977

244. https://www.encyclopedia.com/history/encyclopedias-almanacs-transcripts-and-maps/morale-troop

attitude or mental health of a number of people who are related to each other on some basis'. [245,246]

Viteles states that 'morale may be defined as 'an attitude of satisfaction with desire to continue in and willingness to strive for the goals of a particular group or organisation.' According to Leighton, 'morale is the capacity of a group of people to pull together persistently and consistently in pursuit of a common purpose.' Morale is basically a psychological concept. It is intangible; therefore, it is very difficult to measure the degree of morale accurately. Morale is contagious in the sense that people learn from one another. It is dynamic in nature and cannot be developed overnight. Managers have to make continuous efforts to build and maintain high morale. It is a long-term concept. Morale is the mental attitude of individual or of a group, which enables the employee to realise that the maximum satisfaction of his drives coincides with the fulfilment of the objective or the concern. Morale is a by-product of motivation and employee attitude. Morale is used to describe the overall 'tone' or "climate" prevailing in members of group, society or association. In the context of civil service morale, the term is used to describe the overall attitudes of civil servants collectively towards, all aspects of their work; the job, supervisor, fellow civil servants, working conditions, overall ecology of administration, etc. Morale is a group phenomenon consisting of a pattern of attitudes. It is the sum total of employees' attitudes, feelings and sentiments. Morale is the vital ingredient of organisational success because attitudes and sentiments of employees greatly influence productivity and satisfaction of employees. Morale may be high or low; when the morale of the employees is high, they co-operate fully with the management towards the

---

245. Spriegel, W.R. (1977): "Personnel Management-Principles, Practices and Points of View", New Delhi: Tata McGraw Hill, p.480.

246. Spriegel, William, 1974, Industrial Management & Leadership

achievement of organisational objectives. High morale leads to good discipline, high degree of interest in the job, loyalty to the organisation and high performance. It is 'a composite of sentiments, attitudes, and feelings that grant to general feelings of pleasure and also it is attitude of mental or bearing of a person or group as regards discipline and confidence.'

Approaches to Morale

As indicate earlier, morale is the depiction of emotions, satisfaction, and overall attitude towards a workplace. Productivity, therefore, is directly related to morale. Happy employees have high morale while dissatisfied and unhappy employees have low morale. Linz *et al.* measured employee morale, using job satisfaction, organizational commitment, turnover rates, complaints and employee strikes as a proxy. A high morale means the employee is satisfied with the job, puts in effort, is creative, takes initiative, is committed to the organization and focuses on achieving organizational goals rather than personal goals. Morale is generally referred to as "willingness to work". Bentley and Rempel in the book entitled *Manual for the Purdue teacher opinionnaire*, conceptualized morale as 'the professional enthusiasm and interest that a human being shows towards the group goals and individuals achievement in a given job position. [247] Morale is the degree of willingness and enthusiasm with which the quantity of a group pulls together to achieve group goals. Morale is a symbol of attitudes of employees towards their environment, jobs and superiors. It is the sum total of employees' attitudes, feelings and sentiments towards these variables. Morale is both an individual and a group phenomenon. Job satisfaction and dissatisfaction create the problem of low morale among the

---

247. R.R. Bentley, and A.M. Rempel, Manual for the Purdue teacher Opinionaire (2nd ed.). West Lafayette, IN: Purdue Research Foundation, 1980.

employees. Good motivation leads to high morale. It being a psychological concept, it is not easy to define it precisely.

Different authorities have variously defined morale. Venkatachalam and Sakunthala conceptualises morale in various approaches to its study. According to them, morale is generally referred to as "willingness to work". Job satisfaction and dissatisfaction create the problem of low morale among the employees. Morale is an employee's attitude toward his or her job, employer, and colleagues. Employee morale is the psychological state with respect to satisfaction, confidence and resolve; the attitude of an individual or group of employees, resulting in courage, devotion and discipline; the level of fulfillment one has with intrinsic work aspects, such as variety and challenge, feedback and learning, and space to grow and extrinsic circumstances of employment such as fair and adequate pay, job security, and health and safety. [248] Good motivation leads to high morale. It being a psychological concept, it is not easy to define it precisely. Different authorities have variously defined morale. Different definitions of morale can be classified into three major approaches including Classical, Psychological and Social approaches.

a. **Classical Approach:** Robert M. Guion defined morale as the extent to which individual needs are satisfied and the extent to which an individual perceives that satisfaction stemming from total job satisfaction. According to this approach, the satisfaction of basic needs is the symbol of morale. If the basic needs of the employees are satisfied, their morale will be high.

b. **Psychological Approach:** In the words of Jucious and Slender, "morale is a state of mind and emotions

---

248. Usha Tiwari, A Study On Employee Morale And Its Impact On Employee Efficiency At Jaypee Cement Plant Rewa (M.P.) Abhinav International Monthly Refereed Journal of Research in Management & Technology .Volume 3, Issue 11 (November, 2014)

affecting willingness to work which in turn affects individual and organisational objectives." According to this approach, morale is a psychological concept i.e., a state of mind. Emotions affect the willingness to work which in turn affect individual and organisational objectives. Accordingly, the attitudes and willingness to work is morale. Morale is a mental condition or attitude of individuals and groups, which determine their willingness to cooperate.

c. **Social Approach:** Morale is a social phenomenon, which enables the men to live in a society or group in pursuit of a common goal. According to Blackmanship, morale is the feeling of togetherness. There is a sense of identification with and interest in the elements of one's job, working conditions, fellow employees, supervisor, employer and the company. Broadly speaking, morale is:

    i.   A stimulation of the feeling of togetherness
    ii. An identification of group interest and that of the interest of the enterprise, fellow employees and the requirement of the job; and
    iii. The creation of an atmosphere in the organisation conducive to the achievement of the enterprise.

Morale is an indicator of the attitude of employees towards their jobs, superiors and the organisation's environment. It is a collection of employees' attitudes, feelings and sentiments towards these variables. Morale is a by-product of the group relationships in the organisation. It is a mental process, which, once started, permeates the entire group creating a mood which results in the formation of a common attitude. Generally, the term 'morale' is used to describe an overall climate prevailing among the members of a group. It is not an absolute concept, which can convey a specific meaning. Morale has to be qualified like the word 'health'. Just as good health is essential for any individual, high morale is necessary for any organisation.

Managers cannot establish high morale once and then forget about it for several years. High morale is to be built and maintained by continuous efforts. Morale is multi-dimensional in nature in the sense that it is a complex mixture of several elements. It recognizes the influence of job situation on attitudes of individuals, and also includes the role of human needs as motivational forces. Morale is mostly regarded as a long-term phenomenon. Raising morale to a high level and maintaining it is a long-term measure such as gimmicks, contests or one-shot actions

Characteristics of Morale

Morale is a feeling, somewhat related to esprit de corps, enthusiasm or zeal. For a group of employees, morale, according to a popular usage of the word, refers to the over-all tone climate or atmosphere of work, perhaps vaguely sensed by the members. If employees appear to feel enthusiastic and optimistic about group activities, if they have a sense of mission about their job, if they are friendly with each other, they are described as having good or high morale. If they seem to be dissatisfied, irritated, cranky, critical, rustled and pessimistic, they are described as possessing a poor or low morale. It is a mental condition or attitude of individuals or groups, which determines their willingness to co-operate. Good morale is evidenced by employee enthusiasm, voluntary conformance with regulations and orders, and willingness to co-operate with others in the accomplishment of an organization's objective. Poor morale is evidenced by surliness, insubordination, a feeling of discouragement and dislike of the job, company and associates. Morale is a group concept with five components, namely:

    a.   A feeling of togetherness, i.e., of belonging to a group and not being isolated;

b. A clear goal which will be the target of production set before them;
c. There must be an observed or perceived progress towards the attainment of the goal, i.e., expectation of success;
d. Within the group, each member feels that he has a meaningful task to perform; and
e. A supportive or stimulating leadership.

Features of Morale

Some key features of morale:
a. Morale is a state of mind. It reflects mental health.
b. It is the aggregate of attitudes, feelings, emotions, sentiments, etc.
c. Morale is of two types.
   i. Individual morale-which means a person's attitudes towards life, and
   ii. Group morale, which implies the collective attitudes of a group of persons.
d. Morale is a relative term. It may be high or low.
e. Morale influences human behaviour and performance.
f. Morale is a psychological feeling.
g. Morale is intangible. It cannot be increased directly.
h. Morale is a contagious phenomenon. Individuals transmit their attitudes to each other.

Assumptions in Understanding Morale

The following basic assumptions about people are significant because they are tied up closely with an understanding of what morale is:
   i. There are psychological uniformities which obtain among all tribes, nations and races.

ii. Each psychological uniformity has a range through which it varies. Some variants are characteristic of particular groups of people and form a part of their culture.

iii. Everyone is disturbed by the following general stresses: (a) Threats to life; (b) Discomfort arising from pain, heat, cold, fatigue and poor diet; (c) Loss of the means of subsistence, whether in the form of money, job, business or property; (d) Deprivation of sexual satisfaction; (e) Enforced idleness; (f) Isolation; (g) Threats to children and other members of the family and to friends; (h) Restrictions on movement; (i) Dislike and ridicule to which one may be exposed, and rejection by other people; and (j) Capricious and unpredictable behaviour on the part of those in authority on whom one's welfare depends.

Personnel management carefully analyses these different items of morale because employees vary greatly in their ability to face a situation of stress, and because it is capable of determining the impact which good or bad morale will have on the attainment of organizational objectives. By taking the necessary steps in time, it may improve the attitudes and morale of its employees.

Importance of Morale

Morale can affect productivity. One of the most unpredictable effects of the level of morale is its impact upon employees' productivity. The reviews of the research studies do not show a direct relationship between morale and productivity. Productivity sometimes is high with high morale, but at other times may be low even when morale is high, and vice versa. There can be four combinations of morale and productivity.

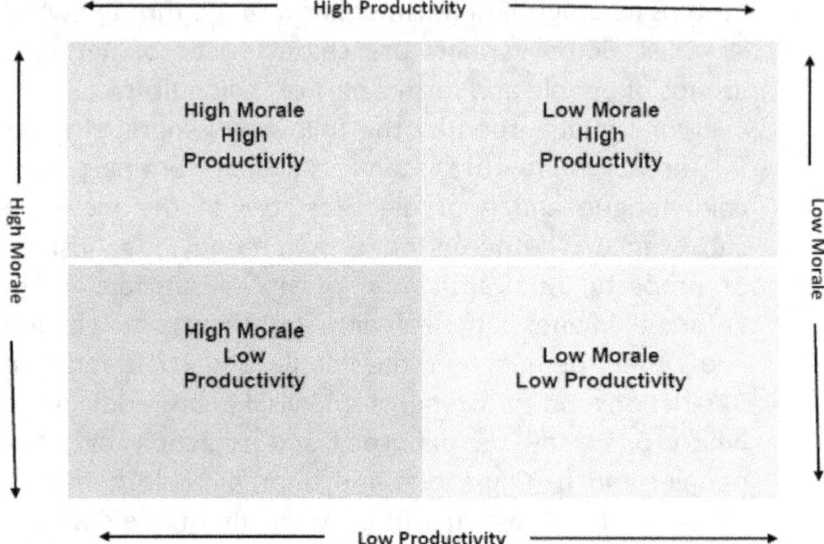

a. **High Morale:**   High morale reflects a predisposition to be more productive if proper leadership is provided. This situation is likely to occur when employees are motivated to achieve high performance standards through financial and non-financial rewards. High morale exists when the employee's attitude is favourable to the total situation of a group and to the attainment of its objectives. It is represented by the use of such terms as, spirit, zest, enthusiasm, loyalty, honesty, dependability, resistance to frustration etc. Possible effects of high morale are:

1. Higher performance
2. Better quality of work
3. Job satisfaction
4. Cheaper goods and services
5. Lower cost
6. Higher profits
7. Better wages
8. Employment stability
9. Low absenteeism
10. Low labour turnover

11. Employees" initiative, regularity and punctuality.
12. Good discipline
13. Fewer industrial accidents
14. Stability and growth of the organisation
15. Sound industrial relation

b. **High Morale/ Low Productivity:** The situation arises when employees spend their time and energy in satisfying their personal objectives unrelated to the company's goals. Faulty machinery, lack of training, ineffective supervision and restrictive norms of informal groups can also lead to low productivity on the part of employees with high morale.

c. **Low Morale/ High Productivity:** Low morale cannot result in high productivity for a long period. However, this situation can occur for a temporary period due to fear of loss of job, exceptionally good supervision and machine paced work in which only a part of employees' capabilities are used.

d. **Low Morale / Low Productivity:** This is a normal relationship. In the long run low morale is likely to result in low productivity. Thus, there is a complex relationship between morale and productivity. This is because morale is only one of the factors influencing productivity. Low morale exists when attitudes inhibit the willingness and ability of an organisation to attain its objectives. If employees seem to be dissatisfied, irritated, cranky, critical, restless, and pessimistic, they are described as having poor or low morale. Effects of low morale are:
    1. Apathy and non-involvement
    2. Fatigue and monotony
    3. High labour turnover
    4. Work stoppages

5.   High rate of Absenteeism
6.   Disciplinary problem
7.   Restriction of output
8.   Increased grievances
9.   Labour unrest
10. Strike
11. Wastage and spoilage

Factors that Influence Morale

Employee morale is a very complex phenomenon and is influenced by many factors on the shop floor. For example, the job, the supervisor, the company and the working conditions pertaining t as well as its policies; the group and inter-personal relations prevailing in that group; salary and other benefits; the employee's family and home life; his social and community life; the policies and attitudes of the top management to its employees and trade unions-all this influence employee morale to a certain extent. Factors influencing employee morale can well be divided into two groups, namely organisational factors and personal factors.

a. **Organisational Factors:** The goals of the organisation influence the attitudes of employees greatly. If the goals set by the management are worthwhile, useful and acceptable, then employees develop a positive feeling towards the job and the organisation. Likewise, a clear structure with well-defined duties and responsibilities encourages people to work with confidence. The reputation of the company is another important factor worth mentioning here. Persons working in a reputed organisation experience feelings of pride and a spirit of loyalty. Employees are highly motivated and their morale is higher if their individual goals and objectives are in tune with organisational goals and objectives. The commonness of purpose will result in high morale. Employees want to be a part of the organisation, which has a worthwhile purpose in which they can believe. Organisational structure has an impact on the quality of labour relations, particularly on the level of morale. Large organizations tend to lengthen their channels of vertical communication and to increase the difficulty of upward communication; therefore, the morale tends to be lower. Against this, a flat structure increases the level of morale. The nature of work is yet another factor. A meaningful and satisfying job helps to improve employee morale. In such a job, each member of the group understands clearly how his specific task contributes to the attainment of group goals. Morale tends to be low when the job provides no challenge and satisfaction and job standards are considered too high.

Many jobs of a routine or specialized nature make for the boredom of the employee, for obsessive thinking and alienation. Dull, monotonous, repetitive work affects employee morale adversely. On the other hand, if an employee is asked to do something interesting and challenging, his morale may be high. The work environment also contributes to morale. The building and its appearance, the condition of machine tools available at the work place, provisions for safety, medical aid and repair to machinery, etc., have an impact on employees' morale. Morale is a direct function of the conditions in the workplace. Clean, safe, comfortable and pleasant work conditions are morale boosters. Added to the above is the working conditions. Physical work environment, job security, wages and other allied factors exercise a significant influence on employee morale. When the wages are fair, job is secure and there are opportunities for promotion, job satisfaction and morale are likely to be high. Reward systems also play a key role in determining the morale of staff. Employees expect adequate compensation for services rendered to the organisation. A good system of wages, salaries, promotions and other incentives keeps the morale of the employees high. One of the requirements of high morale is the possibility and opportunity of progress in any concern. All employees should be given an opportunity to progress and to earn high wages without any discrimination. Another critical factor is leadership. The actions of the management exercise a tremendous influence on the morale of employees. High rates of turn over, for example, indicate that the leadership is ineffective. Competent, dependable and fair-minded leadership can build and maintain high morale. Such a leadership can win the confidence of employees through sympathetic and friendly behaviour. Lines of authority and responsibility are clear and communication system is effective. The actions of managers exert a strong influence over the morale of the workforce. Fair treatment, equitable rewards and recognition for good work affect morale greatly. Employees feel comfortable when they work under a sympathetic, caring leader in place of one who is authoritarian, dictatorial and domineering. Negativism, inconsiderateness and apathy are not conducive to the development of a good work climate.

Tied to leadership is the aspect of supervision. The nature of supervision can better tell the attitudes of employees because a supervisor is in direct contact with the employees and can have better influence on the activities of the employees. There should be an impartial, helpful, and capable team of supervisors and managers and their sympathetic attitude towards their subordinates. The peers and colleagues in the work are also key in keeping morale. Man, being a social animal, finds his work more satisfying if he feels that he has the acceptance and companionship of his fellows. If he has confidence in his fellow employees and faith in their loyalty, his morale will be high. Poor attitude of co-employees influences others. Imagine working with a person who talks about the negative points of an organisation all day long. Such a person can make each workday an unpleasant experience for others. He can cause co-employees to think negatively, and even if they do not, such an attitude is certainly not a morale booster. The confidence of an employee in fellow employees influences morale. When an employee is confident that his co- employees are loyal to him and will provide advice and assistance whenever necessary his morale is likely to be good. A feeling of togetherness (group cohesiveness) and common goals tend to raise employee morale.

How employees perceive themselves influences their attitudes to the organizational environment. For example, the morale of individuals who lack self-confidence or who suffer from poor physical or mental health is generally low. How the employee looks at himself (the self-concept) also influences morale greatly. For example, individuals who lack self-confidence or who suffer from poor physical or mental health frequently develop morale problems. Further, how the employees' personal needs are satisfied can significantly influence their morale. Salary, fringe benefits, daily allowance rates, allowances, may affect employee morale in a positive or negative manner, when they compare themselves with others doing similar jobs. Employees can become disgruntled when they feel that their pay and benefits are not in line with the current industry rates or are not keeping up with rising prices.

The satisfaction, which an individual obtains in his job is largely the result of the extent to which different aspects of his work situations are relevant to his job-related value systems. These include opportunity to learn a job, steadiness of employment, supervision, pay, co-cooperativeness or otherwise of the co-employees, working conditions, cleanliness, working hours, communication, recognition; individual adjustment and group relationship outside the job. If the job factors and the satisfaction they bring are perceived to be favourable to the employees, morale will tend to be higher than if the factors seem unfavourable. If the job gives an employee opportunity to prove his talents, and develop his personality, he will certainly like it and he will have high morale. Related to the above is the availability of future opportunities for rewards. If the employee looks to the future and perceives opportunities for satisfaction and for attainment in the rewards and conditions that lie ahead, morale will tend to be high. If, on the other hand, the rewards and opportunities for the future appear to be bleak, morale will tend to be dampened.

b. **Personal Factor:** The sex, age, education, intelligence of the employees, occupational level, family life of an employee, monthly income, marital status, etc., determine morale. An employee's self-concept, habits and family relations exercise a significant influence on his morale. For some people, it appears most jobs will be dissatisfying irrespective of the organisational condition involved, whereas for others, most jobs will be satisfying only if the organisation condition is right. Personal variables like age, educational level, sex, etc., are responsible for this difference. Until recently, it was believed that there was a "U" shaped relationship between age and morale. Morale was thought to be highest when people started on their job, but subsequently declined until people reached their twenties. Then morale began to rise again. However, today's belief is that age and morale are directly related and that, other things being equal, older employees seem to have higher morale, because perhaps younger employees are more dissatisfied.

They are a "new breed" with higher expectations than their elders. Studies have reported that employers, therefore, hire employees of somewhat higher age, for they perceive in them these qualities: (i) stability that comes with maturity; (ii) a serious attitude towards job; (iii) more reliability, less absenteeism, and proven steady work habits; (iv) a sense of responsibility and loyalty and (v) less tendency to be distracted by outside interests or influences.

Another personal drive is education. An inverse relationship has been found between educational level and employee morale. In other words, the higher the educational level of an employee, the lower his morale because he compares his own attainments with those of others. With occupational level held constant, there is a negative relationship between the educational level and morale. The higher the education, the higher the reference group, which the individual looks to for guidance to evaluate his job rewards. One other personal factor is gender. There is as yet no consistent evidence as to whether women are more satisfied with their jobs than men, holding such factors as job and occupational level constant. One might predict this case, considering the generally lower occupational aspirations of women. The general impression is that married employees and employees who have more dependents tend to be more dissatisfied with greater responsibilities. Nevertheless, such employees may be more satisfied because they value their jobs more than unmarried employees. The occupational level of the employee also influences his level of morale. For example, executives are, on the whole, more satisfied than managers; managers are more satisfied than subordinates; and so forth. Morale tends to increase with increasing years of experience. However, it may decrease after twenty years of experience particularly among people who have not realized their job expectation

Studies suggest that engaged employees work harder, are often willing to take on extra responsibilities and are a positive influence on other employees. Unengaged employees, basically, serve time and do no more and possibly less than required. Employees that are actively disengaged tend to be disruptive and a bad influence on others. However, for those companies with a high-level engagement, benefits include a higher rate of productivity and a lower staff turnover. The degree of morale in any organisation is determined by several factors. Some of them are merely psychological and difficult to identify, however researchers have succeeding in figuring out the following factors:

i. **Confidence in Leadership:** If the leader of the organisation is able to win the confidence of the employees, morale will be high. For employees, the leader being mentioned is the immediate supervisor/superior. If the leader is systematic, fair, honest, helpful and friendly, he may win over the confidence of his subordinates and boost their morale.

ii. **Job Satisfaction:** The morale of the employee would be high if he is satisfied with his job. Hence, right men should be placed in the right job to boost up their morale in their jobs.

iii. **Confidence in Co-Workers:** Mani is a social being and he finds himself more enthusiastic in the company of others. If he finds that his companions or fellow workers are co-operating with him, his morale would be high.

iv. **Sound and Efficient Organisation:** Sound and effective organisation is an important factor affecting the employee's morale. At the same time, the chance of communication should be effective and the personal problems of the employee should be heard and redressed as quickly as possible.

v. **Fair Remuneration:** Fair and reasonable remuneration is essential to secure enthusiasm and willingness of the workers to do the job. The wages should be comparable with those paid in similar concerns. Besides, monetary incentives should be provided to them as and when necessary and possible.

vi. **Security of Job:** If the employee feels secured, they will be willing and co-operative to do the job allotted to them.

vii. **Opportunity to Rise:** The employees should also be made to realize that if they work properly, they will be promoted and adequately rewarded. This feeling of recognition will definitely boost their morale. Leadership should give employees the opportunity to develop their professional skills and their careers.

viii. **Working Conditions:** The conditions of work at which the employees are required to work also affect their morale. Providing safety measures, hygienic facilities, clean workplace, etc., give them satisfaction and boost their morale.

ix. **Physical & Mental Health:** An employee with weak health cannot be co-operative and willing to work. Similarly, his mental strain shall also reduce his motivation of morale. Both physical and mental illness are detrimental to an individual's work and thereby the organisational output.

x. **Good discipline** and conformance with rules, regulation and orders boosts morale.

xi. **Expressing gratitude:** Morale is boosted also by employees feeling that they are valued, with gratitude being expressed and given by superiors proving important.

xii. **Trust:** Trust amongst colleagues is also hugely important to morale, and this is why team work and collaboration in the enterprise should be encouraged.

In his book, *Getting Engaged: The New Workplace Loyalty*, Tim Rutledge explains that truly engaged employees are attracted to, and inspired by, their work ("I want to do this"), committed ("I am dedicated to the success of what I am doing"), and fascinated ("I love what I am doing"). Engaged employees care about the future of the company and are willing to invest the discretionary effort – exceeding duty's call – to see that the organization succeeds. In his book, Rutledge urged managers to implement retention plans so that they could keep their top talent. The need to do so is supported by a 1998 study by McKinsey and others entitled 'The War for Talent' that reported that a shortage of skilled employees was an emerging trend. Today, there is widespread agreement among academics and practitioners that engaged employees are those who are emotionally connected to the organization and cognitively vigilant. Some companies will have to look differently at how they tackle leadership and what types of leaders are in the enterprise. According to *Ivey Business Journal*, there are ten key 'C' words that managers should bear in mind when approaching how they deal with employees, these are:

i. **Connect:** Good relationships between managers and employees are vital to engagement. Those workers that clash with management as they feel undervalued never work at their top capacity for the company.

ii. **Career:** Workers want to feel like they have the chance to advance their career and want challenging and meaningful work that can help them achieve this. It is up to the leader not only to find work that challenges employs, but to also instill the confidence in the employee that they can achieve.

iii. **Clarity:** Leaders need to have vision and this must be communicated to the employee, who wants to know that he is working for a progressive company and wants to fully understand its goals.

iv. **Convey:** Good leaders put in place processes and procedures that allow workers to achieve goals. It is not enough to provide feedback, there must be some facilitation behind driving employees to master tasks and then constructive and encouraging feedback should be given.

v. **Congratulate:** Too many companies are quick to criticize when things go wrong and unwilling to give praise where it is due. This fosters a negative working culture as everyone needs encouragement and is the sign of a bad leader.

vi. **Contribute:** Employees that understand how their work is contributing to the overall company strategy performs better than those who do not. This means that managers have to communicate why a worker's job is important and show them proven results.

vii. **Control**: Workers like to have control over their own lives, as mentioned earlier on, and this can be achieved by flexible working and consulting them over issues that are relevant to their job. The ability for an employee to voice his ideas and opinions is important to this feeling of control.

viii. **Collaborate:** This is something that is seeing a huge rise in popularity within all departments of the enterprise. Teamwork strengthens relationships with both leaders and colleagues, leading to a happier, more engaged and productive workplace.

ix. **Credibility**: People want to be proud of what they do and they want to know that they are working for an ethical and high-performing company.

x. **Confidence:** In order to be proud of the company, an employee has to have confidence is his leaders and the company itself. Scandal, be it of a personal or corporate nature, really tend to damage employee (and consumer) confidence. [249]

Practitioners and academics have argued that an engaged workforce can create competitive advantage. It is imperative for leaders to identify the level of engagement in their organization and implement behavioural strategies that will facilitate full engagement. In clear terms, they describe how leaders can do that. According to the research company, Gallup, engaged employees are committed, love their job and care about what happens to the company they work for. This ultimately leads to higher levels of performance, and as Gallup explains, 'better customer engagement, higher productivity, better retention, fewer accidents, and 21% higher profitability'. Whilst in years gone by the power has been firmly in the hands of the employer, this is no longer the case and companies have to work harder to gain and retain top talent. Flexibility in the workplace is also important to increasing morale, as studies have shown that it produces less absenteeism, higher engagement and productivity. Those employees that are given the opportunity for flexible working feel much more trusted and valued than those who do not. In every organisation, people are working within a subtle environment of attitudes. Each employee has attitudes that range over the entire spectrum of human behaviour. Understanding and managing employee's behaviour in the work organisations become challenging jobs for managers because of complexities involved in the process. The emerging problem of stimulating a feeling of togetherness, a sense of identification with the job has affected the employees' morale. Morale affects output, the quality of a product, costs, co-operation, enthusiasm, discipline, initiative and other ingredients of success. It affects an employee's or a group's willingness to work

---

[249]. Dan Crim, Gerard Seijts, Gerard Seijts, What Engages Employees the Most OR, the Ten Cs of Employee Engagement

and cooperate in the best interests of the individuals, groups & the organisations for which they work. High Morale exists when employee attitudes are favourable to the total situation of a group and to the attainment of its objectives, and this is represented by terms such as team spirit, zeal, enthusiasm, loyalty, dependability and resistance to frustration. Described by phrases such as apathy, bickering, jealousy, pessimism, disobedience of the orders of the leader, lack of interest in one's job and laziness, Low Morale exists when attitudes inhibit the willingness and ability of an organisation to attain its objectives.

Morale, generally defined, is a state of mind that either encourages or impedes action. The greatest combat commanders have always understood that morale reflects the mental, moral, and physical condition of their troops. These conditions, in turn, directly relate to the troops' courage, confidence, discipline, enthusiasm, and willingness to endure the sacrifices and hardships of military duty. Troops with high morale can operate, even succeed against high odds, in all kinds of conditions. Poor morale can lead to failure, even when odds favour victory. At a basic level, good morale allows soldiers to overcome fear. Napoleon Bonaparte was a man of great talent. A skilled general, a cunning politician, and a charismatic leader of men. Another reason why his image is so firmly etched in history is that Napoleon was a great propagandist. According to Napoleon, 'in war, morale conditions make up three–quarters of the game, the relative balance of manpower accounts for the last quarter'. Morale is equally important in management. High morale means willing cooperation and loyalty to the organisation. Employees with high morale take greater interest in the job, feel a sense of identity with the organisation and take pride in it. High morale is an index of sound industrial relations. It helps the management in overcoming labour-turnover, absenteeism, indiscipline, grievances and other labour problems.

Employee morale describes the overall outlook, attitude, satisfaction, and confidence that employees feel at work. When employees are positive about their work environment and believe that they can meet their most important career and vocational needs, employee morale is positive or high. Like employee motivation, you cannot give an employee positive morale. As an employer, though, you do control large components of the environment in which employees work each day. Consequently, you are a powerful contributor to whether an employee's morale is positive or negative. Communication is another significant factor in positive employee morale. Employees want to feel that they are privy to the important information about their company, their customers, and their products. They also need current information so that the decisions they make are congruent with their success in the company. The relationship with their immediate manager and their communication and interaction with the senior managers are also significant. Employees want to feel as if they are valued equally with other employees and held in serious regard by the senior team of leaders.

High morale contributes to high levels of productivity, high returns to stakeholders, and employee loyalty. Low morale may cause high absenteeism and turnover. Respect, involvement, appreciation, adequate compensation, promotions, a pleasant work environment, and a positive organizational culture are morale boosters. Many companies offer diverse benefits to boost morale and satisfaction. [250] Human Resource executives need to consider new strategies for recruiting and retaining the best talents for their organizations. Higher salaries and compensation benefits may seem the most likely way to attract employees. However, quality of the physical workplace environment may also have a strong influence on a company's

---

250. Kongala Ramprasad (2013): Motivation and Workforce Performance in Indian industries. Res. J. Management Sci. Vol. 2(4)pp 25-29.

ability to recruit and retain talented people Some factors in the workplace environment may be considered keys affecting employee's engagement, productivity, morale, comfort level, etc., both positively and negatively. Good management and effective leadership help to develop teamwork and the integration of individual and group goals. Leaders have to sustain performance; sustaining and improving performance for the future is essential for the survival of the organisation. While keeping eyes on performance indicators, leaders encourage creativity and innovation; risk taking and skills for future development. [251]

On any team, in any organization, all responsibility for success and failure rests with the leader-manager. The leader must own everything in his or her world. There is no one else to blame. The leader must acknowledge mistakes and admit failures, take ownership of them, and develop a plan to win. The best leaders do not just take responsibility for their job; they take ownership of everything that impacts their mission. This fundamental core concept enables military units and crew leaders to lead high-performing teams in extraordinary circumstances and win. If an individual on the team is not performing at the level required for the team to succeed, the leader must train and mentor that underperformer. However, if the underperformer continually fails to meet standards, then a leader who exercises ownership must be loyal to the team and the mission above any individual. If underperformers cannot improve, the leader must make the tough call to terminate them and hire others who can get the job done. All that falls on the leader. This is one of the most fundamental and important truths at the heart of team ownership which is indicative of the fact that there are no bad teams, only bad leaders. This is a difficult and humbling concept

---

251. Ngamb H. C.(2011): The Relationship Between Leadership And Employee Morale In Higher Education. African Journal of Business Management Vol. 5(3), pp. 762-776.

for any leader to accept, yet it remains an essential mind-set to building a high-performance, winning team. When leaders who epitomize ownership drive their teams to achieve, a team performs well, and performance continues to improve, even when a strong leader is temporarily removed from the team. Every team must have junior leaders ready to step up and temporarily take on roles and responsibilities for their immediate bosses to carry on the team's mission and get the job done, if, and when the need arises. Leaders should never be satisfied. They must always strive to improve, and they must face the facts through a realistic, brutally honest assessment of themselves and their team's performance.

Summary

Morale is the term usually applied to armed forces during wartime and to sports and athletic teams. It refers to the team spirit and co-operation of people for a common purpose. Human resource on the other hand, considered as the sum of inherent abilities, acquired knowledge and skills represented by the talents and aptitudes of employees, needs to appreciate the concept of morale and its impact of the entity's success. The attitudes, feelings and emotions of employees play a vital role in determining their performance and behaviour. These, in turn, determine the success and growth of the organisation. Morale, therefore, is the description of the emotions, attitude, satisfaction, and overall outlook of employees during their time in a workplace environment. It highlights the fact that, whether good or bad, our performance and actions will depend on the choices, direction and decisions made by leaders. A person's enthusiasm for his job reflects his attitude to work, the environment and to his employer, and his willingness to strive for the goals set for him by the organization in which he is employed. When employees are positive about their work environment and believe that they can meet their most important career and vocational needs, employee morale is positive or high. The chapter in sum, examines the concept of morale, approaches, characteristic features and looks at some assumptions about morale, which, if well understood and harnessed could lead to organisational success.